MAGGIE BEER'S SUMMER HARVEST RECIPES brings together over 100 of Maggie's signature summer recipes, detailed descriptions of her favourite ingredients and inspiring accounts of memorable meals with family and friends.

The recipes highlight Maggie's philosophy of using the freshest and best seasonal produce available in the Barossa Valley, South Australia, and treating it simply, allowing the natural flavours to speak for themselves. Describing herself as a 'country cook', Maggie cooks from the heart and is passionate about instilling in others this same confidence – to use recipes as a starting point, and be guided by instinct and personal taste.

This collection of recipes from one of Australia's best-loved cooks has been taken from *Maggie's Harvest* and is essential for anyone with an appreciation of the pleasures of sourcing, cooking and sharing food.

✦ ✦ ✦

MAGGIE BEER is one of Australia's best-known food personalities. As well as appearing as a guest chef on MasterChef and writing books, Maggie devotes her time to her export kitchen in the Barossa Valley, which produces a wide range of pantry items for domestic and international markets. These include her famous verjuice, pâté and quince pastes, her ice cream as well as her sparkling non-alcoholic grape drinks. Maggie was also recognised as Senior Australian of the Year in 2010 for inspiring joy to many Australians through food.

Maggie is the author of many successful cookbooks, *Maggie's Christmas*, *Maggie Beer* (Lantern Cookery Classics), *Maggie's Verjuice Cookbook*, *Maggie's Kitchen*, *Maggie's Harvest*, *Maggie's Table*, *Cooking with Verjuice*, *Maggie's Orchard* and *Maggie's Farm*, and co-author of the bestselling *Stephanie Alexander and Maggie Beer's Tuscan Cookbook*.

maggiebeer.com.au

MAGGIE BEER'S
SUMMER HARVEST
— RECIPES —

Maggie Beer

with photography by Mark Chew

LANTERN

an imprint of
PENGUIN BOOKS

For Colin

CONTENTS

INTRODUCTION

MY PASSION FOR FOOD HAS GIVEN ME SO MUCH IN LIFE – a sense of purpose, a delicious anticipation of each new day, and gifts of a much deeper kind than financial. Harvesting the bounty from living off the land, sharing the harvest with my family and friends, and being part of a community are incredibly rewarding – I wouldn't swap my life for anything!

Maggie's Harvest, a landmark book when it was first published in 2007, was the culmination of a lot of hard work and highlights my philosophy of using the freshest and best seasonal produce available at my doorstop in the Barossa Valley. These stories of mine are written over many years of great food experiences, some of them sentimental, all of them important in some way so in most cases I have been quite vague about just when they happened.

And while the original *Harvest* edition still lives in its beautifully bound, embroidered cover, for ease of use, what better way to approach each new season than with a paperback edition, exclusively featuring the recipes you'll need for the months ahead. More practical in the kitchen – although you need to know how much I love to see splattered copies of any of my books These seasonal paperbacks celebrate my love for each season and bounty it brings; accentuating the produce available, beginning with winter.

Summer is such a wonderful time; the produce from the garden truly tastes of sunshine. I love the very first of the stone fruit – it is so fragile. A white peach picked ripe from the tree is a revelation of flavour and succulence. The apricots that are fully ripened around Christmas time add so much to the table. On the years when we have a heatwave at the start of January, the apricots are too ripe for anything but jam and we make thousands of bottles of it. I love the first heritage tomatoes from the garden that need nothing more than extra virgin olive oil, basil and crusty bread to be a beautiful lunch. Summer gives so much.

I love and celebrate each change in the season and the food it brings. I hope you love summer too and that, in turn, you'll collect each of the four seasons.

ANCHOVIES

I MUST CONFESS TO BEING PASSIONATE ABOUT THESE salty little creatures. I suspect that those who do not share my enthusiasm tried anchovies as children, when the taste buds are more partial to sweet things, or only know the anchovy fillets that are wrapped around capers and come in little tins of awful-tasting oil. I urge all you doubters out there to give the anchovy another chance.

There is certainly nothing new about anchovies, which have been around for a few thousand years, but what is exciting is that high-quality Australian salted anchovies are once again becoming more available here, due in part to the efforts of the Mendolia family of Fremantle, Western Australia. Even though anchovies have been traditionally associated with the Mediterranean, they have always been abundant in Australian waters but until recently were not caught for anything more than bait, in the main. After some years of problems with supply, Jim Mendolia, who combines traditional European methods of processing and curing anchovies in salt with the latest machinery and equipment, is back in business.

Anchovies are only fished from September to December off the Western Australian coast. Although they are in the waters year-round, they are too small the rest of the year and best left to grow. We have had the chance to learn from the mistakes of others. The Mediterranean has been seriously over-fished and very few anchovies are caught there now; those that are sold for the fresh market come at a high price. Instead, South America supplies the European market with anchovies for salting. The Mendolias keep all theirs for salting, as demand is so high.

If ever you have the chance to buy anchovies fresh, and see anchovies and sardines displayed side by side at a fish market, you will most likely be hard-pressed to tell the difference. A closer look reveals that the anchovy's eyes sit further forward in the head and its mouth is wide open, since its large set of jaws extends past the gills. Both fish are shiny and need to be eaten super-fresh. The fresh anchovy and sardine have white flesh (the red flesh of the salted fish is a result of the curing) and are sold with their guts intact. While the fresh fish

are cooked the same way (grilled with a little extra virgin olive oil and lemon juice is about all you need), the difference is in the entrails. The sardine can be eaten whole, guts and all, but the entrails of the anchovy are very bitter. The trick is to grab the tail and press the sides – the anchovy will split in two and the flesh can be peeled away from the bones. If you wish to gut and fillet a fresh anchovy or sardine, snapping off the head will see most of the innards come away as well. The fish is then split and flattened out and the backbone is peeled away.

Salted anchovies have a firmer, meatier texture than fillets preserved in olive oil and, surprisingly, they taste more of the fish than the salt. When using salted anchovies you must remove the skeleton. I find this most easily done as I am rinsing the anchovies: I simply strip the fillets off the backbone and then pat them dry before sprinkling them with extra virgin olive oil.

Salted anchovies are stunning on their own or they can be used to perk up a dish.

They add bite and saltiness, and, if used judiciously, provide an indefinable dimension without overpowering other flavours. They disappear magically into sauces, providing richness and complexity. Just remember to taste as you go along to ensure balance is maintained. If anchovies are too salty for your purpose, soak them in milk before using.

If you are buying anchovies in oil, consider the oil they are packed in as it will greatly influence the flavour. Only buy in small tins unless you are catering for a crowd as they oxidise soon after opening; whenever I need anchovies, I open a fresh 45 g tin, blotting off the oil they've been stored in before use. A good delicatessen will sell salted anchovies and imported tins of high quality (the Spanish brand Ortiz is worth seeking out). This is a much easier option than trying to find anchovies in good oil.

The Sicilian marriage of pasta with anchovy fillets, sultanas, pine nuts, fennel, garlic, parsley and breadcrumbs produces a dish fit for royalty and can be pulled together at the last moment with the backup of a good store cupboard. If you don't have fennel in the garden or refrigerator, you can use fennel seeds, and you can add tomatoes too, if you wish.

Still talking of pasta, another taste sensation is rape (a variety of *Brassica*) tossed with anchovy fillets, extra virgin olive oil, freshly ground black pepper and lots of fresh Parmigiano Reggiano and served with good-quality dried orecchiette.

For a tomato sauce for pasta, chicken or lamb, sweat chopped onion in a little extra virgin olive oil, then add garlic, chopped canned or really ripe tomatoes, a good dash of verjuice or white wine, a pinch each of sugar and salt and anchovy fillets to taste. Cook until the sauce reaches the consistency you desire, then grind in lots of black pepper, stir in some pitted kalamata olives and lastly drizzle in extra virgin olive oil.

Anchovies are amazing added to eggs in any form. Take soft unsalted butter mixed with finely chopped anchovy fillets, some flat-leaf parsley, a squeeze of lemon juice and some freshly ground black pepper and chill, then top halved hard-boiled free-range eggs with it – better still, pipe it on in a small twirl. Or top the eggs with some tuna and anchovy mayonnaise.

A surprising memory of this mayonnaise came to mind when I was in Tokyo recently on one of my many trips. I went to La Playa, an extraordinary tapas bar run by Toru Kodama (fondly called Carlos), a Japanese chef who had spent seven years in Spain. Every part of the meal was amazing – including the prosciutto Toru had made and matured for five years (the pigs had been fed on acorns!). But the highlight was a tiny variety of capsicum I hadn't seen before that had been roasted and then stuffed with tuna and anchovy mayonnaise. It was simply exquisite.

If you are lucky enough to have fresh anchovies, dust them with seasoned flour and deep-fry them in extra virgin olive oil for literally seconds then serve them hot with a squeeze of lemon juice and a side dish of aïoli.

Anchoïade is a traditional spread from the south of France that is served on croutons. Blend 45 g anchovy fillets, a couple of chopped cloves of garlic, ½ cup flat-leaf parsley, 1 teaspoon red-wine vinegar and some freshly ground black pepper to a paste in a small food processor, then slowly add 80 ml extra virgin olive oil.

At one of our Symposium of Gastronomy evenings held in Adelaide, my friend, chef Cath Kerry, served hot anchovy matches to eat with a glass of champagne before we moved in to view food vignettes from films, both little-known and famous, compiled by Alan Saunders. Cath used a recipe of her mother's to produce a pastry that was as fine as a spring-roll wrapper. A strip of pastry was wound around each anchovy fillet, which was then deep-fried until golden.

Try 1 cm cubes of fresh mozzarella topped with a curled anchovy fillet brushed with extra virgin olive oil, then add a squeeze of lemon juice. Make tiny pizzettas about 4 cm wide from traditional pizza dough, then brush them with extra virgin olive oil and top with a little fresh rosemary before baking at 230°C for 10 minutes. Brush the hot pizzettas with more oil and add a slice of very ripe tomato, a piece of basil and an anchovy fillet. Or serve anchovy fillets with caramelised onion on a crouton or piece of flatbread or in a tart. My favourite is a slab of Sour-cream Pastry (see page 184), pricked and baked on a scone tray and then inhibited during cooking so it doesn't rise too much. Allow to cool for 5 minutes, then top with caramelised onions, anchovies and freshly chopped flat-leaf parsley, and cut into small squares. This is a much less fiddly way of making hors d'oeuvres. Anchovies can also be added to poached chicken, rabbit, tuna or beef.

I so eagerly await that first flush of figs that arrives in December. Once I had masses of garlic that I knew wouldn't last so I roasted the whole heads and then squeezed the garlic out. I chopped anchovies finely and processed them to a paste with the peeled figs and garlic and a squeeze of lemon juice – this was great spread on bread that had been toasted with a smear of extra virgin olive oil.

Croutons with caramelised onion, anchovies and rabbit livers splashed with vino cotto (see page 8)

Where do I begin to choose my favourite anchovy recipes to include here? I love anchovy hollandaise served with rabbit wrapped in vine leaves or with a golden shallot tarte tatin; avocado with a vinaigrette of anchovy fillets, capers and orange rind; guinea fowl in wine with capers, lemon and anchovy fillets – these were all favourites at the Pheasant Farm Restaurant and give an idea of the breadth of the anchovy's repertoire, as do the following recipes.

ANCHOVY MAYONNAISE   *Makes 375 ml*

Try this with poussins that have been barbecued, roasted or poached in stock. I also love it with barbecued kangaroo or pan-fried lamb's brains, but most of all, with veal or rabbit scaloppine.

2–3 anchovy fillets, chopped
2 egg yolks
2 teaspoons Dijon mustard
3 teaspoons white-wine vinegar

1 cup (250 ml) mellow extra virgin olive oil
or half olive and half vegetable oil
sea salt flakes and freshly ground
black pepper

Blend the anchovy fillets in a food processor or blender with the egg yolks, mustard and vinegar for 4–5 seconds or until incorporated. With the motor running, slowly pour in the oil in a thin and steady stream until the mayonnaise thickens and emulsifies. The trick is to do it slowly, so that the mayonnaise doesn't split. Season with salt and pepper and add a dash of hot water to thin and stabilise the mayonnaise, if necessary.

ANCHOVY AND OLIVE BUTTER   *Makes 600 g*

This is an intensely flavoured butter that goes beautifully with quail, rabbit or lamb chops, and keeps for months in the freezer.

1 × 45 g tin anchovy fillets, chopped
300 g black olives, pitted

300 g softened butter
dash brandy

Process the anchovy fillets and olives in a food processor. Add the butter and brandy and blend again to incorporate well. Form the butter mixture into a log, then wrap it in foil or plastic film and chill. Freeze if not using within a few days.

CROUTONS WITH CARAMELISED ONION, ANCHOVIES AND RABBIT LIVERS SPLASHED WITH VINO COTTO *Makes 12 croutons*

If you can't find rabbit livers, you can use chicken livers instead. For this recipe, you'll need 9 chicken livers, as they tend to be smaller than rabbit livers. Remove any greenish bile and cook them whole, then cut them in half once cooked and remove the connective tissue.

125 g unsalted butter

1 French stick, cut diagonally into
    12 × 1.5 cm-thick slices

1 × quantity Caramelised Onions
    (see page 186) *or* 1 × 120 g tub
    Maggie Beer Caramelised Onion

extra virgin olive oil, for drizzling

6 whole rabbit livers, cut in half

sea salt flakes

2 tablespoons vino cotto
    (see Glossary)

6 anchovy fillets, halved

24 sage leaves

freshly ground black pepper, to taste

Preheat the oven to 220°C. Melt 80 g of the butter and brush one side of each bread slice with melted butter, then bake on a baking tray until golden. Meanwhile, gently heat the caramelised onions in a small saucepan over low heat.

Heat the remaining butter in a frying pan until nut-brown, adding a little olive oil to prevent it from burning. Season the livers with salt, then add to the pan with the sage leaves and sear on both sides. Immediately deglaze the pan with the vino cotto.

Quickly assemble the warm croutons. Top each crouton with a spoonful of caramelised onion, place a liver piece on top and brush with the pan juices, then top with an anchovy half, a couple of sage leaves and a drizzle of olive oil and season with freshly ground black pepper.

SASKIA'S FILLET OF BEEF WITH ANCHOVY AND HERB STUFFING *Serves 6*

As a teenager, my daughter Saskia would cook this dish for the whole family on special occasions, and it remains a firm favourite.

2 thick slices white bread, crusts removed
    and discarded

1 large onion, finely chopped

extra virgin olive oil, for cooking

1 × 45 g tin anchovy fillets, well-drained
    and chopped

½ cup flat-leaf parsley, finely chopped

2 sprigs thyme, leaves picked

2 sprigs oregano, leaves picked and chopped

1 sprig rosemary, leaves picked and chopped

1 teaspoon fish sauce

2 teaspoons Worcestershire sauce

75 ml extra virgin olive oil

1 × 1.4 kg fillet of beef

Preheat the oven to 220°C. Toast the bread in the oven until golden brown and leave it to cool. In a food processor, reduce the toast to medium crumbs.

Sweat the onion in a frying pan in a little olive oil over gentle heat until softened. Combine the breadcrumbs, onion, anchovy fillets, herbs, fish sauce, Worcestershire sauce and the 75 ml olive oil in a bowl.

Trim the meat of all fat and sinew and 'butterfly' it open. To do this, cut down the length of the fillet, making sure you only cut halfway through it. Starting at the cut you have just made, turn your knife side on and cut through the fillet towards the edge (but not right through it). Repeat this on the other side, then open out the fillet. Place the stuffing down the middle of the opened-out fillet, then roll the meat back into shape. Tie the fillet with kitchen string, then seal it in a little hot olive oil in a roasting pan on the stove over high heat until browned on all sides. Transfer the roasting pan to the oven and roast the fillet for 12–20 minutes, depending on how well done you like your meat, then leave it to rest for 20 minutes, covered loosely with foil, before carving.

APRICOTS

IT TAKES A LONG WHILE FOR ME TO GET TIRED OF JUST EATING apricots fresh or perhaps poaching them quickly to have with yoghurt for breakfast or as a dessert with cream or ice cream. With soft fruit, the very best way to get it is picked ripe directly from the tree, but buying from a specialist greengrocer or farmers' market that doesn't refrigerate their fruit is the next best thing. Rock-hard stone fruit will soften off the tree and its flavour will develop a little if not refrigerated, though never to its full potential. The taste of refrigerated fruit will always be dulled.

The issue of fruit being picked before it is ripe is a vexed one. Apricots, like other soft fruits, are best when left on the tree to ripen, but the issue of transportation through our vast country and the spoilage that will so obviously occur (when it can take weeks before the fruit gets from farm to final customer) simply means that I suspect the majority of Australians will never truly know how beautiful this fruit can be. Fruit picked under-ripe still develops colour, but only a smidgeon of flavour in comparison – yet how often have I been seduced by the first apricots of the season, large and deep orange (aware of the timing of our own growers' crop, I know these aren't local and so I should resist). Recently, because I needed apricots to make a jam and it was weeks before our local growers would be ready to harvest their perfectly ripe apricots, I bought a box of the 'beautiful looking' apricots and proceeded to try and make a jam, but they were so full of water and lacking in flavour I finished up throwing the jam out. Mental note to myself: follow your nose and wait for the fruit to be perfumed, then flavour will follow.

In late 2012 we bought the orchard across the creek from the Pheasant Farm, from Jim and Margaret Ellis, our neighbours for over forty years. Jim was generous in his advice but it's been a huge learning curve for us as orchards are so much more labour-intensive than the vines. We have 2000 trees now and about one-third of them are apricots, so when a heatwave hits it is all systems go to make as many jars as we can from fruit that has been cut too ripe for drying.

The best jam of all comes from the immediately harvested fruit. Luckily, there are enough trees at different growing stages that we can always find some green-shouldered fruit to add to the overripe so we can get a good set on the jam. The perfume from the jam-making is extraordinary. It's an exciting phase of our life.

The organic movement has been a long time coming and I absolutely applaud it, but my guiding principles are flavour and sustainable agricultural practices, neither of which are exclusive to organic growers. I want to know how my food is grown and, wherever possible, who has grown it. But there has to be balance. Over the years we have had some very wet seasons, when many of our local orchardists would have lost their trees if they hadn't sprayed to combat the diseases brought on by uncharacteristic rain. Growers cannot afford to lose their crops and certainly those I know are only too concerned with doing everything they can to look after their land – this is a vital issue to all.

Here in the Barossa, they often start picking the apricot crop on Christmas Day – which always seemed the height of bad timing. One memorable summer the season was running late, much to the delight of this strong church-going community, who had the rare opportunity to relax and enjoy Christmas Day. That year it took some cajoling to convince a favourite grower to gather the first ripe apricots two days after Christmas! The whole orchard yielded

just half a case of ripe fruit, but the effort was worth it. I piled all the apricots on two oval platters in my kitchen; the perfume of the fruit was so intense there was no way I was going to consign them to the refrigerator. I had special friends for lunch that day and the guest of honour walked in and said, 'Apricots, the smell of South Australia.' Lunch under the willow tree was as simple as lunches always are at Chez Beer, but to everyone's surprise, this time it included dessert (I am not known for my sweet tooth). The apricots had to star, of course, and the dish had to be easy as I was in an unusually relaxed state. So I made an apricot and

mascarpone tart. A bit of planning helped: when I was preparing for Christmas lunch I had made a double lot of Sour-cream Pastry (see page 184) and rolled half of it out to line a tart tin with a removable base, which I then lined with foil and froze. Now I had to remember to have the oven at the right temperature at the right time (which can be a problem if you have had a glass or two of champagne beforehand) to blind bake the pastry at 200°C until golden brown. The halved and stoned apricots, with just a dash of sweet wine poured over them (or just brushed with melted butter), waited in a shallow baking dish ready for the oven to reach 230°C. I baked them for just 4 minutes, then let them cool to room temperature (alternatively, you could place them under a hot grill for 5 minutes). I stirred the juices from the cooled fruit into a cup or two of mascarpone, then spooned this into the prepared tart case. The roasted apricots were positioned rounded-side up and overlapping each other, keeping the mascarpone a secret until the cutting of the tart. A great success!

Having beaten the birds (touch wood) to our apricot harvest this year on our small home block orchard, we haven't yet beaten apricot freckle, which shows up on the fruit's skin as irregular, scaly brown spots. In *The Complete Book of Fruit Growing in Australia*, Louis Glowinski says freckle can be controlled by spraying for brown rot. Next season, I'm going to be armed with an organic spray to try to combat this. All is still not lost, however; the trick is to let the freckly apricots ripen and use them for jam.

Great apricot jam is just one tiny notch under my favourite burnt fig jam. I use 2 kg of the ripest fruit and, to avoid adding any water (which dilutes the flavour of the jam),

I cover the halved fruit with 1 kg sugar and 200 ml lemon juice and leave the mixture overnight. I then cook the jam for as short a time as possible to retain the flavour, taking care that it doesn't burn. Better to have plenty of flavour and sacrifice some of the 'set'.

Apricot jam made like this is a delicacy and should be given pride of place in a more elaborate breakfast: thick pieces of wholemeal toast with lashings of unsalted butter, slathered with jam so full of fruit that you need to squash it down to make it stay on the toast. You do not have to confine it to breakfast: jam like this is worth making scones for and having afternoon tea. A neighbour brought me a flagon of apricot nectar he made from his fruit this season. Expecting it to be super-sweet, I tentatively took my first mouthful, only to find a lovely tartness on the palate. So here is another idea for those apricots that don't make the grade for eating fresh: remove the stones and purée the flesh, then serve the nectar as an aperitif on the rocks, or top with a nice, dry sparkling white wine for a new take on a Bellini.

If you are drawn to the kitchen, Upside-down Apricot Tarts (see page 14) are pretty hard to beat, and make a great summer dessert. I also love the marriage of apricots and almonds, especially in a Crumble (see page 13).

I can't talk about apricots without talking about dried apricots and how wonderful, and endangered, ours are. While I was writing this, my friend Sheri Schubert phoned to organise our annual preserving program, which always starts with apricots. Sheri, an intelligent farmer and committed volunteer in the local Country Fire Service (CFS), always has her finger on the pulse. She told me that the local apricot growers, already hardly making ends meet due to high labour costs, are being paid less again this year for their crop, competing as they are with cheaper imported dried apricots from Turkey. Some are threatening to pull their trees out as they can't afford to stay in business. I urge you to always look to see where your dried apricots come from when you buy. This is not just a matter of buying Australian as a catch-cry, it's about superior flavour and keeping communities and traditions alive.

APRICOT AND ALMOND CRUMBLE
Serves 4

30 large ripe apricots, halved and stoned (about 820g)

sugar, for sprinkling

60 g flaked almonds, lightly roasted

CRUMBLE

125 g flour

100 g sugar

100 g ground almonds

175 g butter

Preheat the oven to 200°C. Arrange the apricot halves in a shallow glass or enamelled baking dish (mine is 25 cm x 16 cm x 3.5 cm). Sprinkle with sugar. Mix the crumble ingredients together in a bowl, rubbing in the butter with your fingers. Spread over the fruit and sprinkle with flaked almonds. Bake for about 30 minutes. Be careful not to burn the flaked almonds – cover with foil or lower the temperature if necessary. Serve warm with cream or ice cream.

HILDA'S APRICOT JAM
Makes about 3 litres

Hilda Laurencis was a very important person to our business and family over almost thirty years. She did everything from dishwashing and food preparation to quail-plucking in the early days of the restaurant, as well as looking after our house. It was Hilda who first made pâté with me using small domestic food processors – we burnt out many a motor together. Hilda retired three times, always deciding to come back, announcing she was bored. This happened in the early days of our export kitchen, where she would lend a hand when we went through the busiest times, and up until three years ago Hilda still helped each week with housekeeping. In all this time she would keep my store cupboard stocked with one of her jams. Just as we finished one, another would appear. Even in her late seventies, Hilda still kept her hand in helping my daughter Saskia one morning a week, and carried on the tradition of bringing the pot of jam, a bag of lemons or a bunch of flowers, that just 'appeared'. Hilda's apricot jam was an undisputed family favourite. We all owe her so much.

5 kg apricots, cut into quarters and stoned   3 kg sugar

Cook the apricots in a large saucepan with 750 ml water on high heat for about 20 minutes or until they are 'all mashed up'. Add the sugar and cook for another 30 minutes, taking care not to burn them. Bottle in sterilised jars (see Glossary).

UPSIDE-DOWN APRICOT TARTS

Serves 2

This is a favourite dish from Jenny Ferguson's book *Cooking for You and Me*. For several years, Jenny ran a wonderful restaurant in Sydney called You and Me and when she finally closed her doors she wrote this book as a record of her time at the stoves. These tarts are extremely versatile. I use two 14 cm tart tins but they can be made smaller or larger, as you please. Plums can be substituted for the apricots, or in winter try rounds of Granny Smith apples.

Rough Puff Pastry leftovers (see page 98)
125 g castor sugar, plus extra, for sprinkling

50 g unsalted butter
6 ripe apricots, halved and stoned

Preheat the oven to 190°C. Roll out your pastry very thinly and cut out 2 circles that are just a bit wider than the tops of your tart tins. Chill the pastry rounds while you prepare the apricots.

Put the sugar and 250 ml water in a frying pan and cook to a light-golden caramel over low–medium heat. Add the butter. Let this mixture bubble for a couple of minutes without stirring, then add the apricots, cooking them for 3 minutes on each side.

Put the apricots, rounded-side down, in the bottom of the tins and cover with the caramel butter. Do not fill quite to the top. Drape a pastry circle over the top of each tin and sprinkle with some of the extra sugar. Put the tins on a baking tray to catch any spills, and bake for about 20 minutes or until the pastry is crisp.

To serve, trim off the excess pastry edges and turn upside-down (so that the pastry is now underneath) on to serving plates. Serve with thick fresh cream or crème anglaise.

DRIED APRICOT AND FRANGIPANE TARTS

Makes 4 × 22 cm tarts

This recipe is great if you are cooking for a crowd as it makes 4 large tarts or between 46 and 48 tiny cocktail tarts. If you wish to make tiny tarts, follow the same process and use smaller tins such as half-moon cake moulds, then press a dried apricot in the centre of each tart and bake for 15 minutes only.

2 × quantities Sour-cream Pastry
  (see page 184)
200 g dried apricots (about 48)
200 ml verjuice
480 g butter

480 g castor sugar
8 free-range eggs
480 g freshly ground almonds
120 g plain flour

Preheat the oven to 200°C. Make and chill the pastry as instructed. Roll out to fill four 22 cm tart tins, then cover and chill in the refrigerator for 20 minutes. Line the pastry cases with foil and weights and blind bake for 10 minutes, then remove the foil and weights and bake for a further 5 minutes.

Meanwhile, soak the dried apricots in the verjuice for 30 minutes.

Reset the oven to 180°C. To make the frangipane filling beat the butter and sugar together until lightly creamed. Beat the eggs in a separate bowl, then stir a little at a time into the butter mixture until all the egg is added, making sure the mixture doesn't curdle. In another bowl, combine the ground almonds and flour, then add this to the butter and egg mixture and mix well.

Drain the apricots, reserving the verjuice. Place the frangipane filling in the tart cases and divide the drained apricots among the tarts, pressing them gently into the filling. Brush the reserved verjuice over the apricots, then bake the tarts on baking trays for 25 minutes or until a toothpick inserted in the centre of the tarts comes out clean.

MUSTARD APRICOTS   *Makes 1 litre*

This recipe uses dried apricots; however it can also be made using very firm fresh apricots, peaches, small figs, cherries or glacé fruit. I serve these mustard fruits with pâtés, terrines, rillettes or cold meats, especially legs of sugar-cured ham or baked hands of pork.

400 g dried apricots	1 cinnamon stick
¾ cup (180 ml) boiling water	3 sprigs lemon thyme
50 g Keen's dried mustard powder	2 cups (440 g) sugar
1⅔ cups (410 ml) lemon juice	1 tablespoon finely grated horseradish
finely grated rind of 1 lemon	

Sterilise two 500 ml-capacity jars (see Glossary). Put the apricots in a bowl with the boiling water and leave to soak for 1 hour. Drain the apricots and transfer to a large bowl, reserving ⅓ cup (80 ml) of the soaking liquid.

Put the mustard powder, lemon juice, lemon rind, cinnamon, lemon thyme, sugar and the reserved soaking liquid in a saucepan and bring to the boil, then simmer over low heat for 10 minutes. Stir the horseradish in to this syrup, and pour immediately over the soaked apricots, then transfer straightaway to the sterilised jars.

Leave to mature for at least 1 week before using. Unopened jars of mustard apricots will keep for up to 12 months, although the apricots will darken a little.

BASIL

IT IS INCREDIBLE TODAY TO THINK THAT BASIL WAS ONCE considered exotic, but I remember well my first encounter with a bunch of basil: it was as large as a bouquet and amazingly intoxicating. It was presented to me by Janet Jeffs in the early 80s after she'd come to work with me at the Pheasant Farm Restaurant. This was a critical and incredibly exciting period – a real coming of age for us. Janet would often walk in with trays of velvety field mushrooms, buckets of watercress and all manner of fresh goodies from our friend Susan Hackett's farm at Ngapala, just north of the Barossa. Janet later gave me the confidence to move from the *table d'hôte* menu to *à la carte* and together we cooked anything that came to hand.

Even though there are many different basils available, I tend to grow and use the well-known sweet basil and the purple-leafed variety known as red or opal-leafed basil. I find that small leaves are packed with more flavour than the huge elephant's ears you sometimes see, and continually picking the basil helps to keep the leaves small. If you have a surplus of basil you can store whole leaves layered with salt and covered with extra virgin olive oil. This keeps the flavour of the basil, but it will lose some of its colour; omitting the salt will keep the colour, but remember that olive oil is not a preservative. When adding basil to a hot dish, tear the leaves and add at the last moment, as the heat reduces the pungency of the herb.

The first time I ever served a cold pasta dish in the restaurant was when we had a wonderful party to celebrate our tenth birthday. It was mid-January 1989, so we were surrounded by ripe, ripe tomatoes, and so much basil had been planted between the roses to keep aphids at bay that we were losing the war of nipping the tops off to save the plants from going to seed. (I've since learnt that growing basil in the shade stops it from going to seed.) As the whole basis of my cooking has always been to use what is in season, basil featured in three dishes that day, and its sweet, spicy perfume pervaded the whole room.

We made Duck Egg Pasta (see page 183), our old staple, in 500 g batches, smothering each cooked and drained batch with extra virgin olive oil to stop the pasta sticking as it cooled.

Salsa agresto (see page 20)

Tomatoes were cut into chunks, neither skinned nor seeded, and left to sit a while with lots of freshly plucked basil, salt, freshly ground black pepper and fruity extra virgin olive oil to make their own highly perfumed juice. (In those days I bought my olive oil by the flagon from Angle Vale in South Australia but for the last twenty years we've had our own olive grove at the farm and another at home.) At the last minute, the lot was tossed with the cooled pasta and served. This sauce is just as good with hot pasta, and can be extended in a number of ways: consider adding finely chopped red onion; or perhaps anchovy fillets and pitted olives; or even fresh ricotta or crumbled feta.

I also chopped up lots of basil to knead into gnocchi dough. After the gnocchi were poached, I pan-fried them in nut-brown butter and added lashings of Parmigiano Reggiano before taking the dish to the table.

For the final basil dish we made a pizza dough, rolled it flat and filled it with pitted black olives, roasted garlic cloves and masses of basil leaves, all anointed with extra virgin olive oil, before pulling it together like a large old-fashioned purse. The first cut after baking released a wonderful aroma as the olives came tumbling out.

It's amazing how smell can trigger evocative memories. All I need to do is brush past a basil plant and its gloriously pervasive perfume takes me straight back to that day. It was a great party and quite a milestone for us.

Jill Stone, who ran Herbivorous, a commercial herb garden in Adelaide, was a great asset to restaurateurs; we could never have grown enough of all the herbs we needed for the Pheasant Farm Restaurant. Basil was, of course, a standard for her, which means she had tremendous amounts of basil wood (the branches that form on commercially grown plants) left at the end of each season. Once Jill and I thought it would be a great idea to use this wood for grilling, but I couldn't find a chipper strong enough to take it without breaking! The basil wood sat in our shed for years; we eventually grilled quail over it and, amazingly, that wonderful perfume was still there.

If you are barbecuing a good piece of rump steak and happen to have a basil plant to hand, pluck a few leaves as you prepare to turn the meat for its final cooking. Brush the meat with extra virgin olive oil, season it with freshly ground black pepper and add a few basil leaves, then turn it over to finish cooking. Allow the cooked meat to rest before eating.

Basil and rabbit have a great affinity. I sometimes buy rabbit fillets off the bone to make a wonderfully quick meal. I arrange three or four large basil leaves, perfect-side down, along a piece of caul fat (nature's Gladwrap, says my friend Cath Kerry!) and place two fat rabbit fillets together end to end on top of the basil leaves to form an even 'log', then wrap up the meat with the caul fat. I pan-fry these tiny parcels for about 2 minutes a side, then allow them to rest before serving them with the sauce from Rabbit Saddle with Basil Cream Sauce (see page 21). I do seem fixated on rabbit, but one of my favourite ever dishes is a fresh pasta I make with black olives speckled through it, served with a rabbit 'sauce'. I pan-fry sliced rabbit fillets with rabbit kidneys and liver for just seconds in nut-brown butter and then set them aside. I add a bit of Dijon mustard to the pan and deglaze with verjuice before returning the rabbit to the pan, throwing in masses of freshly torn basil, seasoning it well and tossing it with the pasta.

I once made an exception to my rule of only adding basil to a dish at the last moment when making a pigeon terrine. I layered the mould with super-fine pieces of smoked pork fat, pigeon, livers and basil. This was then cooked in a water bath at a fairly low temperature and refrigerated to set. The perfume of the basil lingered for the whole week that the terrine stayed fresh enough to use.

PESTO

Makes 375 ml

For an explosion of flavour, float a spoonful of pesto as a raft in a vegetable soup as the French do (they call it pistou), or stir into minestrone like the Italians do. Pesto with pasta is so simple a dish it could almost be labelled convenience food, yet it is healthy and packed with flavour. Pesto can also be tossed with just-cooked green beans: drizzle a dash of extra virgin olive oil over the beans and then sprinkle on a couple of drops of your best balsamic vinegar.

Many years ago I used a mortar and pestle for pounding my basil, but I confess that time and a bad shoulder have the better of me now and I most often make pesto in the food processor. However, whenever I can convince a helper, I am reminded that making it by hand is so worth the effort; it engages you in the aroma from beginning to end, and gives a better texture and colour. Eating pesto the moment it is made is perfection.

I invariably have difficulty preventing my pesto from oxidising after a few days, finding the recommendation to cover it with a film of oil never quite sufficient (although a splash of lemon juice will help if you are planning to store it). For this reason, when basil is abundant, I often resort to making a paste with the basil, pine nuts and oil and then freezing it in tiny plastic pots with a good seal. The pots can be defrosted in hot water and then mixed with the grated cheese and garlic (garlic shouldn't be frozen as its composition will change) and perhaps a little more oil and seasoning.

100 g pine nuts

¾ cup (180 ml) extra virgin olive oil

2 cloves garlic

1 cup firmly packed basil leaves

50 g freshly grated Parmigiano Reggiano

50 g freshly grated pecorino

sea salt flakes and freshly ground
   black pepper

squeeze of lemon juice (optional)

Dry-roast the pine nuts in a frying pan over medium–high heat until golden, tossing frequently to prevent burning. Put ¼ cup olive oil and the remaining ingredients in a food processor and blend to a paste, then check the seasoning and stir in the remaining oil.

SALSA AGRESTO

1 cup (160 g) almonds
1 cup (100 g) walnuts
2 cloves garlic
2¾ cups flat-leaf parsley leaves
½ cup firmly packed basil leaves

1½ teaspoons sea salt flakes
freshly ground black pepper
¾ cup (180 ml) extra virgin olive oil
¾ cup (180 ml) verjuice

Preheat the oven to 200°C. Roast the almonds and walnuts on separate baking trays for about 5 minutes, shaking to prevent burning. Rub walnuts in a tea towel to remove bitter skins, then leave to cool. Blend the nuts, garlic, herbs, salt and 6 grinds of black pepper in a food processor with a little of the olive oil. With the motor running, slowly add the remaining oil and verjuice. The consistency should be like pesto. (If required, thin with more verjuice.)

BASIL, ANCHOVY AND ZUCCHINI PASTA

You could use my Duck Egg Pasta for this dish (see page 183).

400 g (about 12) small zucchini,
   about 8 cm long
sea salt flakes
500 g fresh *or* dried pasta
extra virgin olive oil, for cooking

juice of 1 lemon
freshly ground black pepper
12 anchovy fillets, chopped
20 basil leaves
100 g freshly grated pecorino

Bring a large saucepan of water to the boil for the pasta. Bring another pan of water to the boil, then salt it and cook the whole zucchini for just a few minutes. Remove the zucchini and leave to cool for 5 minutes.

Meanwhile, add 2 tablespoons salt to the pasta pan. Slide the pasta gently into the pan as the water returns to the boil, then partially cover with a lid to bring it to a rapid boil. Cook pasta following the manufacturer's instructions (the cooking times can differ), stirring to keep it well separated (a tablespoon of olive oil in the water can help this too). If using fresh pasta, it only needs to cook for 3 minutes or so. Drain the pasta and transfer to a serving bowl. Reserve a little of the cooking water in case you want to moisten the completed dish. Do not run the pasta under water or you'll lose the precious starch that helps the oil adhere.

Slice each zucchini lengthways into 2 or 3 (depending on their thickness), drizzle with olive oil, squeeze on lemon juice and grind on black pepper, then add to the pasta. Toss the anchovies through the pasta with the basil, pecorino and another drizzle of olive oil. If the pasta needs moistening, add a little of the reserved cooking water. Serve immediately.

RABBIT SADDLE WITH BASIL CREAM SAUCE
Serves 4

Many years ago I read somewhere a recipe of Barbara Santich's for rabbit with basil. I no longer have the notes from that recipe but this is how the dish has evolved over the years.

4 saddles of farmed rabbit (on the bone)	100 ml Golden Chicken Stock
4 golden shallots, thinly sliced	(see page 55)
extra virgin olive oil, for cooking	1 cup firmly packed basil leaves
freshly ground black pepper	⅓ cup (80 ml) cream
100 ml verjuice	sea salt flakes

Preheat the oven to 200°C. Take the sinew off the top of each saddle by slipping the sharpest knife possible (a flexible boning knife, if you have it) under the skin and pulling the membrane away. (This is similar to taking the sinew off a fillet of beef.)

Sauté the shallots very gently in a frying pan in a little olive oil (taking care not to brown them), then paint the saddles with the shallots and oil and sprinkle black pepper over them. Place the saddles in a roasting pan, meat-side up, with a fair amount of space between each one. (If they are too close they will poach rather than roast.)

Heat the verjuice in a small saucepan over high heat and reduce by half. Add the chicken stock and continue to reduce. While the verjuice and stock are reducing, bake the saddles for 8–12 minutes, then transfer them to a warm serving dish and turn them over (bone-side up) to rest, loosely covered. Tear or snip the basil into thin strips. Pour the reduced stock mixture into the roasting pan, place over high heat on the stove and add the cream. Once the sauce is boiling vigorously, add the basil and adjust the seasoning. Serve the sauce over the rabbit saddles with some boiled waxy potatoes and a green salad alongside.

BEANS

THE BEGINNING OF SUMMER IS HERALDED BY THE BEST stringless beans available. Look for specimens that are round, about 10 cm long and bright green (these are not always easy to find). All you need to do is cook them in boiling salted water for a few minutes and then toss them with butter and herbs.

Butter beans are their own taste sensation – a very distinctive flavour. They are a pale, buttery colour and are best when not left to grow too long.

Damper climates may be more successful at growing snake beans than we are in South Australia. They tend to be coarser in Adelaide than in Melbourne, but are still very interesting. They can be found in good greengrocers and in Asian supermarkets. Dark green in colour, they 'snake' over the plate and I love the look of astonishment on people's faces when I serve them.

Flat beans are my beans of the moment – perfectly flat and bright green. I prefer them to any stringless beans I have bought from a greengrocer. If cooked for just a few minutes in boiling salted water and then tossed in preserved lemon butter with some freshly ground black pepper, they are crisp, juicy and delicious.

If truth be told, I wasn't a fan of beans until I fell under the spell of Tuscany, whose inhabitants are known to the rest of Italy as the 'bean eaters' or *mangiafagioli*. The catalyst was a dish of fresh cannellini beans, enjoyed at Cantinetta Antinori in Florence a couple of years ago. They had been simmered for 20 minutes with a bay leaf and garlic, before being strained, then drizzled with new-season extra virgin olive oil. I have to confess that I would never have been seduced if it hadn't been for the extra virgin olive oil. As it made contact with the hot purée, the aromas and flavours exploded; I was hooked. The beans, a creamy light-green colour, were unadorned except for the oil, some sea salt and freshly ground black pepper, and came with crusty bread – a timely reminder of how good 'simple' can be.

Flat green beans with preserved lemon butter and freshly ground black pepper (see opposite)

Broad beans engender passion in some people. There are those who hate them and those who love them. My children hate them – they must have had a deprived childhood!

Growing up, I had two very special 'maiden aunts' who shared a house. Auntie Reta did the cooking, usually a roast, and Auntie Glad was a 'school marm' in the traditional sense. Auntie Glad knew herself to be a good headmistress but a particularly bad cook, so she learnt, practised and delivered a repertoire of just two main courses, chicken casserole and a veal dish, and two desserts. (The desserts were Spanish cream and a very sherried trifle.) Neither of the main course dishes was one that I enjoyed but I did understand the love that went into their preparation, and the saving grace was that she used vegetables in season straight from their back garden. One of Auntie Glad's favourites, and mine, was the broad bean, and they were never double-peeled. It was a long time before I discovered that 'in the very best places' the skin was peeled from the broad beans after podding. To many, the sheer beauty of the surprising bright green of a peeled broad bean might be worth the effort, but the flavour is quite different and, as so many food memories are evocative, I'll stick to them unskinned.

At the restaurant I would often serve a very simple country dish of unpeeled broad beans. With the addition of good extra virgin olive oil and perhaps some Parmigiano Reggiano and crusty bread, I would never even consider peeling the beans as they were so sweet from being freshly picked by my neighbours.

Broad beans eaten fresh from the garden, before their sugar turns to starch and the skins toughen, are a defining flavour worth seeking out. If, when you pod them, the second skin around the bean is quite white, it is a sure sign the bean will be old and tough. If this happens, I would cook them to smithereens, purée them with some fresh herbs, salt and freshly ground black pepper, then add a good drizzle of extra virgin olive oil. In fact, this is also how I handle dried broad beans (see opposite). The purée can then be turned into a soup or the base of a meal – a grilled lamb chop on a bed of broad bean purée, made of either the beans themselves or the beans and pods, sounds pretty good to me. The pods should be bright green, crisp to the touch and without blemishes. It is best to buy them under 10 cm long. If you grow them yourself, try cooking small ones, pod and all, and tossing them with butter and fresh herbs. The smallest ones are also perfect eaten raw.

Fresh, tender broad beans team well with other spring delights such as artichokes, asparagus and fresh peas. Try braising them together in a little extra virgin olive oil and water. Start with the artichokes, then add the asparagus and broad beans. Lastly, you could add some freshly shelled peas. Adjust the flavour with a little verjuice and seasoning and serve warm as a complete dish.

In Tuscany there is a spring tradition of serving broad beans with a fresh pecorino as soon as they ripen. The pecorino is cut into thick slices and served with the beans, and the guests pod the beans as they eat them. There is a saltiness to the fresh pecorino that I imagine beautifully complements the sweetness of the young broad beans.

Broad beans are also called fava beans and are available dried (and sometimes already double-peeled); like other dried beans, they need soaking before use. If soaking dried beans, choose a bowl at least double the volume of the beans you are soaking. Fill the bowl to the top with water and soak the beans for at least 12 hours. If you have left your run too late for that, you can bring them to the boil over high heat in a saucepan of water, then cook for 2 minutes, remove from the heat and let stand for 2–3 hours, before draining and beginning your recipe.

For one of the simplest dishes, try gently sautéing some onions in olive oil with fresh herbs such as bay leaves until the onions are translucent. Season to taste with freshly ground black pepper and add a preserved lemon quarter to the pan (lemon is very much

an extra, but old Florentine recipes often include this, or a dash of vinegar, to add piquancy). Add the soaked and drained broad beans and a few whole garlic cloves and cover with water or light chicken stock and 125 ml extra virgin olive oil. Bring to a simmer and cook very slowly, covered, over low heat for 1½–2 hours or until the beans are totally soft, stirring often and adding more liquid if necessary (a simmer mat placed under the pan helps to control the heat – you want to simmer the beans, not boil them). Drain the beans, reserving a few tablespoons of the cooking liquid. Season with salt and pepper, then either

serve as an accompaniment with a swirl of extra virgin olive oil and freshly chopped flat-leaf parsley, or purée with a few tablespoons of extra virgin olive oil. The amount of oil added depends on whether the purée is to accompany a grill or is to be served as an entrée with crusty bread and a salad – the latter can take a bit more. You can also use this method with haricot, borlotti or cannellini beans.

On days when I feel a bit extravagant, I simmer soaked beans for about 30 minutes, then transfer them to a pot I bought in Tuscany, adding lavish amounts of olive oil. This glazed terracotta vessel is hourglass-shaped, with handles on each side and a tight-fitting lid, and is designed especially for long, slow cooking. Traditionally this would have been used in a wood-fired oven after baking the bread, when most of the heat had dissipated (hence the need to use a simmer mat on the stove). The last time I used this pot I put simmered cannellini beans in with a little chicken stock, some ends of pancetta and a few of the whole garlic cloves that were simmered with the beans, then seasoned it and covered the lot with extra virgin olive oil. It actually did not take an amazing amount of oil (about 190 ml) and I justified using it because it was from the end of a drum. Cooked this way, the beans can take anything from 1–3 hours; and are, by the way, delicious.

This idea can be extended to make a pasta sauce by cooking fennel and pork with the beans, removing them before puréeing the beans, cutting the fennel and pork into pieces

and adding them back to the purée. Or it can be turned into a soup by adding peeled roma tomatoes, using more stock in place of the oil and adding fennel and garlic during cooking. Spoon the soup over a piece of toasted stale (but good) bread and add a swirl of extra virgin olive oil, lots of flat-leaf parsley, sea salt flakes and freshly ground black pepper – you won't need anything more to satisfy your hunger.

Fresh borlotti beans, and perhaps cannellini beans, are often only available to those who shop in autumn markets. Dried beans, however, are widely available, flavourful and inexpensive, yet I suspect are ignored by many who don't realise how wonderful they can be when cooked with care.

DRIED BROAD BEAN PASTE BRUSCHETTA WITH EXTRA VIRGIN OLIVE OIL
Serves 12

It is possible to buy dried fava or broad beans that have already been double-peeled in some Middle Eastern stores. If you can't get these, and you own a mouli, then cook them unpeeled and pass them through the mouli. Alternatively, if you purée the beans in a food processor or blender, then the skins will be part of the dish.

200 g dried broad (fava) beans
1 onion, roughly chopped
2 cloves garlic, peeled
rind of 1 lemon
extra virgin olive oil, for cooking
lemon juice, to taste

sea salt flakes and freshly ground
　black pepper
12 × 1 cm-thick slices sourdough bread
1 clove garlic, halved
½ cup freshly chopped flat-leaf parsley

Put broad beans, onion, garlic and lemon rind in a heavy-based saucepan, then cover with a generous amount of cold water. Simmer over low heat for about 1 hour or until the beans are cooked through. Drain the beans and remove the rind, then pass the beans through a mouli or purée in a food processor, adding enough extra virgin olive oil to form a thick paste. Add as much lemon juice as your taste dictates, then season with salt and pepper. Leave to cool to room temperature.

Just before serving, toast the sliced bread on both sides on a chargrill pan or barbecue over high heat. Immediately rub the cut garlic clove over the toast, then drizzle the toast with olive oil and season to taste with salt and pepper.

Spoon a generous amount of broad bean paste on top of each slice of warm bruschetta, then finish with a final flourish of extra virgin olive oil and lots of chopped flat-leaf parsley.

GREEN BEAN SALAD   *Serves 4*

250 g green beans	sea salt flakes and freshly ground
100 ml walnut oil	black pepper
2 tablespoons verjuice	120 g thinly sliced prosciutto
	80 g walnuts, roasted and skins rubbed

Cook the beans for a few minutes in a saucepan of boiling salted water until they are cooked through but still bright green. Previously I would have said cook until al dente, but my view has changed as truly al dente is undercooked, and the bean only releases its flavour when it is just cooked (this is one vegetable I would refresh under cool water immediately to stop the cooking and keep as much colour as possible). Make a vinaigrette by whisking together the walnut oil, verjuice, salt and pepper. Drape prosciutto over a serving plate. Toss the beans and walnuts in the vinaigrette and pile onto the prosciutto.

BROAD BEANS WITH PASTA AND PROSCIUTTO   *Serves 4*

2 kg fresh young broad beans, shelled	1 cup (70 g) toasted breadcrumbs
½ cup (125 ml) extra virgin olive oil	150 g prosciutto, cut into strips
sea salt flakes and freshly ground	½ cup freshly chopped mint
black pepper	1 tablespoon red-wine vinegar
250 g fresh pasta sheets (I use handmade fine	
ravioli dough cut into 6 cm × 4 cm sheets)	

Bring a large saucepan of salted water to the boil in readiness for the pasta. Simmer the beans in a saucepan with just enough water to cover, a dash of the oil and a pinch of salt for 7–10 minutes or until just cooked. Meanwhile, cook the pasta sheets in the saucepan of boiling water and drain them (do not refresh, as this removes flavour). Put the sheets on to a plate or dish large enough to spread them out and drizzle with a little olive oil to stop any further cooking.

Drain the beans immediately when they're cooked and, while still warm, transfer to a bowl and stir in the breadcrumbs, prosciutto and remaining olive oil. Add the room-temperature pasta. Balance seasoning with salt and pepper, if needed, then add the mint, and perhaps some more olive oil, along with the vinegar. Serve at room temperature.

CAPERS

WHEN I WAS YOUNG I WOULD PICK CAPERS OUT OF A DISH AND put them to one side. Considering my interest in them now, my early dislike of capers might have been an issue of acquired taste, but I think it might also have been because neither they nor the medium in which they were packed were of particularly good quality.

I first found capers to be irresistible when I came across the small ones imported from the Aeolian Islands near Sicily. These intensely flavoured, unopened flower buds of the caper bush comprise almost the entire food production of these islands, where the growers have formed co-operatives to market their capers worldwide. Caper varieties range from these exquisite tiny ones to plumper olive-green buds, and, if packed in the right medium, they can add piquancy to an amazing array of foods.

The caper bush is an attractive plant that thrives in the Mediterranean region, where it can be seen, often straggling and vine-like, growing wild out of old walls, rocks and even piles of rubbish. About a metre high, it has tough, oval-shaped leaves and exquisite pink or white flowers that carry a tassel of long purple stamens. Sadly, the flowers hardly last, but through summer the bush is green and succulent. It is a hardy plant that needs very little water to thrive. Although my six caper bushes give so little in comparison to the volume I devour, they do make a lovely addition to the garden, and bounced back coura-geously one year after having been completely decimated by caterpillars. My sort of plant! They are a great plant for terracotta pots in stone courtyards.

There is a world of difference in the quality of capers brought into Australia – the majority of which are shipped in bulk in brine and bottled here. The most exciting thing for me about capers is that they are now grown commercially in Mannum, South Australia, first by Jonathon Trewartha, a mining engineer-turned-farmer. Jonathon tells me it was one of the articles I wrote on capers during my four-year stint writing a weekly column on food for *The Australian* that inspired him. I threw out a challenge, questioning why we weren't growing capers in Australia when there were many areas with a similar climate to that of the Mediterranean. At the time we imported more than 100 tonnes of capers a year so it was clear that the demand was there. Years later, I'll never forget the day in Mildura when those of us interested in slow food were gathered for the first time. We were sitting on my friend Stefano de Pieri's newly renovated riverboat to hear of his dream of the Murray becoming the 'Slow River' and to hear other speakers on slow food, one of them being Jonathon Trewartha of the Australian Caper Company. When Jonathon and his wife Samantha approached me before proceedings began, and gave me the first jar of salted capers they'd produced, I felt like I'd won the lottery. Taking them home and finding out just how good they were completed the circle. I now only hope that this can be made into a viable agricultural pursuit.

The Australian Caper Company (www.australiancapers.com.au) grow their capers organically using minimal water on the dry rocky slopes of the Murray River near Mannum, combining ancient techniques with modern research. The hardy caper bush, with a deep root system that uses very little water, is grown on land so degraded by salinity it could grow almost nothing else (except saltbush). The capers are picked at first light

every day throughout the hot summer months, and are then cured in their own juices and repackaged in salt, and sold that same season; they are therefore fresher, firmer and more flavoursome than the imported product.

Then there is Brian Noone, a nurseryman formerly of Cottage Herbs in Angle Vale, South Australia, who won a Churchill Fellowship to study caper propagation in the Mediterranean, and in this he found his calling. Since his return, he has successfully bred a caper he's called the 'Eureka', and has protected it with plant-breeder rights.

Brian already supplies the Eureka to the Australian Caper Company, and he also plans to release it to the home gardener as a variety with a long flowering cycle (from early summer through to winter), and a yield of between 5 and 7 kg of capers from each bush. Brian has fielded interest in the plant from as far afield as Morocco, Israel and Syria. Other than the high-end position occupied by the Australian Caper Company, which supplies discerning buyers with the freshest capers, Brian feels that it will be difficult for the Australian industry to compete with cheap imports of bulk capers because of our high labour costs and lack of access to the innovative and very expensive picking equipment used overseas. For more information on Brian's capers, you can visit his website, www.caperplants.com.

Don't ever think farming is easy; Deirdre Baum from Laharum Grover near the Grampians National Park in northwest Victoria, started growing capers to the same organic principles as the olive trees on her farm.

The caper plants were thriving, however flood and fires in the Grampians have meant she is no longer selling capers.

Caperberries, which are also now readily available, are the result of a berry forming when the bud is not picked for capers but left to flower – just like a rosehip. The oval, olive-green caperberry varies from the size of a small fingernail to that of an olive and is sold as a pickle on quite a long stem. They're an acquired taste, combining the flavour of a caper with the crispness of a water chestnut, but they can be a great addition to an antipasto plate or a dish of rich pork rillettes. However, the limiting factor with imported caperberries is that they are only as good as the vinegar and brine mixture they're sold in.

The exciting thing is that the Trewathas have helped to establish a new industry, though small by its nature; so exciting in its value and there are more farmers involved now. The first Australian caperberries, so crisp and slightly sweet, are so much better than anything I've seen imported. Now other growers, some of them inspired by the Trewatha's have used the capers in other products. Kolophon Capers from Berri in the Riverland a few years ago submitted their caper salt and preserved caper leaves to the Delicious Produce Awards and we were delighted by the flavour and the ingenuity of using every bit of the plant.

If you ever get the chance to preserve your own capers, dissolve 125 g salt in 500 ml hot water, then leave the solution to cool before immersing the capers in it for a week. Drain off the brine, then cover with a good-quality vinegar and leave for 4–5 days.

Salted capers need to be washed very gently, in order to eliminate excess salt without breaking the buds. I find using a sieve is the best way – not under running water but by immersing them in a bowl of clean water, which is changed several times between dunks.

Capers are incredibly versatile. They may be most commonly known as an accompaniment to smoked salmon with sliced onion and rye bread, but that is just the beginning. They marry well with pork, their tart saltiness cutting the richness of the meat, and they are a strong contrast to the gentle flavour of veal and rabbit. They are a natural partner to fish, and a vital ingredient in tartare sauce. Boiled vegetables can be taken to another dimension with the addition of some capers, extra virgin olive oil and flat-leaf parsley. Pasta tossed with capers, flat-leaf parsley, roasted garlic cloves, and extra virgin olive oil is a delicious dish that can be prepared in minutes.

If a meal is needed from the pantry in a hurry, just open a can of tuna in olive oil (at present, only Italian tuna in oil is of a quality I would use but perhaps the Port Lincoln fishermen will take a leaf from the caper bush . . .) and a bottle of preserved tomatoes or a can of good-quality peeled tomatoes and reduce them to a sauce with some fresh herbs and extra virgin olive oil. Toss the sauce through hot pasta with some capers: 15 minutes tops, and you're sitting at the table with a glass of red.

Extend mashed hard-boiled egg yolks with mayonnaise, a dash of lemon juice and chopped capers and serve it in the halved hard-boiled egg whites as great finger food. Capers cut up into a good homemade mayonnaise and served with waxy potatoes or tomatoes make a wonderful luncheon dish.

It makes sense that capers combine well with most Mediterranean ingredients – olive oil, eggplants, red capsicums, anchovies and tuna, to name a few. Tapenade, originally from Provence, is a delicious paste made from capers, olives, anchovy fillets, garlic and olive oil that's perfect for spreading on crusty bread or serving with crisp raw vegetables.

Capers are often teamed with anchovies, as in Vitello Tonnato. To make something

a little less complicated to partner a simmering fowl, sweat a finely chopped onion in 1 tablespoon extra virgin olive oil and a knob of butter, then add 4 chopped anchovy fillets, 1 tablespoon capers and 60 ml verjuice and reduce over medium heat until amalgamated. Add a squeeze of lemon juice and some freshly chopped flat-leaf parsley, then season and serve alongside the carved bird.

Many years ago at a Yalumba cooking class, chef Gay Bilson prepared a roulade of eggplant and capsicum with capers. It was such a classically simple dish that I have since made it time and time again – it's so perfect as an entrée or to take on a picnic. She roasted and peeled red capsicums, deep-fried sliced eggplant and chopped lots of flat-leaf parsley. She then laid a large rectangular piece of plastic film on a tea towel and covered it with pieces of eggplant so that they overlapped like roof tiles. Gay then covered the eggplant with the capsicum, laid flat, and sprinkled over the parsley, some salt and pepper and extra virgin olive oil, then scattered on capers and added a touch of balsamic vinegar. Using the plastic film to guide her, she rolled the lot up like a jelly roll, then chilled it before cutting. I like to serve slices of the roll with lots of tiny capers and some extra sea salt flakes alongside. You could also make this into a light meal by serving it with goat's cheese on croutons and a salad of peppery rocket.

Looking through my old menus from the Pheasant Farm Restaurant recently, I relived just some of the dishes in which capers featured: smoked kingfish with capers; tuna pot-roasted in olive oil with tomato, sorrel and capers (a dish by Janni Kyritsis I once had at Berowra Waters Inn); calf's tongue with capers; free-range chicken simmered in stock and served with a caper sauce; rabbit in many guises with capers, olives and anchovies; and, of course, one of the classics, poached brains pan-fried in nut-brown butter with capers and parsley. How could you live without them?

CHICKEN LEGS WITH CAPERBERRIES, RAISINS, GREEN OLIVES AND ROASTED ALMONDS

Serves 6–8

I'm always presented with plenty of chicken thighs and legs by my daughter Saskia who has her amazing chickens, chooks really, raised on the edge of the Barossa to her requirements. There is always more demand for the breast than the marylands, which suits me fine. I much prefer the leg to the breast, and often cook it along with lots of other good ingredients in one of my terracotta pots, and serve it straight from the oven as a complete dish.

I pulled this dish together for one of the early weeks of filming for *The Cook and The Chef* and was thrilled to have at hand some of the best raisins I've ever tasted from Tabletop Grapes in Mildura, along with the first caperberries produced by the Australian Caper Company. Each of the core ingredients – the chook marylands, the raisins and the caperberries – was so special that the dish, as countrified as my food is, was really exceptional.

This is also a fantastic dish served cold the next day, when the juices will have become jellied.

½ cinnamon stick

3 lemons

20 free-range chicken legs (about 2.5 kg)

10 fresh bay leaves

4 sprigs rosemary

extra virgin olive oil, for cooking

80 g flaked almonds

sea salt flakes

80 g unsalted butter

½ cup (125 ml) vino cotto (see Glossary) *or* balsamic vinegar

30 green olives

1 generous cup raisins

½ cup caperberries *or* salted capers, rinsed and drained

finely chopped flat-leaf parsley, to serve

Finely grind the cinnamon stick using a mortar and pestle or a spice grinder. Remove the lemon rind in strips with a vegetable peeler and reserve the lemons for juicing. Marinade the chicken in a bowl with the ground cinnamon, lemon rind, bay leaves, rosemary and enough olive oil to coat the pieces, for at least 1 hour before cooking (overnight is even better).

When ready to cook, preheat the oven to 200°C. Place the flaked almonds on a baking tray and roast for 5 minutes or until golden; set aside. Season marinated chicken legs with salt, then heat the butter and a little olive oil in a flameproof roasting pan on the stove over low–medium heat. Add the chicken and gently seal until golden brown. Transfer the pan to the oven and cook for 10 minutes.

Remove the pan from the oven, then place over high heat on the stove and add a little of the vino cotto at a time to deglaze. Add the olives, raisins and caperberries, then return pan to the oven for another 5–10 minutes (depending on the size of the chook legs), or until the chicken is cooked through.

Toss with the flaked almonds and parsley, then squeeze over at least one of the lemons, adding more lemon juice if needed. Leave for 10 minutes before serving to allow the flavours to meld.

CAPERS AND CHICKEN LIVER CROSTINI   *Serves 10*

During my sojourn in Tuscany, the tradition of serving chicken liver crostini or brus-chetta became part of our standard routine. It was the addition of salted capers that really made the difference – we went through packet after packet. Once again, it was their piquant flavour cutting into the dense liver that made a zesty impact. Rather than mashing the seared livers with a fork or blending in a food processor, we cut them into small pieces, as in this recipe.

1 tablespoon butter, plus extra to melt	¼ cup freshly chopped flat-leaf parsley
250 g chicken livers, trimmed	1–2 teaspoons red-wine vinegar
3 anchovy fillets, chopped	2 breadsticks, cut diagonally into thick slices
⅓ cup (65 g) capers	

Preheat the oven to 200°C. In a heavy-based frying pan, heat the tablespoon of butter until it is nut-brown, then add the livers and turn the heat down to medium. Seal the first side for 1 minute, turn the livers over and cook for about 2 minutes (depending on size), then remove from the heat entirely to ensure they are still pink in the middle. When cool enough to handle, cut the livers into small pieces, then combine with the anchovies, capers, parsley and vinegar.

Brush the sliced bread with melted butter on one side only, then place on a baking tray and bake until golden. Serve the livers immediately, spread on the hot crostini.

SKATE WITH CAPERS AND OLIVES   *Serves 4*

I had skate for the first time in Malaysia, while holidaying on Langkawi Island. It was cooked in a simple Mediterranean style, which seemed rather out of place compared with the rest of the food on offer. On returning home I adapted the following recipe from Ann and Franco Taruschio's *Leaves from the Walnut Tree*, a favourite book. Skate, the wings of a stingray, is inexpensive; in some states it is sold untrimmed, so you may need to clean it.

4 × 225 g pieces skate	handful flat-leaf parsley stalks, leaves picked
plain flour, for dusting	and chopped and stems reserved
sea salt flakes and freshly ground	⅓ cup (65 g) capers
black pepper	⅓ cup pitted and sliced black olives
2 cloves garlic, finely chopped	⅓ cup (80 ml) verjuice
⅓ cup (80 ml) extra virgin olive oil,	squeeze of lemon juice
plus extra for drizzling	

Preheat the oven to 180°C and trim the skate of skin, if necessary. Season the flour with salt and pepper. Brown the garlic in the olive oil in a large, heavy-based ovenproof frying pan, being careful not to burn it.

Capsicums baked with olives, goat's cheese and oregano (see page 38)

plate slows down the process a bit, as the heat is less direct, and results in a wonderfully smoky flavour. My grandchildren love watching when something is burning on the fire – and the deep-red capsicum that chars to black seems to thrill them. Another method is to roast well-oiled capsicums in a sturdy roasting pan in the oven at 230°C for about 30 minutes until blackened (turning them two or three times so that they char evenly). Before putting them in the oven, however, cut the top off each capsicum and pull out the seeds and membrane. This is much less messy than trying to do it later on, and, if you're

careful, avoids the need to run the roasted capsicums under water to clean them, which washes away some of their flavour. Whichever method you use, the blackened capsicums should be left to cool for 5 minutes, then put in a plastic bag to sweat for 10 minutes, after which time the skin will easily slip off. Wipe the flesh clean with a little olive oil, if necessary. The sweet, smoky flavour of roasted capsicum is at its height while the capsicum is still warm. The syrupy juices on the bottom of the roasting pan offer the most intense flavour of all, provided they haven't burnt – you may need to warm the pan and add a little more oil to release the juices.

If you roast a lot of red capsicums, refrigerate any leftovers steeped in extra virgin olive oil, but use them quickly as they will ferment if not totally immersed, and all that effort will be wasted. I find I never have to throw out roasted capsicums that have gone off – they never hang around in our fridge for long enough. Try roasting capsicums with extra virgin olive oil, oregano, olives and goat's cheese or ricotta. A tin of good tuna folded into a handmade mayonnaise with tiny pieces of lemon and parsley can be stuffed inside a whole roasted capsicum and served drizzled with a vinaigrette. You can also purée roasted capsicum to serve as a sauce with grilled or poached fish or chicken; or you could set it into a savoury custard with lots of roasted garlic.

If you want to go that extra step, make Rouille (see page 185). Made like a mayonnaise, but with the addition of garlic, saffron threads, tomato and the all-important purée of roasted capsicum, it is the perfect accompaniment to a fish soup or stew, and is great when served with grilled fish or squid. Try adding it to a stuffing for pot-roasted squid: cook onions in extra virgin olive oil, long and slow so they caramelise, then add rouille, lots of freshly chopped flat-leaf parsley and a chopped anchovy or two. Fill the squid, then seal with toothpicks and braise really slowly. Any leftover rouille can also be added to mashed hard-boiled egg yolks that are then returned to the whites, and piled up high; tossed into a salad of waxy potatoes with extra virgin olive oil and parsley; or added to bocconcini or goat's curd-topped croutons.

Ingredients that have a natural affinity with capsicums include anchovies, capers, eggplants, garlic, goat's cheese, olive oil, olives and tomatoes. A whole roasted red capsicum stuffed with goat's cheese, anchovies and olives – warmed in the oven to melt the cheese a little and served with a crouton of olive bread – makes a great lunch. Sliced roasted red capsicum combined with deep-fried eggplant, capers, lots of nutty flat-leaf parsley, a drizzle of extra virgin olive oil and a thimbleful of great balsamic vinegar is also wonderful.

A finger of grilled polenta about $7 \times 2 \times 2$ cm, made with the addition of milk and cream instead of stock for a change, makes a light and tasty base on which to present other ingredients to begin a meal. Try warm polenta fingers with peeled and chopped roasted red capsicum drizzled with a little balsamic vinegar, caramelised garlic cloves, freshly grated Parmigiano Reggiano and extra virgin olive oil.

Roasted capsicum can be used to make a simple coulis, too: purée the peeled roasted capsicum and add either cream or the appropriate stock. Made with stock, red capsicum coulis is quite a counterpoint to the richness of pan-fried brains or a blue swimmer crab tartlet. If you are making a purée, note that 6 medium capsicums will yield about 500 g purée.

If you want to avoid peeling them, pan-fry sliced capsicums with garlic and thyme in extra virgin olive oil until soft and then add a little balsamic or sherry vinegar to the pan juices. Add onion and tomato to the pan, and finish off with a little chicken stock and perhaps a bit of cream, before puréeing the lot. This coulis goes well with chicken or fish.

Writing this outdoors, just metres away from trays of bright-red capsicums and sliced eggplant, my thoughts turn to drying your own vegetables at home. For those who think sun-dried tomatoes are passé and have moved on to slow-roasted baby tomatoes, I urge you to give sun-dried red capsicum or eggplant a chance; and to please re-visit sun-dried tomatoes, as the only thing that ever spoilt them was indiscriminate use, over-dried or burnt tomatoes, and poor-quality oil.

Ripe red capsicums, so sweet and luscious when grilled or roasted, can be a drag to peel. Drying them produces an incredibly intense flavour and makes peeling easier. Just cut the capsicums into quarters, then remove the seeds but leave the stems in place – they look great later – and sprinkle the cut sides with salt. Place them on wire racks in full sunshine for three days. I bring my racks in each night and return them to the drying location as soon as it is in full sun again the next day. As I look at the capsicums in front of me, after 24 hours drying out, the cut sides have curled towards the sun, so I have turned the quarters over to allow any moisture to escape. The brilliant red skins on the just-turned pieces are already delightfully crinkled and I can see they will slip off with the slightest pressure when the drying is complete – perfect.

Because mould is the enemy of dried vegetables, and comes from exposure to air, it is a good idea to store home-dried delicacies in sealed airtight containers. I prefer to steep them in extra virgin olive oil, which does not preserve the vegetables but instead keeps the oxygen out. Don't be tempted to add garlic as spores under its skin can spoil the dried product. Properly sun-dried capsicums and other vegetables such as tomatoes and eggplant do not need to be soaked before use, but they do need to be checked for mould. They will last for months if dried and stored well. Use sun-dried capsicums wherever you might use sun-dried tomatoes. If you have steeped your capsicums in oil, use this when making a vinaigrette or toss it through pasta – but please, use really good oil!

I am looking forward to enjoying these flavours of summer long after the season has drawn to a close, when I am back inside working at my desk, with only the wintry view of the willow tree to remind me of those warm days in the garden.

SWEET ROASTED RED CAPSICUM PÂTÉ   *Serves 6*

So here you have it – the basic recipe for my totally vegetarian pâté. It started as a dish for six and we used to make it by the hundreds, starting every batch from scratch. We tried to see if we could make it more cost-effective by buying in the capsicums already cut, but this meant we lost control over the quality and ripeness, and the cutting by a commercial operation on the other side of Adelaide meant the capsicums had to be cut the day before they were cooked, so all those lovely juices and oils were lost. It was a lot more expensive to produce than our liver-based pâté but I wanted to be able to offer an 'off the shelf' pâté for not only the vegetable lover but also the vegetarian, who up until now has had a very limited range of top-quality commercially produced foods to choose from.

However, as I refused to take any shortcuts, we were unable to sustain it as one of our products, so I am sharing this recipe with you.

½ cup (125 ml) extra virgin olive oil	4 egg yolks
12 cloves garlic, peeled	120 ml thickened cream
3 sprigs thyme	sea salt flakes and freshly ground
6 red capsicums	black pepper

Preheat the oven to 230°C and use a little of the olive oil to lightly grease six 150 ml dariole moulds (ovenproof rounded coffee cups will do the job, too). Caramelise the garlic cloves very slowly in the remaining olive oil with the thyme in a saucepan over low heat, taking care not to burn them, then set the pan aside. Roast and peel the capsicums as described on page 38, coating them with the oil used to caramelise the garlic (reserve the garlic but discard the thyme). Reduce the oven temperature to 200°C.

In a food processor, purée the roasted capsicums with the juices from the roasting pan and the reserved caramelised garlic (you need 50 g purée). Blend the egg yolks and cream into the purée and season, then transfer to a bowl. Spoon the pâté into the prepared moulds, then stand them in a roasting tray of warm water (the water should come two-thirds of the way up the sides of the moulds) and bake for 45 minutes. If serving as a pâté, then cool to room temperature in the water bath and refrigerate until required. This dish can also be served hot as an entrée with hollandaise sauce, in which case it is called a mousse.

SQUAB WITH RED CAPSICUM PANCAKES

Serves 6

These capsicum pancakes can also be served with goat's cheese warmed over them or as an adjunct to a dish of ratatouille.

sea salt flakes and freshly ground
   black pepper
6 × 450 g squabs
1 lemon
butter, for cooking
50 ml balsamic vinegar
600 ml reduced Golden Chicken Stock
   (see page 55)

PANCAKES
6 deep-red capsicums
squeeze of lemon juice
1 tablespoon extra virgin olive oil
1 free-range egg
200 ml milk
135 g self-raising flour
sea salt flakes and freshly ground
   black pepper
butter, for cooking

Preheat the oven to 230°C. To prepare the pancake batter, roast and peel the capsicums as described on page 38, then increase the oven temperature to the highest possible. Squeeze a little lemon juice over the roasted capsicums and purée them in a food processor with the olive oil (you should have 500 g purée). In a large bowl, mix the egg and milk, then add the flour. Stir in the capsicum purée, then season the batter very well and leave it to stand in the refrigerator while you prepare and cook the squab.

Season the cavity of each bird and squeeze in a little lemon juice. Heat a little butter in a frying pan until it is nut-brown and add a dash of olive oil to inhibit burning, then seal the birds on all sides over medium heat and transfer to a roasting pan. Roast for 8–10 minutes, then remove from the pan and leave to rest, breast-side down, for a good 10 minutes before serving.

While the squabs are roasting, cook the pancakes one at a time in a little melted butter in a heavy-based frying pan over low–medium heat. These pancakes need to be cooked very slowly, so that the outside is nut-brown and the inside is cooked. The batter makes 6 thick rustic pancakes. Wipe out the pan and add more butter each time before cooking the next pancake.

Drain the fat from the roasting pan, then deglaze the pan with the balsamic vinegar and reduced stock and boil vigorously until the sauce reaches your desired consistency. I prefer to serve each squab sitting on a pancake rather than carving the birds. Pour the sauce over the birds and serve any extra in a jug at the table.

Cherry clafoutis (see page 47)

CHERRIES

THE MENTION OF CHERRIES MAKES ME THINK IMMEDIATELY OF Cherry Ripe. Nowadays this has a double meaning, since one of our great food commentators and author of *Goodbye Culinary Cringe* shares that name with the childhood-favourite chocolate bar I would eat furtively from the corner shop. I always claim that I don't have a sweet tooth, but each time my children hear me saying so, they chorus derisively, 'and she only listens to the ABC too!', as they think these are my catch-cries in life. But it's exactly what my mother used to say, and yet when needing a sugar fix it was a Cherry Ripe she would reach for; it's the same for me, and it's the same for my children. All of us without a real sweet tooth.

Cherries have also always meant Christmas to me. One year when I was very young and money was scarce, my mother explained in advance that there would be nothing under the Christmas tree that year, but she surprised us with huge bunches of cherries, a bottle of Coca-Cola and a small box of Old Gold chocolates each. Unbelievable treats for a child of five in 1950! Coca-Cola and chocolates aside, I have never had a Christmas since without bowls of ripe, juicy black cherries.

Cherries are graded by size, and size is related to price. A retailer will often have cherries at two or three prices, and you get what you pay for. Interestingly, retailers tell me they sell equal numbers of dear as cheap cherries, as the consumer is becoming more demanding. It's important for the industry to find a use for inferior cherries rather than selling them fresh for the table. This is more difficult now that the canning of cherries is almost non-existent in this country, but there are other possibilities, such as making liqueurs and chocolates.

The first cherries of the season always command a premium price simply based on supply and demand, and as cherries do not colour up or get any sweeter after picking, they should always be picked ripe. So getting those cherries to market is a race against the weather. Perfect hand-picked cherries will always demand a premium too, and so they should; the cherry grower has more chance of being wiped out by unseasonal storms than possibly any other fruit grower.

How I love the large juicy black ones to eat. There are many varieties to choose from and although at present only the more serious greengrocer or farmers' market will name the varieties, we the consumers can do our bit to change that by asking for more information. Some of the old-fashioned varieties of large black cherries like St Margaret or William's Favourite are still quite common. The American varieties such as Van and Stella, both of which have large blood-red fruit, and Bing, which has large bright-red fruit, have also become well established. These varieties are less acidic and their sweetness is more attractive to many, particularly the lucrative Asian export market.

As cherries have such a short season from flowering to maturity, fewer chemicals are used on them than any other fruit tree. But the risk in growing cherries commercially is

great. At the end of October the farmer assesses what their crop will be based on how each tree has 'set'; yet so many things can go wrong at the last moment that this prediction is often way off the mark. Too much rain can result in fruit splitting, and in forty-eight hours a wonderful crop can be lost; then there is the potential for hail, frost and strong winds to contend with. The early fruit is subject to bird attack and, other than netting, there is not much one can do. (Netting brings the potential for other problems: keeping predatory birds out means you also keep the helpful insect-eating birds away.)

A number of years ago I had organised to buy a small crop of morello cherries to pickle for Stephanie Alexander, who was having difficulty finding enough fruit. Everything was arranged – the ingredients, the jars, the staff – and then I had a call from the grower. The crop was lost virtually overnight in a storm. It's a very vulnerable position to be in as a farmer, particularly if the crop is your sole source of income. Having learnt from Stephanie just how good sour morello cherries are for pickling, and, even with good weather conditions, finding it very difficult to buy them commercially, I finally have quite a mature morello cherry tree whose small fruit hangs defiantly against the birds (it's obvious they don't have my palate). Sadly, our only access to morellos commercially is the imported 4.25 kg tins. The other cherry tree in my orchard is the first tree to ripen each year, but I seldom get to beat the birds.

While being parochial, I think the best cherries in Australia come from the Adelaide Hills (I know other areas would dispute that, but for me it is an issue of access to fruit with minimal transportation time). But now that chilled and cushioned transport is available, cherry-growing regions are being selected for their climate rather than their proximity to markets. In South Australia, cherries are also grown in the southeast of the state and in the Riverland, where the fruit is ready weeks ahead of Adelaide's. In Victoria, there are cherry orchards in the foothills of the Dandenongs and near Wangaratta in the northeast, while Young and Orange are the major cherry-growing areas in New South Wales and, of course, they are grown around most of Tasmania.

For years I have used a dehydrator, originally bought decades ago to dry a glut of strawberries. Whilst I love morellos dried, because of their smaller size it is easier to pickle them, but any dried cherry is such a treat to add to cereal, muffins or any number of desserts – perhaps even homemade Cherry Ripes! Dried cherries are now available in some organic markets and top grocery shops.

I have to admit that I am far more likely to cook with dried cherries than fresh ones. Fresh cherries are in season for such a short time that I relish eating them with no adornment. However, I have enjoyed fresh cherries poached in red wine with sugar, cinnamon and lemon rind, much as one cooks pears. I also love using fresh cherries in a Clafoutis (see page 47). I remember well the first years of the Pheasant Farm Restaurant when it was just me and an apprentice. I had no skill or interest in making desserts, so I enlisted the help of a local cook to teach me. We tried a cherry clafoutis – and nothing sold. The next day we made another batch but called it cherry pudding. Nothing was left.

Brandied cherries are worth having in the cupboard: the cherries and their juice can be spooned over vanilla ice cream or used in a rich chocolate cake. Bill Bishop, who was a driving force in the early stages of Adelaide's cherry industry, recommends layering sugar, brandy and cherries, a third of a cup at a time, in a sterilised preserving jar and then screwing down the lid tightly before leaving to mature for three months. Bill says the juice is also delightful to drink!

In late 1996 I was planning a banquet to be held at the Park Hyatt in Tokyo to launch our products in Japan. The very Australian menu featured our pâté, smoked kangaroo, marron, venison, Woodside goat's cheese, Heidi Gruyère and Farmers Union matured cheddar with our quince paste, and was to end with a fresh cherry tart. Our distributor and host Toshio Yasuma had chosen Mountadam wines to accompany each course. The night before my departure I was told that the cherry crop in Tasmania had been affected by an outbreak of moth and my cherries couldn't be air-freighted to Tokyo – disaster! In a flash of inspiration I remembered the buckets of pickled morello cherries from the previous season. I had them vacuum-sealed and packed them in my suitcase (I declared them!). I made an almond tart and layered the pastry case with the cherries before adding the filling, for which I was given a 1935 brandy to use. This was served with a choice of Mountadam's ratafias: the chardonnay ratafia tasted of almonds and the pinot noir version tasted of cherries – the perfect accompaniments.

LEW KATHREPTIS'S PICKLED CHERRIES   *Makes 1 litre*

I like to pickle fresh cherries, a simple process, and prefer to use morello cherries for their sharpness and because they shrivel less during pickling. I used to follow a recipe in *Jane Grigson's Fruit Book* until I found another from former Adelaide chef Lew Kathreptis in *Stephanie's Australia*. I make jars and jars of these each year, leaving them for about six weeks to mature. Occasionally I find a jar in the back of the cupboard that is more than a year old – and the cherries are always still good! Pickled cherries are great to serve with pâté, duck or pork rillettes, terrines, hams or pickled pork. I also serve pickled morello cherries with pheasant roasted with rosemary and pancetta – the tartness of the morellos offsets the richness of the dish. If you want to use the cherries in a sweet dish, just leave out the garlic.

850 ml white-wine vinegar	6 bay leaves
700 g sugar	1 clove garlic
24 black peppercorns	1 kg morello cherries
12 cloves	

Boil all ingredients except the cherries in a stainless steel saucepan for 10 minutes, then leave to cool completely.

Meanwhile, wash and dry the cherries thoroughly, discarding any that are bruised or marked. Trim the stalks to 1 cm long, then pack the fruit into a sterilised 1-litre preserving jar. Pour the cold syrup over the cherries, then seal and store for at least a month (I use mine after six weeks, but they will keep indefinitely).

CHERRY MUFFINS   *Makes 12*

135 g plain flour	1 egg
2 teaspoons baking powder	1 tablespoon walnut oil
pinch salt	185 ml buttermilk
2 heaped tablespoons brown sugar	300 g fresh cherries, washed, stemmed
90 g rolled oats	and pitted *or* 150 g dried cherries
100 g unsalted butter, melted and cooled	

Preheat the oven to 180°C and lightly grease a 12-hole muffin tin. Combine the flour, baking powder, salt, sugar and oats in a bowl and make a well in the centre. Mix the cooled melted butter into the flour with the egg, oil and buttermilk. Fold in the cherries, then two-thirds fill the holes of the muffin tin. Bake for about 20 minutes or until a fine skewer inserted into a muffin comes out clean, then cool the muffins on a wire rack.

CHERRY CLAFOUTIS

Serves 6

I prefer not to pit cherries when making a tart such as this, as the stone helps keep the shape and flavour of the fruit intact. Be sure to warn your guests, though, before they tuck in.

500 g fresh dark cherries

1 tablespoon castor sugar

2 tablespoons kirsch

CUSTARD

2 large eggs

¼ cup (55 g) castor sugar

¼ cup (50 g) plain flour

½ cup (125 ml) crème fraîche

or sour cream

½ cup (125 ml) cream

grated rind of 1 lemon

butter, for baking

icing sugar, for dusting

Preheat the oven to 200°C. Place the cherries in a shallow baking dish and sprinkle the castor sugar and kirsch over them. Bake for 5–6 minutes or until the cherries are cooked but still firm. Set the cherries aside and reserve the cooking juices.

For the custard, beat the eggs in an electric mixer, then add the castor sugar and beat until frothy. Carefully add the flour and combine, then add 1 tablespoon of the reserved cherry cooking juices, the crème fraîche, cream and lemon rind.

Dot a gratin or small baking dish with a little butter (I use a 30 cm oval copper baking dish), then spread half the custard over the base of the dish. Spoon in the cooked cherries to cover the custard, then add the remaining custard. Bake for 25–30 minutes; the top will be golden and the cherries will appear as little mounds in the custard. Serve warm, dusted with icing sugar.

CHICKEN

 THOSE OF YOU WHO ARE AROUND MY AGE WILL REMEMBER JUST how good chicken used to taste when we were children. I know it's difficult for young people to imagine, but roast chicken on Sunday was a very special treat. Added to that was the fact that the only way you had such a meal was if you had a chook pen in the backyard and were up to performing the necessary tasks to bring the bird to the table yourself. Of course, that meant that the bird was hand-plucked, which added to the flavour – something I never realised at the time.

It was in 1991 that I discovered the difference dry-plucking makes during a short stint in the Hyatt Hotel's kitchens in Adelaide, when Urs Inauen was in charge of the now-defunct Fleurieu Restaurant. Urs and I, together with fellow chefs Cheong Liew and Tom Milligan, were preparing our challenge for the Seppelt Australian Menu of the Year and all game to enter the kitchen was dry-plucked by the cooks and apprentices. The resulting guinea fowl, and the stock made from the bones, had a flavour superior to anything I had ever tasted – due, I believe, to the dry-plucking. To compound my belief, during a holiday in Umbria I was struck by the amazing flavour of the poultry. I'm sure it was the result of the birds being raised by small-scale breeders who dry-plucked them. It makes sense when you think about it: dry-plucking leaves the layer of fat under the skin intact. Fat means flavour, and, as you know, you can always take both the skin and fat off after cooking (if you are strong-willed enough).

I decided to test this new-found theory of mine at home. I roasted two well-brought-up chooks – one corn-fed and dry-plucked and the other free-ranged but wet-plucked – side by side for flavour comparison, using the basic method in Stuffed Roast Chicken on page 56 (I didn't stuff the corn-fed bird, which took about 10 minutes less to cook). Both were excellent, but the corn-fed, dry-plucked chicken was both sweeter and more intense in flavour and seemed to have a tighter, or denser, texture. The corn-fed bird certainly released a lot more fat than the other, so next time I would sit the bird on a trivet (a small

Roast tarragon chicken (see page 51)

cake rack would do the trick). The breast browned extraordinarily well; in fact I considered putting a buttered brown-paper 'hat' over the breast to protect it (much as my mother would have put a herbed and buttered piece of cheesecloth on the breast of a turkey).

Don't hold out hopes of seeing a rash of dry-plucked birds on the market, however, as the procedure is incredibly labour-intensive and it is hard to get producers to commit to it; but if you get the opportunity, it is worth paying extra for. Any farmer specialising in delivering poultry to a niche market should consider this process.

Time has marched on incredibly since my childhood, and we can now see both ends of the quality spectrum in the chicken market. Today we can conveniently buy chicken in every conceivable form and cut, yet sadly the majority is mass-produced. Whilst it's great

to be able to buy just the breast or the legs, or bones for stock as it suits, the compromise in flavour is one I will not accept. And the current fashion of selling breasts and legs skinless is deplorable. The fat from the skin of the chicken does *not* permeate the meat during cooking. In other words, cook with the skin on and, if you are worried by the fat, take the skin off afterwards. The skin provides the meat with natural protection, and cooking without it makes achieving a succulent piece of chicken almost impossible.

But thankfully there are real exceptions to this and in each state there are specialist free-range poultry producers raising birds whose flavour is so superior to the mass-produced birds they almost need another name to identify them. And of course that is what happens – these farmers 'brand' their produce. In South Australia we first had Kangaroo Island chook, a really great product, and of course my daughter Saskia's chooks. Ian Millburn of Glenloth Game in northwest Victoria has long been providing wonderful corn-fed chickens to the restaurant industry, as well as his fabulous squab. There is a smattering of these top-class producers in every state. Your first move is to find a quality butcher and ask the right questions. Are their chickens free-range? What are they fed on? Are they grown slowly and naturally to maturity without preventative doses of antibiotics?

I have a lot to share about my daughter Saskia's chooks. Eating them now is almost an everyday matter, as it would be for the families of any of the handful of great poultry producers who grow what I have long called 'well-brought-up chooks'. I certainly urge anyone who has the opportunity to purchase any of these birds to do so, as the difference between these and their intensively farmed cousins is as chalk to cheese. Even among the best of the producers there are quite specific points of difference, and certainly one that I know from my close association with Saskia's – no secret here – is that they are reared on a totally vegetarian diet. The legume, wheat and corn mix the chooks feed on results in such a profound difference in flavour from that of chooks fed on protein derived from fish- and meat-meal. There is no doubt that the corn in the diet results in greater amounts of fat under the skin and a lot more marbling than other diets – but what flavour it produces.

It has been a bit of a standing joke in our family that, when the girls were growing up, I would never cook a roast dinner. Years ago I had a real reminder of how easy it can be when Saskia asked Colin and I to dinner one night while her then-husband, Greg, was away. Despite working all day, with her youngest Rory only nine months old, Lilly five years old and Max seven, Saskia cooked a roast chook – one of hers – so delicious and so evocative of my childhood, but with an absolute minimum of fuss. The 2.3 kg chicken had been stuffed under the skin with butter and lots of tarragon from the garden. Red onions, young carrots, waxy potatoes and pumpkin had all been cut into large chunks – none of them peeled – and scattered around the chook in the roasting pan, then a cup of verjuice (but it could easily have been wine) was poured into the base of the pan. The lovely thing about this meal is that it took 1 hour and 10 minutes in a hot oven without even being looked at; a truly beautiful roast chook, full of memories of the time when this was the most special meal we would ever have – those tastes, those feelings were all there and I absolutely loved it!

That perfect, simple meal reminded me of the first time I ever dined with my friend Stephanie Alexander, around twenty years ago; we had roast tarragon chicken. It was so wonderful I suspect it must have come from Ian Millburn, even in those days. To make the tarragon butter for a 2.2 kg chook, mix together 1 tablespoon freshly chopped tarragon leaves and 100 g unsalted butter, add a squeeze of lemon juice and season with sea salt and freshly ground black pepper. Spread the butter under the skin of the chook before roasting.

So here we have a call for the return of roast chook as the pièce de résistance. Stuffed Roast Chicken is such a family favourite – see the recipe on page 56. But if you don't have time to make a stuffing, tuck three squashed garlic cloves, rosemary, thyme and a good squeeze of lemon in the bird's cavity. Drizzle the skin with extra virgin olive oil and rub sea salt flakes all over, then cook it exactly as for the stuffed chook. Remember, the quality of the chook makes all the difference in the world.

My friend Damien Pignolet has been so generous with his knowledge over the years, both with the recipes he sends me on a whim (simply because he knows I would love to hear of yet another way in which he's using verjuice in his cooking), and as a sounding board for new products I have developed (he always comes back to me with an incredibly detailed and considered opinion). One very special memory was when Damien asked me to cook a course for his 50th birthday celebrations, at an intimate luncheon for around 30 people at his home. The very fact that Damien – such a perfectionist, and a chef of immense techni-cal ability and 'feel' combined – had asked me, an absolutely haphazard cook, to contribute was a great feeling. I remember his incredibly compact kitchen, with everything you could possibly need to hand, but not that much space (especially with a couple of cooks/chefs in the kitchen, each of us presenting one course) and feeling nervous as anything. Somehow I managed to bring it all together – a ballottine of boned Barossa Chook stuffed with livers, onions, bacon and herbs, baked slowly and already resting well before the guests arrived, so I could enjoy the party too. Simple as it was, I was inordinately proud that Damien loved the dish.

Carving at the table may be a lost art to many, but there is nothing wrong with using kitchen scissors to divide the spoils. I've yet to see a family that doesn't fight over the breast and leg meat! My mother always pinched the wings before they came to the table, just as I always commandeer the pope's nose (although if Saskia is here, there's a fight for it). My favourite bits of all are the pickings from the bones. I would actually prefer to make a meal of them, but it doesn't seem right if everyone else is being delicate. Besides, I'd probably have to share my tidbits in this family. I have often delighted in the Italian tradition where the carcass of the carved bird is brushed with olive oil and put back onto the spit for a few minutes before it is gnawed at by all and sundry. My kind of food!

It's important to cook chicken just perfectly, so that it's not pink at the bone when you are serving it, but only just cooked. To achieve this, the bird should be removed from the oven while the meat is, in fact, still pink at the bone, then left to rest for 20–30 minutes, turned upside-down so that the juices run down over the breast (don't worry, the bird will stay warm for this length of time). It is this resting period that finishes the cooking. Overcooking means a dry and stringy bird, no matter how good its credentials are.

If you wish to have some sort of juice to serve with your roast chicken without actually making a sauce or gravy, the trick is to 'wet-roast' the bird by adding 125 ml verjuice, water, stock or wine to the roasting pan at the start of cooking, and spooning an extra 60–125 ml of it over the bird as it comes out of the oven to rest. A delicious jus forms in the bottom of the pan, especially if the bird was initially smeared with butter and had a couple of rosemary sprigs placed across its breast and the juice of half a lemon squeezed into the cavity before roasting. Another alternative is to make a warm vinaigrette. Cook 6 finely sliced shallots in 80 ml extra virgin olive oil in a small saucepan over very low heat until translucent (or I often use a nut oil such as almond). Deglaze the pan with 2 tablespoons sherry vinegar, then add a little lemon rind and thyme and whisk in 100–120 ml jus from the roasting pan after separating the fat from it.

Don't think, however, that roasting or pan-frying are the only ways to go with chicken. I love a chook (always with giblets) simmered in stock and left to cool until it becomes jellied, and even now I turn to chicken noodle soup when I'm feeling below par – and whenever my younger daughter Elli is feeling unwell she still comes home and asks for it too. It's such wonderful comfort food.

I also like to grill or barbecue chicken. To do this I 'spatchcock' the bird by cutting out the backbone with kitchen scissors or a sharp knife, then I marinate the flattened bird breast-side down. Try a marinade of extra virgin olive oil, thyme, freshly ground black pepper and strips of preserved lemon or slices of meyer lemon, or perhaps just extra virgin olive oil, sprigs of rosemary and slivers of garlic. I season the chicken just before cooking and position it about 15 cm from the heat source. The chicken is grilled skin-side up for about 5 minutes to brown it, then turned over and brushed with more marinade and grilled for about 4 minutes. The skin side is grilled again for 3 minutes, making the cooking time 12 minutes in all. Then I leave the bird to rest, breast-side down, for at least 10 minutes before serving. To cook the same bird on the barbecue, the chicken needs to be turned every minute or two after the skin has caramelised for 10 minutes, so that the skin doesn't char to oblivion.

Chicken on the barbecue is especially good, particularly poussin weighing between 400 and 500 g. 'Spatchcock' or butterfly each bird as described above then place in a marinade of extra virgin olive oil, fresh herbs (particularly rosemary or basil) and some thin slices of lemon. Shake off any excess oil before barbecuing as it tends to make the flames flare. Chicken takes a little longer to cook than most meat (this size bird should take about 20 minutes) and must be turned halfway through cooking, or earlier if it starts to burn too much on one side. Always test chicken for doneness by inserting a skewer into the thickest part – if the juices run clear, it should be cooked. It is essential to rest the cooked bird for at least 10 minutes, so keep the hungry hordes at bay.

Give barbecued chicken another dimension by using a post-cooking marinade instead of a pre-cooking one. In a flat dish, place grapes, grape or lemon juice, extra virgin olive oil and some sea salt, plus any roasted nuts you might have, or sliced fresh figs, then toss the cooked chicken with this and leave for about 15 minutes before serving. The resting chook will soak up all these flavours. The meat won't go cold and will be succulent and juicy – everyone will want to suck on the bones.

If butterflying poussins seems like too much trouble, thighs with the skin and bones intact are the easiest alternative, as each piece will be of relatively even thickness. Cook as per the poussin, but for about 10 minutes in all, and rest in the same way.

The best way I have found to cook chicken breasts is to seal them gently in nut-brown butter in an ovenproof heavy-based frying pan over low–medium heat, then to put them into a hot (230°C) oven for 4–6 minutes, depending on their thickness. Check the cooking by lifting up the little under-fillet; the flesh should be pink but not at all raw. Rest the chicken, turned over, for the same length of time it took to cook – the cooking will continue while the breast is resting and the meat will no longer be pink but lovely and moist. Degrease the browning pan and deglaze it with verjuice, then serve the chicken with these juices and a savoury jelly such as the cabernet or vino cotto jelly we make for our Farmshop.

Golden chicken stock

For a truly great sandwich, combine leftover chicken with a verjuice mayonnaise. In an electric mixer, food processor or, if you are really keen, a non-reactive bowl, mix 2 egg yolks with 60 ml verjuice and 1 teaspoon of your favourite mustard. Whisk until emulsified and then slowly drizzle in a mixture of 125 ml extra virgin olive oil and 125 ml grapeseed oil to combine and emulsify; you may need a little more oil to reach the desired consistency as the egg yolks' ability to take the oil will vary, but 250 ml should be close. Season to taste with 1 teaspoon salt, ¼ teaspoon freshly ground black pepper and ¼ teaspoon castor sugar, then stir in 1 dessertspoon freshly chopped tarragon. Fill slices of good-quality bread with diced chicken breast mixed with the mayonnaise and either watercress sprigs or shredded iceberg lettuce.

I cannot write a chapter on chicken without mentioning offal. Other than an orange cake I made for my grandmother on my eighth birthday, offal was the first meal I ever cooked. I remember clearly my dish of chicken livers: they were done in butter with herbs (most likely dried). I also remember being so thrilled with the flavour that my lifelong habit of picking as I cooked was established that day!

At the Pheasant Farm Restaurant I always kept emergency rations for when other dishes were in short supply. My secret was confit. I confited the hearts, giblets and livers of good free-range chooks separately and stored them immersed in duck fat in the cool room. If I ran out of a dish on what was always a very limited menu, I would offer a *salade gourmande*, which consisted of these delicacies offset by preserved lemons or pickled green walnuts and bitter greens. It was a beautiful dish and worth having in reserve because anyone who had it (given they loved offal) never regretted that their original choice had been unavailable.

GOLDEN CHICKEN STOCK   *Makes about 2 litres*

I just can't cook without a good stock, and a chook stock is the one I use most of all. While there are a few good stocks on the market, usually made by small producers and these days we make one commercially too, for me nothing touches the homemade. There is something incredibly rewarding about having a pot of stock simmering on the stove, especially knowing that, either reduced or frozen, it might keep you going for a month. It takes so little work and adds so much to your cooking that I urge you to do it.

The better the quality of the original chook the better your stock will be. The skin and bones (with a generous amount of meat still attached) of a mature, well-brought-up bird has not only better flavour but more gelatinous quality. It's truly important not to overcook a stock; your benchmark should be that the meat on the bones is still sweet. An overcooked stock has all the goodness cooked out of it, and the bones have a chalky flavour.

I tend to make my stock in a large batch and then freeze it in 1-litre containers. Using fresh 'bright' vegetables rather than limp leftovers, and roasting the bones and veg before simmering them, gives the stock a wonderful golden colour and a deeper flavour. You only need use enough water to cover the bones and veg by about 7 cm in your stockpot (this way in most cases your stock won't need reducing). Never allow your stock to boil, just bring it to a good simmer, and don't skim it as you'll take the fat – and the flavour – off with it (you can remove the fat easily after the cooked stock has been refrigerated.) Don't let the stock sit in the pan once it is cooked: strain it straight away, then let it cool before refrigerating.

1 large boiling chicken (about 2.2 kg), cut into pieces (if you are using bones only, you will need 3 kg)	1 stick celery, roughly chopped
	1 bay leaf
	6 sprigs thyme
2 large onions, unpeeled and halved	6 stalks flat-leaf parsley
1 large carrot, roughly chopped	1 head garlic, halved widthways
extra virgin olive oil, for cooking	2 very ripe tomatoes, roughly chopped
100 ml white wine (optional)	
1 large leek, trimmed, cleaned and roughly chopped	

Preheat the oven to 200°C. Place the chicken pieces, onion and carrot in a roasting pan and drizzle with a little olive oil. Roast for 20 minutes or until chicken and vegetables are golden brown.

Transfer the chicken and vegetables to a large stockpot, then deglaze the roasting pan with wine over high heat, if using. Add the wine with the remaining vegetables and herbs to the pot, and cover with about 2.5 litres water. Simmer, uncovered, for 3–4 hours.

Strain the stock straight away through a sieve into a bowl, then cool by immersing the bowl in a sink of cold water. Refrigerate the stock to let any fat settle on the surface, then remove the fat.

The stock will keep for up to 4 days in the refrigerator or for 3 months in the freezer. To reduce the stock, boil in a saucepan over high heat until it is reduced by three-quarters. When the reduced stock is chilled in the refrigerator, it should set as a jelly; if not, reduce again. Jellied stock will keep in the refrigerator for 2–3 days, and in the freezer for 3 months.

STUFFED ROAST CHICKEN   *Serves 6*

If you are roasting a supermarket chook, I'll warrant that this recipe for our family stuffing will be serious competition for the chicken itself. I really urge you, however, to seek out birds grown to maturity by small producers – then the combination of succulent, flavoursome flesh and our stuffing will return roast chicken to its place of honour on the table!

I have a variety of timers in my kitchen that I use constantly, and you might find one useful for this recipe. I'm always doing six things at once and it's all too easy to get distracted and forget to turn the chook or put the vegies on.

100 g bacon, rind removed, meat cut
  into matchsticks

1 large onion, finely chopped

¼ cup (60 ml) extra virgin olive oil

120 g chicken livers, trimmed

3 cups (210 g) coarse stale breadcrumbs

1 sprig rosemary, leaves stripped and
  finely chopped

¼ cup flat-leaf parsley leaves

2 teaspoons thyme leaves

1 × 2.4 kg free-range *or* corn-fed chicken

sea salt flakes and freshly ground
  black pepper

1 lemon

butter, for cooking

Preheat the oven to 180°C. Cook the bacon in a dry frying pan over high heat. Sauté the onion in the same pan over medium heat in half of the olive oil, then drain the excess fat from the frying pan. Sear the livers on both sides in the same pan for 2–3 minutes over medium heat, then rest them for a few minutes before slicing (the livers should still be pink in the middle).

Toast the breadcrumbs with the remaining olive oil in a roasting pan in the oven until golden, watching that they don't burn. Mix all the herbs in a bowl with the onion, bacon, livers and breadcrumbs.

Season the inside of the chicken with salt, pepper and a squeeze of lemon juice, then fill the cavity with the stuffing. Smear the outside of the chicken with butter and sprinkle with salt and pepper. Squeeze the rest of the lemon juice over the bird.

Roast the chicken on one side in a roasting pan for 20 minutes. (If the bird is browning unevenly, you may need to use a trivet or a potato to raise the unbrowned end. You may also find that a splash of water or stock needs to be added to the pan to prevent the juices burning.) Turn the bird over onto its other side and cook for another 20 minutes. Turn the chicken breast-side up and cook for another 20 minutes.

Once the chicken is cooked, remove it from the oven and turn it breast-side down to rest, covered, for at least 20 minutes before carving.

CHICKEN BREASTS WITH ROSEMARY, PINE NUTS AND VERJUICE

Serves 4

⅓ cup (55 g) raisins

¼ cup (60 ml) verjuice

2 sprigs rosemary

⅓ cup (80 ml) extra virgin olive oil,
  plus extra for drizzling

freshly ground black pepper

4 free-range chicken breasts, skin on

⅓ cup (50 g) pine nuts

1 tablespoon butter

sea salt flakes

Salsa Agresto (see page 20), to serve

Soak the raisins in the verjuice overnight. (Alternately, microwave the raisins and verjuice on the defrost setting for about 5 minutes, then leave to cool.) »

Strip the rosemary leaves and reserve for another use. Place the stalks in a bowl with 60 ml of the olive oil and a little pepper. Add the chicken breasts and marinate for at least 1 hour.

Preheat the oven to 220°C. Moisten the pine nuts with a little olive oil and roast on a baking tray for 5 minutes or until golden brown; keep an eye on them as they burn easily.

Heat the butter until golden brown in a frying pan large enough to accommodate all the chicken breasts with lots of space between them; otherwise, cook the chicken in batches. Add the remaining tablespoon of olive oil to the pan to inhibit burning, then salt the chicken breasts and pan-fry, skin-side down, over medium heat for 6–10 minutes or until well sealed and golden. Turn and cook on the other side for 3–4 minutes or until cooked through. (The total cooking time will depend on the thickness of the breasts, but as a rule, two-thirds of the cooking should be done on the skin side.) Season the chicken with salt and pepper, then rest in a warm place, skin-side down.

Discard any butter left in the pan and toss in the raisins and the verjuice, then deglaze the pan over high heat until the liquid has reduced by half. Stir in the pine nuts.

Pour the sauce over the chicken and serve with Salsa Agresto. If serving for lunch, then accompany with a salad of peppery greens. For an evening meal, serve with soft polenta (see page 60) or potatoes mashed with extra virgin olive oil.

BONED CHICKEN STUFFED WITH GIBLETS AND PROSCIUTTO

Serves 4

½ cup (125 ml) verjuice

4 litres reduced Golden Chicken Stock
(see page 55)

1 × 1.6 kg boned free-range chicken
(ask your butcher to do this)

sea salt flakes

STUFFING

100 g chicken giblets, cleaned and
sliced widthways

100 g chicken hearts

butter, for cooking

2 tablespoons freshly chopped herbs
(preferably rosemary and marjoram)

freshly ground black pepper

1 large onion, roughly chopped

2 cups (140 g) coarse stale breadcrumbs

extra virgin olive oil, for cooking

200 g thinly sliced prosciutto, finely chopped

1 teaspoon Dijon mustard

Preheat the oven to 220°C. To make the stuffing, cook the giblets and hearts in a small frying pan over medium heat in a little butter with the herbs and a grind of black pepper, then chop them finely and set aside in a medium-sized bowl. Sweat the onion in some more butter over low heat, then add it to the giblet mixture. Toast the breadcrumbs with a little olive oil in a roasting pan in the oven until golden, watching that they don't burn. Add the prosciutto, mustard and breadcrumbs to the giblet mixture.

In a deep saucepan over high heat, reduce the verjuice by half. Add the stock to the pan and heat until warm. Flatten out the boned chicken, skin-side down, and spread it with the

stuffing, then roll up the chicken and season with salt. Wrap the chicken in a double thickness of muslin (or an old tea towel or large Chux), then secure each end with kitchen string so it is shaped like a bonbon.

Put the stuffed bird into a large saucepan with the warm stock mixture – it is important that at least three-quarters of the bird is immersed. Poach for 20 minutes over low heat at a very gentle simmer, then turn the bird over and poach it for another 20 minutes. Remove the bird and wrap it in foil to rest for 30 minutes. Reduce the poaching liquid over high heat to a sauce consistency.

Slice the stuffed chicken and serve it with the sauce and a dollop of Salsa Verde (see page 185).

FREE-RANGE CHOOK WITH GREEN OLIVES, FENNEL AND SOFT POLENTA

Serves 6–8

I love to use my daughter Saskia's chooks for all my chicken dishes. Her chickens are reared free-range, on a vegetarian diet; you can really taste the difference this makes.

1 × 2.3 kg free-range *or* organic chicken,
  cut into 12 pieces
1 cup (250 ml) extra virgin olive oil,
  plus extra for drizzling
½ cup (125 ml) verjuice
2 pieces preserved lemon, flesh removed,
  rind rinsed and chopped
1 sprig rosemary
1 large fennel bulb, diced
1 large onion, diced
1 clove garlic, finely chopped
sea salt flakes and freshly ground
  black pepper
1 cup (250 ml) Golden Chicken Stock
  (see page 55)

1 × 400 g can crushed tomatoes *or*
  400 ml tomato sugo (see Glossary)
  with basil
120 g green olives

POLENTA
2 cups (500 ml) milk
1 cup (250 ml) Golden Chicken Stock
  (see page 55)
100 g butter
125 g fine polenta
sea salt flakes and freshly ground
  black pepper
¼ cup freshly grated Parmigiano Reggiano
  (optional), to serve

Marinate the chicken pieces in a large bowl with the olive oil, verjuice, preserved lemon and rosemary in the refrigerator for a few hours or overnight.

Preheat the oven to 180°C. Transfer the chicken to a roasting pan, reserving the marinade. Add the fennel, onion and garlic to the pan, drizzle with a little olive oil and season well with salt and pepper. Brown the chicken and vegetables in the oven for 10–20 minutes. Remove the pan from the oven and reset the temperature to 160°C. Deglaze the pan with a little of the reserved marinade over high heat on the stove, then add the chicken stock, tomatoes and olives. Turn the chicken pieces and roast for another 20 minutes, then turn them to the other side and roast for another 20 minutes. Remove from the oven and rest the chicken pieces, skin-side down, in the tomatoey juices.

Meanwhile, to make the polenta, bring the milk, stock and butter to scalding point in a saucepan over medium heat. Whisk in the polenta, then reduce the heat to low and season with salt and pepper. Stir the polenta for 30 minutes; there is no other way to get a creamy result, and under-cooked polenta is a pale imitation of its perfectly cooked cousin! When it is ready, stir in the Parmigiano Reggiano, if using.

Spoon the soft polenta onto a platter and top with the rested chicken and sauce. Sautéed spinach or silverbeet is a great accompaniment to this meal.

CHICKEN BREASTS STUFFED WITH
APRICOTS AND GREEN PEPPERCORNS
Serves 4

8 dried apricots

verjuice, for soaking

160 g unsalted butter, at room temperature,
    chopped

2 teaspoons chopped green peppercorns

2 tablespoons freshly chopped
    flat-leaf parsley

2 teaspoons chopped thyme

4 × 250–300 g free-range chicken breast
    fillets, skin on

sea salt flakes and freshly ground
    black pepper

extra virgin olive oil, for frying

Preheat the oven to 180°C. Place the apricots and a little verjuice or water to cover in a small saucepan and simmer over low heat until apricots are plump and hydrated. Remove from the heat and leave to cool, then drain and roughly chop.

Mix the butter, apricots, peppercorns and herbs in a bowl with your hands; this stops the ingredients from breaking up too much. Divide the butter mixture into quarters. Push one quarter of the mixture gently under the skin of each breast, then run your hand over the skin to create a smooth surface.

Heat a little olive oil in a large frying pan over medium–high heat, season each breast with salt, then sear until golden on both sides. Transfer chicken to a baking tray and roast for about 9 minutes or until cooked through. Remove from the oven and leave to rest in a warm spot for 10–15 minutes, then serve with steamed broccolini and smashed waxy potatoes with extra virgin olive oil.

ROAST CHICKEN WITH FIG, GRAPE,
WALNUT AND BREAD SALAD
Serves 6–8

My first trip to San Francisco was for the 'Fancy Food' Trade Show. As trade shows are notoriously exhausting, standing for between eight and ten hours a day, talking to every potential customer and telling the same story over and over again, there had to be some treats to keep me going. I was travelling with Wayne Lyons, my General Manager at the time, who had never been to the States. He was most amused that I had a list of restaurants to visit as he expected neither of us would have the energy to do anything more than grab a bite to eat by dinnertime. However, I had my priorities, and so on our only free night we managed to get a very late booking at Zuni Café. When we arrived at about 10 p.m. and our table wasn't quite ready, I suspect we were almost past hunger. I gave Wayne no choice at all and ordered the roast chicken with bread salad for two – it was very simple and just so remarkable.

I have used the principle of the way I think they cooked it in many different forms ever since. The essentials are firstly to have a great chook, and secondly to use great bread.

1 × 2 kg free-range *or* organic chicken, cut into 12 pieces	SALAD
sea salt flakes	6 preserved vine leaves, patted dry
½ cup (125 ml) Golden Chicken Stock (see page 55)	2 tablespoons unsalted butter, chopped
2 tablespoons verjuice	½ cup chopped walnuts
	⅓ cup (80 ml) olive oil
MARINADE	3 thick slices wood-fired bread, crusts removed, cut into chunks
2 cloves garlic, thinly sliced	8 figs, halved
⅓ cup (80 ml) verjuice	1½ tablespoons red-wine vinegar
⅓ cup (80 ml) extra virgin olive oil	¼ preserved lemon, flesh removed, rind rinsed and thinly sliced
4 sprigs tarragon	1½ cups seedless green *or* black grapes
freshly ground black pepper, to taste	2 tablespoons freshly chopped flat-leaf parsley

Mix the marinade ingredients together and place in a sealed container with the chicken pieces. Refrigerate for 2–4 hours, turning once.

Preheat the oven to 200°C. Place the drumsticks in a roasting pan, season with salt and bake for 7–10 minutes. Remove the remaining chicken pieces from the marinade, add to the pan, season and bake for another 10 minutes or until golden and cooked through. Heat the stock in a small saucepan over high heat, then add to the roasting pan along with the verjuice. Cover with foil and leave to rest while you make the salad.

Reduce the oven temperature to 180°C. Place the vine leaves on a large baking tray, dot with butter and roast for 2 minutes or until crisp. Place the walnuts on another baking tray and lightly roast in the oven. Heat 2 tablespoons of the olive oil in a frying pan over medium heat, then add the bread and fig halves and fry until golden. Mix the vinegar and remaining olive oil in a large salad bowl, tasting to check that the flavour is balanced. Toss the bread, figs, walnuts, preserved lemon and grapes in the bowl with the dressing and season to taste. Add the chook pieces, pan juices, vine leaves and flat-leaf parsley and serve.

CHICKEN PIECES ROASTED WITH OLIVES, PRESERVED LEMON AND FENNEL

Serves 6

2 kg chicken thighs, skin on, trimmed
    of excess fat
2 preserved lemons, flesh removed,
    rind rinsed and cut into long strips
1 tablespoon fennel seeds *or* 1 fennel
    bulb (when in season), cut into
    1 cm-thick slices
freshly ground black pepper

extra virgin olive oil, for cooking
24 black olives (do not pit or the flavour
    will leach out; simply warn your guests)
sea salt flakes
1–2 tablespoons verjuice
lots of freshly chopped flat-leaf parsley,
    to serve

Toss the chicken (always with the skin on, even if you are strong-willed enough to take it off after cooking – it keeps the chicken moist) in a bowl with the preserved lemon, fennel seeds or fennel, some pepper and enough extra virgin olive oil to coat the ingredients. Leave to marinate for 1 hour.

Preheat the oven to 220°C. Divide the chicken and marinade between 2 shallow roasting pans, then add the olives and season with salt. Make sure the pans are large enough so that none of the pieces overlap and there is just enough oil to coat all the chicken. Roast for about 10 minutes.

Turn the chicken over and reset the oven to 180°C, then cook for another 10 minutes or until the chicken is cooked through, keeping an eye on it to make sure the marinade ingredients are not burning.

Remove from the oven, drizzle with verjuice and a tablespoon or two of good extra virgin olive oil and leave to rest, covered, for 15 minutes. Just before serving, add the parsley and use the pan juices to moisten the chicken.

CHOKOS

I'M SURE THAT MY AUNT'S GARDEN IN ASHFIELD WAS THE norm when I was growing up in Sydney: chokos grew rampant through the compost, and the vines rambled over the back fence and into the lane behind. The humid climate obviously suited them, and as a child it seemed to me that jungles of chokos grew wild everywhere.

I'm talking of a long time ago, in the post-war period, when there was a limited range of vegetables on offer. I don't remember chokos being for sale in shops but there was such a glut of them every summer, and no one wasted anything in those days, so they were a staple. Not only that, but as the choko readily picks up the flavour of other foods it was often used to extend jams, which were themselves part of the breakfast ritual in most families then.

Few of my contemporaries share my positive memories of chokos, with my husband Colin going so far as to say they are a waste of space – however, I love them. I find them delicate, whereas others describe them as tasteless. I suspect it is a simple matter of the offending chokos having been cooked until they became grey and watery. I was lucky in that as bad a cook as my aunt was in general, she cooked two things to perfection: chokos and broad beans. She was a passionate gardener, so these vegetables went straight from the plant to the pot. Although she always peeled chokos (under running water so the sticky milk they exuded could be washed away), we ate them so often they were always quite small when picked; at this size their skin is hardly spiky at all and their flavour is more pronounced. My aunt usually steamed the chokos in a small wire basket in her pressure cooker, which meant they didn't become waterlogged.

These days, if I ever find tiny apple-green chokos in the market I rush home and steam them whole, then cut them in half and add lashings of butter, freshly ground black pepper and lemon juice and eat the lot – skin, seeds and all. If they are slightly larger, but still unmarked and bright green, I peel them, then sauté them in extra virgin olive oil with fresh thyme and garlic. For a speedy result, cook peeled and quartered chokos for 8 minutes in barely boiling, salted water before slicing them. I have also tried baking a large choko stuffed with spicy minced meat, but it's like cooking an overgrown zucchini: the vegetable is really just a tasteless vehicle cooked only so as not to be wasted. The secret is to relish tiny chokos in season – and to compost the rest.

As the choko is seldom written about, and even less frequently honoured, I remember clearly an article written years ago by Melbourne food teacher Penny Smith. In it she revealed that it had taken an overseas trip for her to realise the potential of a vegetable in her own backyard. She had ordered a salad of crab meat and coconut in Madagascar; a shredded, pale-green crunchy vegetable was a wonderful part of the dish. It was raw choko. Since reading Penny's article, raw choko has become part of my salads – but the choko must be young.

I wrote ten years ago that, of the ten specialised vegetable books I owned, only three mentioned chokos. Jane Grigson had once again not disappointed me, as in her *Vegetable Book* she devoted a chapter to it – under the name 'Chayote', as it is more commonly known elsewhere.

Jane had written of an Australian friend of hers who picked a huge choko weighing over a kilogram (I'm sure it would have made the *Guinness Book of Records* and the front pages of the local newspapers, but only as a curiosity). The friend took it into her kitchen where, I quote, 'it soon started to wander. A long pale stem with rudimentary leaves and clinging tendrils burst through the choko from the single flat seed, and explored every cranny of the room, a triffid of a plant, until it found the door. Then she disentangled it carefully and cradled the shrunken parent to a hollow she had made by the trellis, where it could take root and rampage fruitfully.'

Much closer to home, and so important in so many ways, is Stephanie Alexander's updated edition of *The Cook's Companion*, the book I go to first these days. Stephanie has the most encyclopaedic knowledge of food, and her book has a chapter on chokos full of all the information you could want – on the varieties and season, selection and storage, preparation and cooking, as well as recipes.

I wouldn't swap my Mediterranean climate for anything, but I occasionally long for a choko vine. I cannot resist buying a choko that is going to seed and am full of optimism as I plant it, but sadly I've yet to succeed.

CRAB AND CHOKO SALAD INSPIRED BY PENNY SMITH *Serves 4*

While my copy of Penny Smith's article is long gone, I still have my notes, and the few times I've been able to get young chokos by some fluke, have made the recipe using our

South Australian blue swimmer crabs. Even though you can buy already picked crab meat, it will never be as good as crab you catch yourself. If you do find good-quality picked crab meat make sure you take it out of its vacuum packaging an hour in advance to rid it of any plastic smell – check that no bits of shell remain and moisten the crab meat with a little extra virgin olive oil.

4–6 tiny chokos	sea salt flakes and freshly ground
1 tablespoon coconut milk	black pepper
2 tablespoons lemon juice	250 g cooked crab meat, freshly picked
100 ml fruity extra virgin olive oil	1 cup coriander leaves

Peel the chokos and then slice them finely lengthways (I use a Japanese shredder), seeds and all. To make the dressing, mix the coconut milk, half the lemon juice and ¼ cup (60 ml) of the olive oil, then season with salt and pepper and adjust with more lemon juice, if necessary.

Sprinkle the crab meat with the remaining lemon juice and olive oil, then season and let stand for a minute or so. Toss the crab meat carefully with the dressing, coriander and choko and serve on a large plate.

CHOKO SALAD   *Serves 4*

6 tiny chokos	2 plump witlof
2 tablespoons lemon juice	1 × 150 g piece bacon, rind discarded,
1 teaspoon Dijon mustard	meat diced
200 ml extra virgin olive oil	1 large clove garlic, crushed
sea salt flakes and freshly ground	1 thick slice white bread, crusts removed,
black pepper	cut into small cubes
1 tablespoon freshly chopped chervil	

Peel the chokos, then slice them finely lengthways (I use a Japanese shredder), seeds and all. (If your chokos aren't tiny, boil them whole in their skins for 20 minutes and then slice them finely.)

For the vinaigrette, mix the lemon juice and mustard, then whisk in 125 ml of the olive oil and season with salt and pepper. Mix the chervil into the vinaigrette, then toss it with the choko slices and set aside.

Separate the witlof leaves without using a knife (to do so will cause discolouration), discarding any damaged outer leaves. Render the bacon in a hot, dry frying pan over high heat until cooked. Meanwhile, gently heat the remaining olive oil with the garlic in another frying pan over low heat and fry the bread cubes until golden brown, then drain on kitchen paper. Toss the croutons with the witlof, bacon and dressed chokos and serve.

CHRISTMAS

THERE ARE SO MANY OPTIONS FOR CHRISTMAS LUNCH BUT, for me, the best is a lunch of simplicity and style with people I care about. I feel strongly about family traditions and somehow, in my family, all our traditions come back to food. The difficulty arises in a partnership when you suddenly find you have two differing sets of traditions.

There are two alternatives. One is to compromise to keep the extended family together; the other is for each family, at some stage, to begin their own set of traditions. When children are young, nothing is more fun than gathering together all the cousins and sharing the presents under the tree. As the children grow up, they start to want their 'special friends' to join them on Christmas Day. So, either the family gathering becomes larger (as long as each contributing family can find common ground to enjoy the day) or an alternative day is found for the extended family get-together, and new traditions develop that will probably stay in place for the next generation. Whatever path is chosen, the most important thing, as far as I am concerned, is the sharing of good food.

When I was a child in Sydney, our Christmas lunch was casual but wonderful. Both my parents were great cooks but very little work was done on Christmas Day. We shared the day with relatives and friends and the common theme was always a large table laden with food. Sometimes this would be inside, sometimes in the garden – and several times, actually on the beach.

When I was very young, the pride of the table would be a roast chook. It's hard to remember just what a luxury that was, though I do remember the kerfuffle when Dad killed it in the backyard, which my brothers delighted in – but Mum and I always had the job of plucking and cleaning it. A pretty typical household of the time!

Our food became more lavish as the years progressed, and goose became the star of the table. For me it has been so ever since – Christmas without goose just doesn't seem right. There was sometimes duck or chook as well, depending on how many people there were to feed. We often began with fresh Hawkesbury River oysters, and I do remember having wine with the meal (but never champagne, as we might today). There would be lots of salads on the table – simple things like fresh tomatoes and beetroots cooked and sliced into vinegar with onion, and lovely fresh potato salad. I think the mayonnaise was made

with condensed milk and vinegar then, but I remember it tasting wonderful at the time. The only thing we would actually cook on the day was the potatoes – even the goose would be cooked on Christmas Eve and kept in the food safe. We would also have a ham or a hand of pork, and a wonderful brawn (see opposite), which filled the crispers of our old fridge.

Having inherited the tradition of a feast of beautifully simple food from my own parents, it is so important to me to continue that tradition for my children, and now my grandchildren. We keep it really simple so there is no stress, with much of the preparation being done the night before. The cooking of the goose, though, is always done on Christmas morning now, these days in an oven bag, while we have drinks with our friends the Schuberts who host open house.

But our favourite Christmas times are when we all sit outside, either under the pear tree at the bottom of our garden, or in the courtyard under the umbrella of what must be a one-hundred-year-old wisteria tree.

While I now make the Christmas pudding (not just one but by the thousands!) I truly can't remember ever serving it on Christmas Day. These days we're more likely to have a jelly of sparkling shiraz set with raspberries for the adults, and our vanilla bean and elderflower ice creams for the kids, and leave the pudding for the Boxing Day supper to have with the leftovers.

BRAWN   *Makes enough to fill a large mixing bowl*

Making brawn, as my parents did every Christmas, is not a task to be undertaken lightly. Firstly, you need a most co-operative butcher, and you may need to place your order at least a week in advance. Often the tongue is sold separately from the pig's head, so you'll need to make a separate order, or you can use 4 sheep's tongues instead. Ask for brined trotters, which give the dish that extra saltiness. Most of all, be prepared to pitch in and 'get your hands dirty' to pull all the meat away from the bone once it is cooked – not for the squeamish. For me, it's a labour of love.

1 pig's head, cut into 4 (the tongue was not present in the one I bought)	2 sprigs thyme
	10 crushed juniper berries
4 sheep's tongues, brined	10 allspice berries
2 brined pig's trotters (they are not salty enough if not brined)	¼ cup (60 ml) white-wine vinegar
	1 cup (250 ml) white wine
1 veal knuckle	sea salt flakes and freshly ground black pepper
3 onions, chopped	
2 carrots, chopped	juice of 1 lemon
3 leeks, white part only, chopped	rind of 1 lemon *or* orange
5 stalks flat-leaf parsley	½ cup freshly chopped flat-leaf parsley
2 fresh bay leaves	

Remove the brain from the pig's head, otherwise it will limit the life of the finished brawn. Wash all the meat and vegetables well. Put the meat into a large stockpot. Add the chopped vegetables, herbs and spices. Just cover with water, add the vinegar and simmer very, very slowly (over the lowest heat possible) until the meat falls off the bone. This takes about 5 hours, with a simmer pad under the pot to slow the cooking. (Brawn, like stock, can be cooked too much so that all the goodness is cooked out of it.) Skim occasionally as it cooks, and when cooked, pick through the meat whilst still warm, rejecting any skin, bone or gristle, and put the meat into a bowl. (I prefer to leave some meat whole or in large chunks, such as the tongues and cheeks. There should be a mixture of sizes and textures in the finished brawn.) Refrigerate the cooking liquid to easily remove any fat residue – it will jelly once cold.

Bring the cooking liquid to the boil and strain immediately. Take 2 cups of the strained liquid and the wine and boil it, reducing it by half. Taste and add salt, pepper and lemon juice, as required. Add the meat pieces and simmer for just a few minutes, then re-check the seasoning. Remember that the brawn will be eaten cold, so it will need to be more highly seasoned than usual. Add lemon or orange rind and freshly chopped parsley. Pour into a glass bowl and leave to set in the fridge. Serve cold with crusty bread and home-made pickles.

The following is the menu for a
simple sort of lunch for Christmas Day.

———— ◆ ————

Yabbies with Walnut Dressing

Roast Goose with Apple, Onion and Sage Stuffing

Apple Aïoli

Aunt Reta's Christmas Pudding

YABBIES WITH WALNUT DRESSING   *Serves 4*

16 live yabbies (4 per person)

fresh dill (wild dill, if you can get it),
    for cooking

caraway seeds, for cooking

DRESSING

150 g walnuts

1 slice white bread, crust removed

2 tablespoons milk

2 cloves garlic

¼ cup (60 ml) lemon juice

70 ml walnut oil

sea salt flakes and freshly ground
    black pepper

First stun the yabbies by placing them in the freezer for 20 minutes. Bring a saucepan of salted water to the boil and throw in the yabbies, along with some dill and caraway seeds. Boil them rapidly for 3 minutes. Drain and leave to cool.

Preheat the oven to 200°C. For the dressing, roast the walnuts on a baking tray in the oven until they just begin to colour. While still warm, rub their skins away in a tea towel then, using a sieve or colander, shake the discarded skins away and leave the nuts to cool. Use a mortar and pestle or food processor to grind the walnuts to a fine paste. Soak the bread in the milk, squeezing out as much liquid as possible by hand. Crush the garlic cloves with a little salt under the wide blade of a chef's knife. Blend with the soaked bread and lemon juice in a food processor to make a smooth paste. Add the walnut paste and continue blending in the food processor, adding the walnut oil slowly as if making a mayonnaise, and season to taste with salt and pepper if necessary. Chill the dressing before serving.

To serve, peel the yabbies and serve with the chilled dressing.

ROAST GOOSE WITH APPLE, ONION AND SAGE STUFFING   *Serves 6*

A goose doesn't have a huge amount of meat on the breast, but what it has is incredibly rich, so a bird this size will easily feed six people. Using an oven bag to stop the meat drying out is a measure worth taking no matter the age of the goose, but an older goose requires a much longer cooking time and a very slow oven to become tender. The most important factor in achieving success is to know the age of your goose, so ask the supplier; only roast a goose without an oven bag if you are assured the goose is no older than twelve to fourteen weeks.

1 × 3.5–4 kg goose
extra virgin olive oil, for cooking
verjuice *or* lemon juice, for cooking
sea salt flakes and freshly ground
    black pepper

STUFFING
1 cup walnuts
80 g butter
250 g dried apples, minced

30 sage leaves
¼ cup (60 ml) verjuice, plus extra if needed
1 cup chopped pale-green celery leaves
100 ml extra virgin olive oil
4 small onions, finely chopped
freshly grated nutmeg, to taste
2½ cups (175 g) stale grated breadcrumbs
sea salt flakes and freshly ground
    black pepper

Preheat the oven to 200°C. For the stuffing, roast the walnuts on a baking tray in the oven until they just begin to colour. While still warm, rub their skins away in a tea towel then, using a sieve or colander, shake the discarded skins away and leave the nuts to cool. Finely chop the walnuts and set aside. Heat the butter in a frying pan, then sauté the apples and sage and, when almost cooked, deglaze the pan with verjuice, add celery leaves and transfer to a bowl. Heat the olive oil in the pan, then sauté the onions over low heat until cooked. Add a little nutmeg to taste.

While the onions are still hot, add the breadcrumbs, walnuts and apple and sage mixture, then moisten with a little extra verjuice if needed. Stuff the bird with this mixture and secure the cavity; either sew it up or plug with a whole apple to stop the stuffing escaping. When I use an apple, I find sealing the cavity with a metal skewer sufficient to keep the stuffing from falling out. Reduce the oven temperature to 160°C.

Coat the stuffed goose with a little extra virgin olive oil and verjuice or lemon juice (this will caramelise the skin as the goose cooks), season well, then place in an oven bag and transfer to a large roasting pan. For a young goose, cook for 45 minutes, then turn the bird over and cook for another 45 minutes or until the legs come away easily from the bone (with an older goose, it could take twice as long for this to occur). For an older goose, turn the oven down to 120°C after the first 45 minutes and cook for another 2 hours 15 minutes (about 3 hours in total).

When cooked, open the oven bag and increase the temperature to 210°C, then return the goose to the oven to brown the breast skin for 10 minutes.

For a casual meal, I would serve the goose with Apple Aïoli rather than a sauce (see page 72). An alternative would be a jar of quality cranberry jelly or the cabernet jelly I make at the Farmshop.

APPLE AÏOLI

1 Granny Smith apple

juice of 1 lemon

4 egg yolks

2 cloves garlic, crushed

2 cups (500 ml) extra virgin olive oil

sea salt flakes and freshly ground
black pepper

Grate the apple and immediately soak in the lemon juice. Process the yolks in a food processor with the garlic, grated apple and lemon juice. While processing, add half the oil in a thin stream and then the rest more rapidly, until emulsified. Season to taste.

AUNT RETA'S CHRISTMAS PUDDING

Most families have pretty entrenched Christmas traditions surrounding food, and in ours these were definitely the province of my Aunt Reta, whose role in the household all her life was to make both the Christmas pudding and cake. The pudding was a major hit, moist and luscious, and so full of rum and threepences and sixpences that we thought it terribly daring. This pudding is a source of great nostalgia for me, so I include it here for sentimental reasons. The quantities can easily be halved for a smaller pud, and you can use brandy instead if you find the rum too strong. The Christmas pudding in *Maggie's Table* is closer to the one I make commercially; the percentage of fruit is so high it needs no sugar at all.

500 g dried currants

400 g sultanas

200 g muscatels

200 g mixed peel

200 g glacé cherries

1½ cups (375 ml) overproof rum

380 g butter

380 g dark-brown sugar

8 eggs

1 tablespoon mixed ground nutmeg
and cinnamon

675 g self-raising flour, plus extra
for dusting

salt

Mix the fruit in a large bowl and soak overnight in the rum.

Cream the butter and sugar then mix in the eggs, one at a time. Stir in the fruit, rum and spices. Sift in the flour with a large pinch of salt and mix well. Dust a square of washed calico (approximately 70 cm square) with flour. Spoon the pudding mixture into the centre of the cloth, pull the corners and edges to the centre and tie well with kitchen string to secure.

Bring a large saucepan of water to the boil. Immerse the pudding, bring the water back to the boil and let it bubble quietly over low heat for 6 hours, keeping the pudding completely immersed. When cooked, hang in a well-ventilated place to dry until required.

Before you wish to serve, boil the pudding again in a large saucepan of water for 1 hour. Unwrap and serve.

Aunt Reta's Christmas pudding

CURRANTS

IT IS SO RARE TO SEE FRESH CURRANTS IN THE MARKETPLACE. AS a fresh fruit they are almost forgotten, yet if there's any chance at all of finding them fresh it will be between February and March. I suspect your best chance will be in organic or farmers' markets, but the flavour of the tiny, almost-black currants is so wonderfully intense that it's a shame they are not much more accessible. If you're lucky enough to find them, eat from the bottom of the cluster up, holding the stem way above your mouth – a little like the fox in *Aesop's Fables* – and just lie back and enjoy them.

There are two main varieties of currant. The zante, the one I sometimes find, is an early and very fragile variety; its thin skin and intense, sweet flavour make it perfect for eating fresh. The more commonly seen carina, the most prevalent variety planted for drying, has a tougher skin and a longer bunch than the zante, and crops twice as heavily.

Many farmers believe that currants became unfashionable as the demand for bigger and bigger grapes increased. The fresh currants I buy are about double the price of sultana grapes, but they are worth every cent. As the soft-skinned zante is so vulnerable to damage as a growing crop (rain can cause enough damage to spoil a crop two years out of three, and spoilage in transport is a real issue too), it's difficult for farmers to justify growing currants unless a real premium is paid for them. They need to target the specialty market, and even that can be too small to sustain production.

I'm often driven by romantic ideas of gardening, such as one I had of planting twenty zante currant vines to grow over a glasshouse frame. The idea was that the resulting 'tunnel' would be wide enough to hold a large refectory table, yet low enough for the hanging bunches of ripe currants to be within reach. Well, I planted them on a slope and soon realised I had them in totally the wrong position for the final part of the plan – the long table. I moved them the next year to a more appropriate place but the spark must have gone out of the idea by then and after a year of very low rainfall and with no irrigation to aid my 'folly', I lost them all.

I now have a currant cutting given to me by a reader from a one-hundred-year-old vine of hers. I planted it on a post of the chicken shed and its crop will, I hope, be ready within weeks. Planting it by the chook shed means I go past it every day, so it doesn't get forgotten.

It was actually the currant that gave me my first true taste of the Barossa. In 1973 we started to look at properties from afar, buying the South Australian papers every week while still living in Sydney. One place sounded so promising I made the journey down by bus to look at it. I have never been particularly practical, and I fell in love with a currant vine that was laden with fruit ripe for eating, which hung down through the criss-cross of a very established trellis at the back door of the kitchen. Colin, hearing my report on the telephone that night, suggested I had another, more objective look. I would have bought the property just for that old vine, but sadly the house was a bit ramshackle in the harsh light of the next day.

Of all dried fruit, the currant is my favourite because it seems to have a higher acidity, which serves savoury food well (of course, the use of dried currants in cake-making is well established). If dried currants are to be added to rich game dishes such as hare, they are particularly good if soaked in verjuice or even red-wine vinegar beforehand.

If you want to dry your own currants, the fresh bunches can be strung across the ceiling in a draught-free pantry, each bunch out of reach of the next; it will take 5–10 days, depending on the weather. Bunches of currants can also be dried in the sun: arrange them side by side on black plastic, leaving enough plastic free so that it can be folded over the currants at night to keep out any moisture. If this process is carried out between the vines, as it often is, a lot of dust accumulates and the dried currants need to be washed. Handle the bunches very gently once they're dried to keep them intact, and spray them with olive-oil cooking spray to retain their moistness.

TUNA ROLLS WITH CURRANTS, PINE NUTS AND BAY LEAVES

Serves 8

This recipe came about when I was asked to do a cooking school at Accoutrement, a cookware supply store in Sydney. Owner Sue Jenkins knew of my plans to holiday in Italy and thought I should hold a school inspired by the food of Tuscany, Umbria and Sicily upon my return. Then frosts and drought all but decimated our grape crop at home, so my Italian travel plans were cancelled, but I was still committed to the classes. Luckily for me, books on Italian food form the major part of my library, such is my passion for Italy, and so my research for the classes came from these: I simply looked for recipes that would work best with my local ingredients.

I based the following recipe on one in Mary Taylor Simeti's wonderful book *Pomp and Sustenance*, although my method differs, and I use tuna rather than swordfish. I choose whichever tuna is in season: bluefin if you can find it, of course, but yellowfin is also well worth it. If you cannot buy tuna trimmed of its skin and bloodline, allow an extra 150 g to ensure you end up with 1 kg trimmed weight.

1 × 1 kg piece tuna, skin removed and
    bloodline trimmed
1 large red onion, cut into quarters
32 fresh bay leaves
extra virgin olive oil, for cooking
lemon wedges, to serve

FILLING
¼ cup (35 g) dried currants
2 tablespoons verjuice

16 bamboo skewers *or* rosemary sprigs,
    leaves stripped
¼ cup (40 g) pine nuts
1–2 tablespoons extra virgin olive oil
1 cup flat-leaf parsley leaves
5 cloves garlic
sea salt flakes and freshly ground
    black pepper
120 g freshly grated pecorino

For the filling, soak the currants in the verjuice overnight or heat on the defrost setting in a microwave for 5 minutes to reconstitute. Meanwhile, soak bamboo skewers or stripped rosemary stalks for 30 minutes in water to prevent them burning during cooking.

Preheat the oven to 200°C. Moisten the pine nuts with a little of the olive oil and roast on a baking tray for about 5–8 minutes or until golden brown. Keep an eye on them as they burn easily. Chop the parsley and garlic together well, then add the pine nuts and the reconstituted currants and roughly chop. Season to taste, then thoroughly stir in the pecorino and 1 tablespoon of the olive oil.

Keep the tuna chilled until you are ready to use it. Cut the tuna into 24 thin slices about 10 cm × 7.5 cm and about 3 mm thick. Gently flatten any smaller slices by placing between two pieces of plastic film and gently tapping with a soft mallet, as you would for scaloppine.

Separate the onion into crescents. Place 1 teaspoon of the currant filling on one end of each slice of tuna and roll it up as neatly as possible, then spear it a couple of centimetres off-centre onto a skewer or rosemary stalk with a piece of onion. Follow with a bay leaf, then another roll of tuna, then onion, and so on until 8 of the skewers have been filled (3 rolls and 4 bay leaves per skewer). Run a second skewer through the rolls parallel to the first skewer, but a couple of centimetres apart, and repeat this process with the remaining skewers. Make sure the skewers aren't packed too tightly; otherwise the fish will stew rather than grill or roast.

If grilling the rolls, heat the griller as high as it can go, otherwise roast at 230°C. Cook them in batches if your grill or oven is small – it is important that the tuna parcels don't touch, again to prevent stewing. Brush the tuna rolls with olive oil and grill for 2 minutes on the first side and 1 minute on the second, or roast for 5 minutes. The tuna should be only just seared and the onion needs to be nothing more than warm. Serve with extra virgin olive oil and lemon wedges. Any leftovers are delectable the next day, when the flavours have had time to meld.

SPINACH WITH CURRANTS AND PINE NUTS   *Serves 6*

175 g dried currants

½ cup (125 ml) verjuice

225 g pine nuts

1 kg spinach, carefully washed

sea salt flakes

¼ cup (60 ml) extra virgin olive oil

freshly ground black pepper

Soak the currants in the verjuice overnight or heat on defrost in a microwave for 5 minutes.

Preheat the oven to 200°C. Moisten the pine nuts with a little olive oil, then roast them on a baking tray for about 5–8 minutes or until golden brown; keep an eye on them as they burn easily. Plunge the spinach into a saucepan of boiling salted water and blanch for 30 seconds. Strain the spinach in a colander, pressing down very firmly to release as much water as possible. Strain the currants.

Heat the olive oil in a large, heavy-based frying pan and toss the drained spinach until warmed through, then add the pine nuts and currants and season with salt and pepper. Serve with grilled meat or fish.

AUSTRALIAN HERRINGS (TOMMY RUFFS) WITH CURRANTS   *Serves 12*

The first time I made this dish I used 10 kg of tommy ruff fillets. As the 1990 Adelaide Symposium of Gastronomy coincided with Writers' Week, we planned a 'fishes and loaves' luncheon after a forum at which Stephanie Alexander, Michael Symons (author of *One Continuous Picnic*) and Don Dunstan were speaking. The luncheon was fairly loosely arranged: it was advertised very minimally as a meal to be shared by everyone, and we had no idea how many would come.

I headed off from the Barossa with my van laden with trays and trays of freshly baked bread; the tommy ruffs with currants were on the floor of the van on butcher's trays covered with plastic film. On the outskirts of Adelaide is a tricky piece of road where the speed limits change. I was deep in thought about how we'd feed the multitude if they turned up when a policeman walked out onto the road. I only just saw him in time and jumped on the brakes, which sent the bread flying off the trays, while the fish marinade spilled everywhere. I was very upset – at the policeman and my own stupidity – and said, nearly in tears, 'I'm going to a miracle with Don Dunstan, please let me go!'

Speeding fines aside, the lunch was a great success. We laid all the food out in the writers' tent in the park and people seemed to come from everywhere. It was a great example of community faith and sharing. But because I'd been so worried about not having enough food, we had far too much, so we took the leftovers around to the Salvation Army, where a gentle giant of a man called Tiny thanked us, but said he'd make soup to go with it so it wasn't too rich a feed.

Tommy ruffs are a much under-utilised small oily fish a little like a plump, sweet herring – in fact, their name was officially changed to Australian herrings in July 2006. This dish makes for great al fresco eating as the fish is three-quarters cooked beforehand (the marinade completes the cooking) and is served at room temperature with crusty bread. If tommy ruffs are not available, the flavours in this dish complement almost any oily fish.

130 g dried currants	plain flour, seasoned with salt and freshly
1 cup (250 ml) verjuice	ground black pepper
butter, for cooking	3 large red onions, sliced into rings
1 cup (250 ml) extra virgin olive oil	rind and juice of 3 lemons
500 g tommy ruff (Australian herring) fillets	3 sprigs thyme

Soak the currants in verjuice overnight or heat on defrost in a microwave for 5 minutes.

Heat a knob of butter with a little of the olive oil in a heavy-based frying pan over medium heat until nut-brown. Dust each fish fillet with seasoned flour just before adding it to the pan and seal for 30 seconds on each side. Add more butter as needed before cooking the remaining fish, watching the temperature of the pan so that the butter is kept nut-brown.

Arrange the fillets in a serving dish in a single layer, topping and tailing them so that they are not on top of each other. Toss the onions in a little of the olive oil in a saucepan over medium heat for just long enough to soften, and then add the lemon juice and rind (this will change the colour of the onion from pale to deep pink or burgundy). Add as much of the remaining olive oil as required to balance the vinaigrette, then add the reconstituted currants and the thyme and warm gently over low heat. Pour the hot vinaigrette over the fish in the serving dish, where the 'cooking' will be completed. The fish can be eaten 15 minutes after the vinaigrette has been added or it can be left at room temperature (providing it isn't too hot) for eating later in the day. If refrigerating, bring back to room temperature before serving.

EGGPLANT

THERE ARE MANY MORE VARIETIES AVAILABLE THAN THE COMMON but beautiful glossy dark aubergine-coloured vegetable we call eggplant. (What came first – the colour or the vegetable?) When I bought my first really special car, I had to wait for my colour of choice to become available: the deep, lustrous purple of aubergine. The colour, shape and flavour of this fruit are all very special to me. I know most people call it eggplant, but old habits die hard, and while I still use both names, I always think 'aubergine'.

The long thin eggplants called Japanese eggplants are readily available; sometimes they are the same dark glistening aubergine colour and other times they are striped mauve and cream. There is also a variety that is similarly shaped but totally green, almost apple-green, and which makes for wonderful eating. Then there are tiny Thai eggplants I know little about. But the creamiest of all eggplants I've encountered is the Violetta di Firenze eggplant, introduced to me by Michael Voumard, a great chef and gardener, who was then living in the Barossa. They are round, about the size of a tennis ball, and the mauve and cream of their skin is intermingled rather than striped. These are a true taste sensation, particularly if you get the chance to enjoy recently picked ones. Michael also grew a long thin apple-green variety called Thai long green or Louisiana green – also creamy and just superb.

When shopping for the dark-purple variety, choose those with the darkest, shiniest skins with no shrivelling evident. I prefer the smaller fruit, as very large eggplant have big seeds and can be bitter. Such specimens are generally only to be seen late in the season and are large simply because they are older (although bear in mind that seasons differ Australia-wide and that larger specimens may reach you from further afield earlier than those produced locally).

I have learnt that the older, larger and literally seedier ones are also paler, as if the sun has bleached their colour. In my experience, young eggplants definitely do not need salting (contrary to what is widely advised) and, in fact, can easily become soggy with salting. While I seldom remove the skin, I have discovered that some members of the family who previously found it difficult to eat eggplant because it made their mouths sting quite badly had no trouble once it was peeled.

However, there is another reason to salt: it rids the eggplant of excess moisture and so reduces the amount of oil it soaks up as you pan-fry it. If you do salt eggplant, cut it the way you wish to use it and then sprinkle the exposed flesh with a little salt and leave it in a colander for 20 minutes to drain. The salt will leach out the juices, ridding a larger egg-

plant of bitterness, and revealing a mild, sweeter taste. Rinse off the salt and pat dry with kitchen paper before proceeding to cook the eggplant.

During the time of the Pheasant Farm Restaurant, I was lucky to have fantastic growers like the Fanto family on my doorstep. Like all good growers, the Fantos love to eat their own produce and Rose Fanto did not hesitate when I asked for her favourite use of their main crop. The Fantos eat a mainly vegetable-based diet and during the season eggplant fritters are a staple. Rose cuts smallish eggplants in half or sometimes quarters and then boils them briefly until they are soft right through. After leaving the eggplants to cool, she chops them with basil (she only uses basil), then adds breadcrumbs and eggs and rolls the mixture into balls, which she chills to ensure they hold their shape when deep-fried just before serving.

Recently picked ripe young eggplants have a marked sweetness about them, so chargrilling slices on the barbecue for a few minutes introduces a special flavour. Serve these as a side dish to meat or as a meal on their own, dressed with extra virgin olive oil, roughly chopped flat-leaf parsley, freshly ground black pepper, sea salt flakes and a touch of vino cotto or good balsamic vinegar.

I see no need to deep-fry eggplant, finding shallow-frying or sautéing in extra virgin olive oil best. Don't use your estate-bottled oil for this as there is no doubt it loses flavour upon heating, but extra virgin olive oil gives a crispness tinged with the fruity flavour of the olives. My next alternative would be a quality vegetable oil. A deep-sided heavy-based frying-pan works well, but handle it with care and make sure the pan is only half-filled with oil, since it will foam when you place the eggplant in. To test if the oil is hot enough, put a small piece of bread crust in the oil and if it sizzles around the crust, it is just about there. Take care that the oil is not so hot that it is smoking. Do not fry too much at a time as the temperature will drop too quickly and the eggplant will be saturated instead of crisp. Lift out when golden brown and place on crumpled kitchen paper to drain.

If you want to avoid using too much oil when cooking eggplant, you can brush slices with a little oil, sea salt and stripped rosemary and either dry-bake them until they collapse in an oven dish just big enough to fit them, or chargrill them. They can be served as an accompaniment to lamb chops, roast kid, or grilled chicken, quail or fish.

To prepare an eggplant as a meal in itself, cut a medium to large eggplant in half, spoon out the flesh and then refill each half with a mixture of breadcrumbs, beaten egg, tomato, grated cheese such as Parmigiano Reggiano, fresh herbs and the chopped eggplant flesh. This can be stewed, baked or barbecued and served with a salad or fresh tomato sauce for dinner.

Eggplant marries wonderfully with anchovies, pesto, goat's cheese, labna, garlic, tomatoes and oregano. But that's just the beginning. There are so many wonderful dishes with eggplant from so many cultures – Moroccan, Greek, Italian and French – that once you feel comfortable with this great vegetable you should search further into the dishes of these countries.

The Middle Eastern specialty baba ghanoush was probably my first-ever taste of eggplant, more years ago than I care to remember. Much later, when I was in Tasmania at a Symposium of Gastronomy, I tasted the benchmark of this classic dish at an eggplant feast prepared by Ann Ripper. Ann's former in-laws, the Haddad family, ran the Ali Akbar restaurant in Hobart, and she used dishes from their repertoire. This dinner was the most amazing statement of simplicity, with offerings arranged on platters for everyone to share. The six or seven dishes included: eggplant with red capsicum and garlic; a delicate and easy-to-handle rolled eggplant slice filled with goat's cheese and walnuts; an omelette with eggplant pasta; baba ghanoush – and oh, how I wish I could decipher the rest of my notes written on a paper serviette!

This experience took my love of eggplants to another level altogether; I couldn't wait to get home to try and replicate Ann's baba ghanoush, featuring smoked eggplant. I waited patiently for late summer, when eggplants are at their best. Success! Since then, I have had wonderful results with smoking eggplant on racks in my oven or following the method below, using a small fish smoker which can be bought from some hardware stores or the Queensland-based company Togar Ovens. Otherwise you can improvise using a barbecue with a hood.

MY TIPS FOR SMOKING EGGPLANT AND OTHER INGREDIENTS

+ My smoker works with any sawdust that is free of contaminants. Rosemary stalks added to the sawdust give extra flavour to whatever you are smoking. Or instead of sawdust, you can use lemon tree leaves or even a mixture of brown sugar and orange pekoe tea. If using sugar, place it on a sheet of heavy-duty foil so you don't have any mess to clean up later.

+ I find it handy to stand the smoker on a fire-resistant surface so it is high enough for me to be able to see if the flame is still burning. If the smoker is located out of the wind it will burn more slowly, which increases the intensity of the flavour.

✦ My instructions say a teacup of methylated spirits will burn for 25–30 minutes, but this depends a great deal on the conditions. Place the methylated spirits in the base of the windshield (a perforated metal ring).

✦ Make sure you use gloves or an oven mitt to lift the lid off the smoker as it gets very hot.

✦ If smoking eggplant over a naked flame, you should scrape off the charred skin before eating. Following the manufacturer's instructions, I place 2 tablespoons of sawdust and 6 rosemary stalks in the stainless steel tray, then light the methylated spirits. I then place 2 small–medium eggplants (halved lengthways), cut-side up, on the wire rack that sits above the sawdust (a second tray is used when smoking a larger quantity). With the lid on, I smoke the eggplants for 20 minutes, then turn them over, adding more methylated spirits and lighting the fire for another 10 minutes. By this time, the eggplants are perfectly cooked. I then use them to make Smoky Eggplant with Tahini (see below).

✦ Smoking food gives it a strong colour as well as flavour. You can enhance this even further by brushing the food with oil before smoking.

✦ Smoking is also suited to oily fish such as tommy ruffs (Australian herrings), while salmon fillets, particularly with the fatty belly attached, make a great and simple dish – leave the skin on to retain the moisture.

✦ The smoker is best cleaned with hot, soapy water soon after use.

SMOKY EGGPLANT WITH TAHINI
Makes about 500 ml

It is most important to use small to medium-sized eggplants that have no green tinges, as this indicates a lack of ripeness. Make sure too, that your tahini isn't past its use-by date, is of a good quality and is used at room temperature. This dish is delicious served warm or chilled on hot toast or flatbread.

2 small–medium eggplants,
   halved lengthways
1 clove garlic
¼ cup (60 ml) extra virgin olive oil
¼ cup freshly chopped flat-leaf parsley

juice of ½ lemon
150 ml tahini
sea salt flakes and freshly ground
   black pepper

Smoke the eggplants following the instructions given above. Leave the eggplants until cool enough to handle, then chop them roughly before pulsing them in a small food processor with the garlic, adding the olive oil in a thin stream. Stir in the parsley, lemon juice and tahini, then check the seasoning.

Grilled eggplant with herbs (see page 83)

ROSE'S PRESSED EGGPLANTS

Makes 2 litres

One year, my Barossa eggplant supplier, Rose Fanto, was persuaded to sell her produce at the Yalumba Harvest Picnic, held during the Barossa Vintage Festival. While Rose was sure of her own culinary traditions, she was less certain of how they might be received by the general public. Included in her selection were my favourite – pressed eggplants. Her recipe for salting, drying and pressing eggplants is worth the effort involved. Rose collects fennel from the roadside, where it grows wild, but you could use dill as an alternative.

1.5 kg eggplants, peeled and cut widthways
into 5 mm-thick slices
2 cloves garlic, thinly sliced

1 stalk fresh wild fennel *or* dill
salt
extra virgin olive oil, for drizzling

Layer the eggplant slices with the garlic and fennel in a large rectangular glass or ceramic dish. Top with a handful of salt, put a similar-sized tray on top and weigh down with a very heavy weight, then place in the refrigerator.

Pour off the liquid which collects every 2 days, until all the moisture from the eggplant has been drained or evaporates; this may take up to 6 weeks. The only way to be sure the eggplant is ready is to taste it – take a slice and drizzle it with really good olive oil, then eat it!

If ready, pack the pressed eggplant into sterilised preserving jars (see Glossary), top with olive oil and seal. These are so more-ish that you won't keep them long, but I would store them in the refrigerator where they'll last for months.

EGGPLANT WITH VINO COTTO

Serves 4 as an accompaniment

This dish makes an excellent accompaniment for grilled meats or whitefish – or simply serve it at room temperature with slabs of grilled wood-fired bread and a small rocket salad.

¼ cup (60 ml) extra virgin olive oil
1 onion, chopped
2 eggplants, cut diagonally into
5 mm-thick slices
sea salt flakes and freshly ground
black pepper

¼ cup (60 ml) vino cotto (see Glossary)
1 tablespoon freshly chopped
flat-leaf parsley

Heat the olive oil in a frying pan over medium heat, then add the onion and sauté for 5 minutes or until transparent. Season the eggplant with salt and pepper and add it to the pan to brown. Increase the heat to high and deglaze the pan with the vino cotto, cooking until the vino cotto is syrupy.

Fold through the flat-leaf parsley and serve.

VICTORIA'S STUFFED EGGPLANT WITH VERJUICE, ROCKET AND PRESERVED LEMON SAUCE

Serves 8 as an entrée or 4 as a main

Victoria Blumenstein worked for me for three years at the Farmshop after closing her own establishment, Blumenstein's, in Adelaide. Like so many of the people who have given so much to me while we've been working together over the years, Victoria has a passion for produce and cooking, coupled with a keen intelligence. I think how lucky I am that Victoria was with me at a time when I needed to devise ways of cooking with our new products, especially verjuice for the Japanese market. Never short of ideas, it was such a buzz working with her, as two minds approaching a challenge from slightly different directions are always more powerful than one. Victoria continually developed dishes for the Farmshop, using verjuice and vino cotto in ever-changing ways and recording these recipes for our customers. Here is one of her classic recipes using eggplant and verjuice.

2 eggplants, cut lengthways into
   2 cm-thick slices

STUFFING
⅓ cup (65 g) barley (to yield 1 cup
   cooked barley)
2 tablespoons chopped pitted kalamata olives
1 small red onion, finely chopped
2 tablespoons freshly chopped
   flat-leaf parsley
2 teaspoons chopped mint
finely chopped rind and juice of 1 lemon

½ cup (125 ml) extra virgin olive oil
sea salt flakes and freshly ground
   black pepper

SAUCE
3 quarters preserved lemon, flesh removed,
   rind rinsed and roughly chopped
⅓ cup (80 ml) verjuice
1 cup (250 ml) extra virgin olive oil
2 cups rocket leaves, trimmed
½ teaspoon sugar, or to taste (if needed)

For the stuffing boil the barley in water for 20 minutes. Combine the cooked barley with the remaining ingredients in a bowl and season to taste.

Meanwhile, if necessary, salt the eggplant slices, and place in a colander to drain for 20 minutes. Wash them and pat dry with kitchen paper. Heat a chargrill plate over high heat, then chargrill the eggplant slices and let cool.

Preheat the oven to 180°C. Place spoonfuls of stuffing at the widest end of the eggplant slices and roll up. Place the stuffed eggplant, seam-side down, in an oiled shallow baking dish, then bake for 12 minutes.

Meanwhile, to make the sauce, place the preserved lemon and verjuice in a blender or food processor and blend until lemon is finely chopped; the appearance should be slightly gelatinous. Add olive oil, then rocket, a little at a time, blending well before adding the next batch. The olive oil must cover the blade or the sauce will oxidise. If the sauce is a bit too sharp, adjust by adding sugar. Serve the stuffed eggplant with the sauce.

FRIED EGGPLANT WITH GARLIC, PARSLEY AND YOGHURT *Serves 4*

A dish similar to this was made for me about 20 years ago by a marvellous Frenchwoman, Kiki (who worked for me for a short period), the mother of Cath Kerry, a great cook, caterer and restaurateur for many years at the Adelaide Art Gallery. I use eggplant so much now that it seems strange to think I knew so little about it until then. Try moistening freshly cooked pasta liberally with extra virgin olive oil, then tossing this eggplant mixture through.

3 medium eggplants, peeled and cut into
    1 cm × 2 cm pieces
1 tablespoon salt (optional)
¼ cup (60 ml) extra virgin olive oil
3 cloves garlic, finely chopped

2 tablespoons freshly chopped
    flat-leaf parsley
freshly ground black pepper
1 cup (250 ml) yoghurt, crème frâiche
    or sour cream

If necessary, salt the eggplant slices and place in a colander to drain for 20 minutes. Wash them and pat dry with kitchen paper. Heat the oil in a frying pan over medium–high heat and fry the eggplant in small batches until golden brown. Place on kitchen paper to drain. Combine the garlic, parsley and pepper and scatter over the cooked eggplant. Toss with the yoghurt, crème frâiche or sour cream or serve the eggplant with the dressing on the side.

RABBIT SCALOPPINE WITH EGGPLANT *Serves 4*

Unless I'm using anchovies from a freshly opened tin, I always soak them in milk before use. This minimises the saltiness and counteracts a little of the oxidisation that generally occurs.

6 double rabbit fillets
3 medium eggplants, cut into 1 cm-thick
    slices, ends discarded
extra virgin olive oil, for frying
plain flour, for coating
sea salt flakes and freshly ground
    black pepper
butter, for frying

VINAIGRETTE
8 anchovy fillets
milk, for soaking
¼ cup (60 ml) extra virgin olive oil
1 clove garlic, chopped
2 tablespoons red-wine vinegar
3 large green olives, pitted and sliced
1 tablespoon flat-leaf parsley leaves

Place the anchovy fillets in a bowl, cover with milk and soak for 20 minutes. Drain and set aside.

Using a sharp knife, remove the sinew from the rabbit fillets as you would for a beef fillet. Wrap each fillet in plastic film and gently pound it into a scaloppine shape (flat and roughly oval).

Salt the eggplant slices if necessary; if they are in season and not too large, you shouldn't need to. In a heavy-based frying pan, heat some olive oil on high until very hot and fry the eggplant slices until brown on both sides. Drain on kitchen paper.

For the vinaigrette, heat the olive oil in a small saucepan and gently warm the garlic in the oil. Add the anchovies, red-wine vinegar, olives and parsley. Keep the mixture just warm while you cook the rabbit.

Preheat the oven to 150°C. Season the flour. Heat a little butter until nut-brown in a heavy-based frying pan, then remove from the heat for a second while you toss the rabbit fillets in the seasoned flour. Put the pan back on medium heat for a moment and then seal each fillet for about 30 seconds on each side. Remove the fillets and rest them for a minute or so.

Warm the eggplant slices on a tray in the oven, then interlay the rabbit fillets with the eggplant on a serving platter, using 3 eggplant slices to 3 rabbit scaloppine. Serve immediately with the warm vinaigrette drizzled over. This is also good with Anchovy Mayonnaise (see page 7).

GOOSEBERRIES
AND ELDERFLOWERS

GOOSEBERRIES ARE BECOMING MORE READILY AVAILABLE. THEY are picked whilst half green and half ripe, and their sharpness of flavour is a wonderful accompaniment to game. Their flavour softens somewhat when sugar is added to them for use in desserts. Eventually, green gooseberries will ripen to red, even if kept in the refrigerator, and will become much sweeter.

The gooseberry is a delicate-looking fruit, with its translucent, finely veined yet 'hairy' skin. It is naturally tart and, unless picked from your own garden, I doubt many would like to eat gooseberries raw; they're definitely an acquired taste. Having said that, gooseberries are wonderful added to moist puddings; or cooked and served with really rich poultry such as goose, duck or pheasant, where the sharp flavour cuts through the richness of the meat.

I've always known that gooseberries have a lyrical connection with elderflowers, but it wasn't until my first trip to Ireland in 2003 that I realised how extraordinary these flavours could be. I was there to conduct a verjuice masterclass at Ballymaloe Cooking School in County Cork, which was founded by Darina Allen. I had known of Ballymaloe forso many years before the opportunity for me to go there arose. In a magazine article I happened to read, Darina had thrown down the gauntlet from afar to see if I'd be interested in teaching there. When Darina was invited to Adelaide by Tasting Australia in October 2001, we finally met and my commitment to visiting Ballymaloe was cemented.

We arrived in that hot northern summer of June 2003, stopping first for a quick trip to Inverness, Scotland, before flying on to Ireland. In both places it was similarly warm and wild elderflowers were everywhere you looked, from country lanes to arterial roads; it was running rampant. No wonder elderflowers are such a part of the country cooking traditions of England, Ireland and Scotland.

Ballymaloe House and Ballymaloe Cooking School were more than I had dreamed of: such beautiful grounds, with seven gardeners, and a kitchen and herb garden that was

mind-blowing. Every day, baskets of fresh vegetables, herbs and fruits would be picked for me to choose for my classes.

I loved the many and varied ways that Darina used the wonderful resource of elder-flowers. At dinner in her home one evening she and her husband Tim served a glass of champagne with elderflower cordial to start the meal, then a gooseberry and elderflower compote to finish. What's more, on the Ballymaloe House menu they offered elderflower cordial, elderflower sorbet with pomegranate and champagne and, naturally enough, Darina's compote.

Elderflowers so invaded my senses that I returned home to make vanilla and elderflower ice cream to serve with elderflower heads in champagne batter early that southern summer, but the magic of the combination of elderflower and gooseberry still transports me straight back to a hot summer's night in County Cork.

I've always had elderflowers growing at the farm, and, in the Pheasant Farm Restaurant, I would use them to decorate dessert plates – their lacy heads look so beautiful. I also cooked the flower heads in a light batter and dusted them with icing sugar to serve with the first of the season's raspberries and vanilla ice cream. Never seeming to have enough, I planted six bushes at home last year. They're often found in old-fashioned gardens and, when planted in the right spot, with a mixture of shade and sun, and given plenty of water, they grow enthusiastically and look beautiful.

Jane Grigson's Fruit Book inspired my version of gooseberry and elderflower jelly, which follows her procedure exactly, except I halve the amount of sugar. I'm not sure whether this is a reflection of our practice of allowing the gooseberries to ripen more, or the English palate. The elderflower gives a wonderfully fragrant note to the jelly, and when some of the tiny lacy flowers are scattered on top of the almost-set jelly, it shimmers as it quivers.

GOOSEBERRY SAUCE FOR GAME   *Makes about 300 ml*

The amount of sugar used here will depend on the ripeness of the gooseberries. Red gooseberries will be riper and therefore much sweeter than green gooseberries.

45 g butter

20 g sugar

250 g punnet gooseberries, washed,
    topped and tailed

280 ml Golden Chicken Stock (see page 55)
    or game stock

Melt the butter and sugar in a saucepan over medium–high heat and add the gooseberries. Simmer for about 3 minutes. Add stock and reduce to a sauce. The seeds are very soft and it is optional whether you strain the sauce through a sieve or not.

GOOSEBERRY AND ELDERFLOWER COMPOTE   *Serves 6*

I have re-created this recipe from the wonderful and evocative memories of my trip to Ireland.

1 cup (220 g) sugar

250 ml water

4 elderflower heads, washed well, *or*
    1 tablespoon elderflower cordial

1 kg gooseberries, topped and tailed

Make a sugar syrup by combining the sugar, water and elderflower heads or cordial in a saucepan. Bring to the boil and simmer over low–medium heat until syrupy. Add the gooseberries and simmer for about 5 minutes or until tender. Remove from heat and leave to cool, then remove the elderflower heads.

Serve the compote with pouring cream.

MACADAMIA MERINGUE WITH WHITE
CHOCOLATE MOUSSE AND GOOSEBERRIES

Serves 6

Make sure when buying white chocolate that it contains cocoa butter, as some inferior brands contain vegetable fat.

¼ cup (35 g) macadamias

2 egg whites

100 g castor sugar

GOOSEBERRIES

600 g gooseberries, washed and stemmed

½ cup (110 g) sugar

1 tablespoon elderflower cordial

MOUSSE

200 g white chocolate, chopped

50 g unsalted butter

2 teaspoons finely chopped lime rind

1 cup (250 ml) 35 per cent fat cream
 (see Glossary)

Preheat the oven to 150°C. Roast the macadamias on a baking tray until just golden, then leave to cool. Roughly chop and set aside.

Line a baking tray with baking paper. Using an electric mixer, whisk the egg whites until soft peaks form, then slowly add the sugar, continuing to whisk until it is completely incorporated. Spread the meringue in a rectangle evenly over the baking paper on the baking tray, then bake for about 1 hour. Turn the oven off and leave the meringue inside to dry out slightly; the centre should still be a little chewy.

Meanwhile, for the mousse, melt the chocolate and butter in a small heatproof bowl over a saucepan of gently simmering water; the bowl should not touch the water. Once the chocolate melts and the butter is incorporated, add the lime rind, then remove from the heat and leave to cool. Whip the cream until stiff peaks form, then fold into the cooled chocolate mixture. Cover with plastic film and refrigerate until ready to use.

For the gooseberries, place the fruit in a small saucepan with the sugar and elderflower cordial and cook over low heat, stirring occasionally, for 10–12 minutes, or until the gooseberries are tender but still retaining their shape. Drain and leave to cool.

To assemble, trim the meringue into two pieces to fit into a deep rectangular serving dish. Place one piece of the meringue on the bottom of the dish. Spread half the mousse over the meringue, then scatter with half the gooseberries. Lay the second piece of meringue on top of the gooseberries, then repeat the layering with the remaining mousse and gooseberries. Top with chopped macadamia nuts, then chill well before serving.

GOOSEBERRY PAVLOVAS

Serves 10

Savour New Zealand, an annual three-day masterclass held in Christchurch for food and wine lovers, puts on some quite amazing shows for such a small committee. I've been invited to attend several times, and each visit has been a standout, but one lasting memory is of this gooseberry pavlova that Tina Duncan of White Tie Catering (and one of the prime movers behind the event) made for the Gala Dinner of the inaugural Savour New Zealand in 2001.

With such a large audience attending, Tina wanted to be prepared and so made individual pavlovas in advance. On the night she placed some stewed gooseberries in each bowl, topped with a layer of whipped cream, on top of which she served the meringue like an upside-down pavlova. This allowed the desserts to be served quickly and efficiently to such a large crowd.

This is such a fantastic combination of texture and flavour – one which Tina tells me she has fond memories of her mum serving after the Sunday roast. I can still taste this wonderful dessert as I pen this; it reminds me that gooseberries deserve so much more attention.

3 egg whites

1½ cups (330 g) castor sugar

1 teaspoon cornflour

1 teaspoon vanilla extract

¼ cup (60 ml) boiling water

2 cups (500 ml) 35 per cent fat cream
(see Glossary)

GOOSEBERRIES

1½ cups gooseberries

⅓ cup (75 g) castor sugar,
or more to taste

Preheat the oven to 150°C. Place the egg whites, sugar, cornflour and vanilla extract in the bowl of an electric mixer. Start to beat, gradually adding the boiling water, then beat for about 15 minutes or until stiff and satiny. Drop large spoonfuls onto a baking tray lined with baking paper – don't worry about the meringues being too perfect.

Bake the meringues for 20 minutes, then reduce the oven temperature to 100°C and cook for another 30 minutes. Cool on wire racks.

Meanwhile, for the stewed gooseberries, place the gooseberries and sugar in a small saucepan and simmer on low heat for 10 minutes or until cooked through. Leave to cool.

Whip the cream until soft peaks form.

If you're catering for a crowd and want to assemble dessert in advance, place a spoonful of stewed gooseberries in the bases of 10 bowls, top with whipped cream, then finish with a meringue. Otherwise, spread the cream generously on each of the meringues and top with stewed gooseberries.

NECTARINES

IF I HAD TO NOMINATE MY FAVOURITE STONE FRUIT ABOVE ALL others, hard though it is to better a perfect white peach plucked ripe from the tree, I would have to give my vote to the old-fashioned white nectarine. Forget about fancy fruit such as peacharines – give me a ripe nectarine in its perfect state and I am in heaven.

The many varieties of nectarine mean that the season is quite a long one. But, like all stone fruit, it is only when they are picked ripe that I can wax lyrical about them. If not, then I advise you to cook them rather than eat them as is. Nectarines must also be handled carefully as they bruise particularly easily. A nectarine picked green will never ripen properly and will have a bitter taste to it. Choose your greengrocer carefully: once you are familiar with ripe fruit fresh from the tree it is difficult to accept anything less.

Actually a smooth-skinned peach (not a cross between a peach and a plum, as is often erroneously thought), the nectarine has a tarter and spicier taste than the peach. As such, nectarines make great tarts or pies, whereas peaches do better simply baked or poached. Try adding ground roasted almonds to the pastry when making a nectarine tart, since almonds and nectarines are such a good duo. Or you could half-fill a pastry case with a frangipane filling of ground almonds, butter, sugar and eggs, and arrange nectarine segments on top, before baking. An old-fashioned crumble can be made in a flash with nectarines. The crumble mixture can be kept, well sealed, in the refrigerator for weeks, and dessert can then be a spur-of-the-moment idea.

The nectarine has very thin skin, which makes peeling easy. Simply pour boiling water over the fruit and leave for 15 seconds, then strip off the skin. You will find the blush that appears on the skin will also be present on the flesh. Soft-skinned fruit is wonderful poached in a verjuice or light sugar syrup, and with the nectarine you have the added bonus of that sunset-coloured blush. Blanch and peel the nectarines, then add the skin to the poaching liquid with the fruit to give it a rosy hue. A jelly can be made from the

Nectarine frangipane tart (see page 95)

poaching liquid, too, and poured over halved nectarines in a mould. Five Alba Gold gelatine leaves will be just enough to set 500 ml jelly so that it quivers when it is brought to the table, if it is made the day before and left to set. An old-fashioned jelly mould would be perfect for this: invert the jelly onto a platter and serve with dollops of Kangaroo Island or other thick cream. However, if you plan to serve this outside on a hot summer's day, then play it safe and add an extra gelatine sheet.

I often serve the wonderfully moist olive oil and sauternes cake from Alice Waters' *Chez Panisse Cooking* with poached nectarines at room temperature. I reduce the poaching liquid to a glaze and pour it over the nectarines and the cake for a great dessert.

Preserving nectarines is well worth the trouble, as long as they are ripe and not bruised. Nectarines can be pickled or spiced in the same way as peaches and served with terrines or barbecued quail. Bottled nectarines make a great difference to muesli on a winter's morning, and can be served simply with ice cream or cream for a last-minute dessert. I don't know of anyone drying nectarines commercially (apart from my neighbours, the Ellis family, who sell at the Barossa Farmers' Market every Saturday), but they have a very special flavour that teams well with a soft brie.

If you have a glut of nectarines and wish to freeze them, blanch and peel the fruit, then discard the stones and purée the pulp. Add 2 tablespoons lemon juice (this stops the fruit discolouring) and 1 cup sugar to each 2 cups purée, then freeze. One of the best ways to use the purée is to fold it, partially frozen, into a good vanilla bean ice cream just as you are serving it.

NECTARINE CRÈME PÂTISSIÈRE TART   *Serves 6–8*

1 × quantity Sour-cream Pastry (see page 184)	CRÈME PÂTISSIÈRE
8 nectarines, stoned and sliced	6 egg yolks
20 g butter	100 g castor sugar
1 tablespoon brown sugar	2½ tablespoons plain flour
	2 cups (500 ml) milk
	1 vanilla bean

Make and chill the pastry as instructed, then line a tart tin with it. Chill the pastry case for 20 minutes. Preheat the oven to 200°C. Line the pastry case with foil, then cover with pastry weights and blind bake for 15 minutes, then remove the foil and weights and bake for another 5 minutes. Set the baked pastry case aside and increase the oven temperature to 250°C.

Arrange the nectarines in a baking dish. Heat the butter with the brown sugar in a small saucepan over medium heat until melted, then brush over the nectarine slices. Bake the fruit for 15 minutes, just enough time to caramelise it, then set aside and leave to cool to room temperature. »

For the crème pâtissière, beat the egg yolks and castor sugar until creamy, then add the flour and beat to a smooth paste. Heat the milk with the vanilla bean in the top of a double boiler over low heat. (If you don't have a double boiler, use a heatproof bowl that fits snugly over a pan of boiling water.) Remove the vanilla bean (cut it in half and scrape the seeds into the hot milk, if you wish). Whisk half the milk into the egg mixture until smooth, then whisk in the remainder. Pour the mixture back into the double boiler and stir over low heat with a wooden spoon until thickened. Cook for another 2 minutes, stirring, then remove the pan from the heat and set aside to cool. Press a buttered piece of baking paper on top of the crème pâtissière to prevent a skin forming.

Fill the pastry case with the cooled crème pâtissière and top with the nectarine slices, overlapping them like roof tiles. Serve immediately.

FRENCH-STYLE NECTARINE TART   *Serves 6–8*

I am a great lover of puff pastry but rarely take the time to make it. Instead, I make a rough puff pastry as described by Jacques Pepin in his *La Technique* (he calls it fast puff pastry). This method uses the same ingredients as puff pastry but puts them together differently and takes half the work. The resulting pastry isn't as refined as classic puff – which is probably why it suits my cooking style – but has almost as many applications. It is particularly good for pie tops.

The weather (more specifically, the temperature and humidity), and flour you are using affect how much liquid you need each time you make pastry, bread or pasta. Always reserve a little of the specified liquid in case not all of it is needed. I use cream rather than water when making pastry for a dessert. This recipe makes about 500 g pastry – it doesn't seem to work as well when made in small amounts. Freeze any leftover pastry: pat it into a flat 'cake', then wrap it well in plastic film the day it is made, to avoid oxidisation.

750 g ripe nectarines
1 tablespoon sugar
2 tablespoons loquat *or* apricot jam
1 teaspoon kirsch

ROUGH PUFF PASTRY
450 g plain flour, plus extra
    for dusting
450 g chilled unsalted butter, cut into
    1.5–2 cm cubes
1 teaspoon salt
1 cup (250 ml) water *or* 300 ml cream

To make the pastry, tip the flour onto a cool bench and make a well in the centre, then add the butter and salt. Using the tips of your fingers or a pastry scraper, rub or cut the butter into the flour. Add three-quarters of the water or cream and mix into the flour mixture, but do not knead it. Add the remaining water or cream if necessary; the dough should still be lumpy with small knobs of butter.

Generously flour the bench and roll the dough out to a 1.5 cm-thick rectangle. Use your hands to even up the rectangle to make folding and rolling easier. Brush any flour from the pastry, then fold one end into the centre (brushing the flour off is important, as any extra flour will toughen the pastry). Repeat this on the other side, then fold the dough in half, creating four layers of pastry. This is your first double turn. Roll out the pastry and repeat this process twice more. If the dough becomes too difficult to manage, refrigerate it for 15–20 minutes between turns. Wrap the finished dough in plastic film and rest it in the refrigerator for 20 minutes.

Roll out the chilled pastry and use it to line a 20 cm tart tin with a removable base. Prick the base of the pastry case all over with a fork. Refrigerate the pastry case for at least 20 minutes.

Preheat the oven to 220°C. Wash and dry the nectarines, then cut them in half and remove the stones. Cut each half into 3 segments and arrange in circles over the chilled pastry case, with the slices just overlapping one another. Sprinkle the sugar over the fruit and bake for 30–35 minutes or until the fruit is cooked and the bottom of the pastry case is well browned (you may need to cover the edges of the pastry with foil during cooking to prevent burning). Carefully remove the tart from the tin and slide it onto a wire rack to cool a little. Gently warm the jam and kirsch in a small saucepan over low heat, then brush over the fruit. Serve warm with ice cream or cream.

PASSIONFRUIT

WHEN I WAS A CHILD GROWING UP IN SYDNEY, THE PASSIONFRUIT vines were as luxuriant and plentiful as the chokos that grew over most back fences, including my aunt's. We used to sit among the vines attacking the fruit with a penknife before sucking the skins dry. In the years I spent travelling through Europe and North Africa in my twenties, I never once came across passionfruit (although I'll admit I didn't go to any of the fabulous food shops of Paris). Then again, I wasn't really looking: I mistakenly thought passionfruit was a peculiarly Australian delicacy, as it seemed linked to childhood memories and Australian country cooking in a way no other fruit is.

In fact, passionfruit originated in South America. It's not hard to see how the Spanish missionaries there came to name the plant, finding that the various parts of its beautiful, complex flower reflected the sufferings of Christ. As Jane Grigson says in her *Fruit Book*, 'they believed the Creator had thoughtfully arranged the Passion Flower, the *Flos Passionis*, in this way, and had planted it in the New World ready to help in the conversion of the Indians'.

Passionfruit season can be confusing because the fruit is among the increasing number of those almost always available, particularly in hot climates, even if in reduced quantities. In warmer climes they crop lightly all year, with a flush at the end of summer and then again towards the end of winter. In cooler climates you are more likely to see a vine fruiting in late summer or early autumn. In the Barossa, passionfruit is very much a late summer fruit.

After many false starts, we had brief success with passionfruit at home by planting the vine with an ox heart at its base on the advice of a neighbour. Rumour has it that the iron from the ox heart helps the passionfruit to grow, and in this case it worked. However, the vine was close to a rainwater tank that subsided and collapsed when one of our ancient pear trees fell down, taking with it everything in its path, including the passionfruit. Refusing to give up, we've finally established one in the Pheasant Farm garden, this time using left-over livers as a source of iron. It is now bearing well against all odds, as the farm's only water comes from a bore and is higher in salt than most plants can tolerate; this makes the garden at the Pheasant Farm a continual struggle.

The fragrance and bittersweet flavour of the common, round purple passionfruit is without peer. (I once successfully planted a banana passionfruit but couldn't be bothered to eat the fruit much. I feel the same about the very large red passionfruit, which is too sweet for my taste.) No aroma can fill the senses more than a freshly opened, fully ripe passionfruit. Of all the ways to enjoy it, serving the fresh pulp with a little cream tops them all. Don't be tempted to strain the seeds away: I believe that the seeds and the pulp are not to be separated, so ignore any recipe that tells you otherwise!

When choosing passionfruit, be careful to reject those with smooth, shiny skins. Don't let their rich shades of purple seduce you: such fruit can be under-ripe and will lack the sweet counterpoint of ripe passionfruit, as well as having almost no fragrance. If the fruit is light, the pulp will have dried up. Choose instead the less vibrant, old and crinkly passionfruit that feels heavy in the hand and whose fragrance declares its readiness. Passionfruit can be stored at room temperature if the weather isn't too hot, and they keep well in the refrigerator (the pulp can be frozen, too).

The mere scent of passionfruit dolloped onto a tiny cream-filled shortcrust pastry tart sends me into orbit; that intense whiff carries its promise through to the finish. I always say I don't have a sweet tooth, but suddenly I find myself thinking about passionfruit soufflé, passionfruit butter (so rich yet tangy enough to soothe my guilt), and pavlova topped with cream, sliced ladyfinger bananas and passionfruit (a classic, whether we acknowledge it or not). The flavour of this remarkable fruit heightens the taste of anything you put it with.

Dinner parties were part of our early married life, and everyone expected dessert. I remember a time when the only piece of furniture we had was a mattress, and yet we still had dinner parties, our guests sitting uncomfortably on the floor, with plates balanced on knees. Cooking meat, fish and vegetables seemed natural to me, but desserts were another deal – so once I had perfected the pavlova it featured every time we had people to dine. I always like sneaking the leftovers the next morning, when the pavlova is moist from the fridge and the flavour of the passionfruit has really infused the cream.

It was one of my staff, Julie, who insisted on proving to me that you could make a pavlova using Muscovy duck eggs, even though I had read Harold McGee's advice in *On Food and Cooking* that duck egg whites don't beat well because they are short on the globulins that make hen egg whites foam so well. Always happy to test a theory (and knowing that Julie had a real menagerie at home and wouldn't waste anything), I was willing to try it. The resultant pavlova actually had a lighter, fluffier meringue, so these are the perfect choice for someone who prefers a marshmallow-like pavlova. We used 7 duck egg whites to 375 g castor sugar, 3 teaspoons cornflour and 1½ teaspoons white-wine vinegar (instead of lemon juice) and cooked the pavlova at 150°C for 45 minutes only.

PASSIONFRUIT BUTTER   *Makes 475 ml*

While I use a saucepan to make passionfruit butter, it can also be made in a double boiler, but it takes more time. I love passionfruit butter with biscuits warm from the oven, on toast, or to sandwich between melting moments or sponge cakes.

10 large passionfruit	30 g unsalted butter
3 eggs	⅓ cup (80 ml) lemon juice
200 g castor sugar	

Cut the tops off the passionfruit with a sharp, serrated knife and extract the pulp. Beat the eggs, then tip them into a stainless steel or enamelled saucepan and add the passionfruit pulp, sugar, butter and lemon juice. Stir over low heat until the mixture comes to the boil, then keep the mixture at a simmer for 15 minutes, being careful it doesn't burn or reduce too much. By the end of the cooking time the mixture will seem quite thick, but it will only set properly when cool. While the passionfruit butter is still hot, ladle it into clean, warm sterilised jars (see Glossary) and seal. Once opened, store jars in the refrigerator.

PASSIONFRUIT AND BANANA PAVLOVA   *Serves 6*

My pavlova is of the chewy variety: the outside is crisp and the inside is still moist.

4 egg whites (at room temperature)	8 passionfruit
190 g castor sugar	3–4 ladyfinger bananas
1 teaspoon cornflour	300 ml thickened cream, whipped
juice of 1 lemon, strained	

Preheat the oven to 130°C. Beat the egg whites on high speed in an electric mixer until fluffy. Still beating, slowly add the sugar until the mixture is thick and glossy, then beat in the cornflour and 1 teaspoon of the lemon juice (reserve the rest).

Line a baking tray with baking paper. Pile on the meringue, hollowing out the centre to form a 'nest'. Bake the pavlova for 1 hour 40 minutes until quite firm. Turn the oven off but leave the pavlova inside to cool completely.

Just before serving, cut the tops off the passionfruit with a sharp, serrated knife and extract the pulp. Peel and slice the bananas, then toss with the remaining lemon juice to prevent discolouration. Spread the pavlova with the whipped cream and cover generously with passionfruit and banana.

PASSIONFRUIT SPANISH CREAM   *Serves 6*

When my aunts made Spanish cream or angel's food for me as a child it always separated, with a layer of jelly on the bottom and fluff on top. But years later I read in *The Schauer Australian Cookery Book* that it 'should be a sponge right through. If the gelatine is added too hot, the jelly part will sink to the bottom and the sponge will be on top, which is not correct.' I followed this advice when making my passionfruit version, but I found that family tradition was too strong – I missed the familiar separation of the custard and jelly! In the following recipe the gelatine is not cooled and the result is as I remember – my aunts' Spanish cream.

While I usually prefer to use gelatine leaves (see Glossary), in our family this dessert would have only ever been made with gelatine powder. If you wish to use leaves, soften them in the warm water, then squeeze them well before stirring them into the custard.

6 passionfruit	3 eggs (at room temperature), separated
600 ml milk	100 ml warm water
2 tablespoons castor sugar	9 teaspoons gelatine powder

Cut the tops off the passionfruit with a sharp, serrated knife and extract the pulp. Fill the bottom half of a double boiler with water and bring it to the boil. (If you don't have a double boiler, use a heatproof bowl that fits snugly over a pan of boiling water.) Put the milk and sugar into another saucepan and bring to boiling point, stirring until the sugar dissolves.

Beat the egg yolks in the top half of the double boiler off the heat. Whisk the hot milk mixture slowly into the egg yolks, beating the whole time. Stand the egg yolk mixture over the boiling water in the double boiler for about 2 minutes, stirring with a wooden spoon to slowly thicken the custard. Remove the custard from the heat and cool a little, then add the passionfruit and leave to cool further.

Put the warm water (it should be quite warm) into a small stainless steel bowl and sprinkle the gelatine powder on top – as if you were sprinkling sugar onto the *crema* of a short black. The idea is for the warm water to absorb the gelatine without any need for stirring (this won't happen if you use cold water). Stir the gelatine mixture into the custard, then pour the custard into a glass bowl. Beat the egg whites until stiff, then fold them into the custard and leave it to set in the refrigerator – this should take less than an hour.

PEACHES

THERE IS NOTHING TO COMPARE WITH THE PERFUME AND BLUSH of a freshly picked peach, as James de Coquet reflects in the 'Peach and Nectarine' chapter of *Jane Grigson's Fruit Book*:

Renoir used to say to young artists longing to paint – like him – the pinkish-brown tones of an opulent breast: 'First paint apples and peaches in a fruit bowl.' My greengrocer sold me worthy models for painting. Their curves were perfect and graceful. Their grooves were in exactly the right place. Their gradations of colour were an art school exercise, and as for the velvety down of their skin . . . 'It's the left cheek of my girl', as the Japanese poet has written.

Ripe peaches bring to mind that wonderful burden of having an abundance of fruit – when the whole tree ripens at once, the spoils must be shared. Each peach variety has such a short season that often you will find you have a glut with which to make jam or preserve.

Should one eat the skin or not? I once asked some fellow cooks this and they were adamant that eating peaches skin and all is the go. In contrast, my husband Colin said that the very idea made the hairs on his arms stand on end. Skin or no skin, it is difficult to eat a peach delicately. I love the juice running down my arm as I strive to savour every mouthful.

It is almost too tantalising to talk about the precious white peach, as it is so difficult to find a perfect specimen, unless you have access to a tree, a growers' market or a great greengrocer, or are prepared to order them from a mail-order company such as Snowgoose (www.snowgoose.com.au), who specialise in supplying premium-grade fruit. A perfect white peach is picked fully ripe, but such peaches bruise easily and have a limited shelf-life. The temptation to pick peaches before they are ripe is not worth it, as they will never offer the rich, sweet acidity of naturally ripened stone fruit, yet transporting these peaches correctly is the challenge. There is quite a tradition of pick-your-own berry farms – what we also need are pick-your-own stone fruit orchards.

Baked peaches with almond and ginger butter (see page 108)

If you are lucky enough to have your own tree, you will have experienced the other extreme of having too much fruit ripening all at once. I am often in this position, but enjoy the glut while it lasts. This is when I enjoy sliced white peaches over cereal, or sometimes I cut up a huge bowl of white peaches and large yellow Million Dollar peaches, then sprinkle the fruit with a little cereal, add a great dollop of yoghurt and start the day with a veritable feast.

Poaching white peaches leaves a blush on the flesh that is revealed after the skin is removed. Try them with raspberries or set them in a Sauternes jelly. Yellow peaches present more possibilities to the cook as they preserve well. While you do not need to add sugar to the bottling syrup, yellow peaches do need to be peeled as the skin dulls with cooking.

I finally made it to Harry's Bar in Venice in 2006, and even with the history attached to it and the beauty of the city, I could not hide my disappointment with their Bellinis. I much prefer the ones we make ourselves – the trick is to squeeze the white peaches by hand.

BELLINI

Here is the recipe for the Bellini from Harry's Bar. Use white peaches only, and, rather than a food mill or meat grinder, use your hands to squeeze them. Alternatively, you can buy imported white peach purée from specialty importers.

white peaches	**Prosecco (Italian sparkling wine)**

Squeeze the white peaches to a pulp by hand, then force through a fine sieve. If the peach purée is very tart, sweeten it with just a little sugar syrup (a syrup made from equal amounts of sugar and water). Refrigerate the purée until it is very cold, then mix with chilled Prosecco, in the proportion of 1 part peach purée to 3 parts wine or, for each drink, 30 ml peach purée and 100 ml wine. Pour the mixture into well-chilled glasses.

PEACH CHUTNEY   *Makes 750 ml*

The flavour of the peaches is paramount in this chutney – the old-fashioned, firm cling-stones have the right amount of punch.

100 g butter	**100 g dried currants**
1 large onion, roughly chopped	**175 g dark-brown sugar**
9 clingstone peaches, peeled and cut into eighths	**300 ml red-wine vinegar**

Heat the butter over medium heat in an enamelled or stainless steel saucepan and cook the onion until softened, then toss in the peaches. Add the remaining ingredients and stir well.

Bring the chutney to the boil, then cook just above a simmer, stirring occasionally, until it thickens. This will take between 45 minutes and 1 hour. Fill hot, sterilised jars (see Glossary) with the chutney and seal them.

GRILLED PEACH SALAD WITH PROSCIUTTO   *Serves 2*

One of the great challenges of making the television show *The Cook and The Chef* on the ABC is featuring produce that will be available in the markets when the episode is screened. This is not always the easiest of logistical exercises, but I am adamant about this detail, as I am determined to highlight produce that is fresh and in season.

This is one of the dishes we cooked when we were filming the series right in the middle of peach season.

3 yellow peaches, halved and stoned	¼ cup (60 ml) extra virgin olive oil
45 g butter, chopped	3 teaspoons balsamic vinegar *or* vino cotto
1½ tablespoons brown sugar	(see Glossary)
6 slices prosciutto	2 handfuls witlof and rocket leaves

Preheat the grill to 240°C or high. Place the peach halves, cut-side up, on a rack lined with baking paper over a grill tray. Place a cube of butter into each peach half, sprinkle with sugar, then cook under a hot grill until they caramelise and are cooked. When cool enough to handle, slip skins off peaches.

Lay 3 slices of prosciutto on 2 plates. Combine the oil and balsamic vinegar to make a vinaigrette. Bundle half the witlof and rocket in the centre of each plate and drizzle with a little of the vinaigrette, then place 3 peach halves on top. Drizzle the remaining vinaigrette over the peaches and prosciutto and serve.

PEACH AND AMARETTO JAM   *Makes 3 × 380 ml jars*

Use a mixture of really ripe peaches (for flavour) and less ripe peaches (which have higher levels of pectin). Don't keep the peaches in the fridge as this reduces their pectin levels.

1.5 kg peaches, skin on, cut into chunks	750 g castor sugar
and stones reserved	juice of 2 lemons
rind of 1 lemon	2 tablespoons Amaretto

Put the peaches and lemon rind into a large heavy-based saucepan and simmer over very low heat for 20 minutes or until tender. Tie some of the stones in a clean Chux and add to the pan, then continue to simmer for another 20 minutes, stirring occasionally to prevent the bottom of the pan burning. When the fruit is cooked, remove the bag of stones and stir in the sugar.

Add the lemon juice and check the flavour, adjusting with more lemon juice if desired. Cook for another 20 minutes or until the jam begins to thicken and set. To test whether setting point has been reached, take out a spoonful of jam and place on a white saucer. Place the saucer in the fridge for a few minutes, then test the jam by pushing it with your finger – if it wrinkles, the jam is set. As soon as it reaches setting point, stir in the Amaretto.

Immediately fill three 380 ml clean and dry jars to the top, then seal with a lid and invert them so that the hot jam sits in the lid; all sides of the jars will be 'sterilised' by the hot jam. Leave to cool then turn right-way up. Opened jars should be stored in the refrigerator.

BAKED PEACHES WITH ALMOND AND GINGER BUTTER   *Serves 10*

120 g glacé ginger

200 g almonds

100 g sugar

200 g unsalted butter

10 peaches, stoned and cut in half

Mix the ginger, almonds and sugar together in a small bowl, then combine with the butter, and chill in the refrigerator for 20 minutes. Preheat the oven to 200°C. Hollow out the peaches slightly to make a bigger hole, and bake for 10 minutes, then allow to cool slightly before adding a large dollop of butter to each and baking for 10 more minutes.

VERJUICE-POACHED PEACHES   *Serves 6*

Peeling the peaches after poaching is optional; bear in mind that the skin of some varieties of yellow peach will be difficult to remove.

2 cups (500 ml) verjuice

2 cups (500 ml) water

700 g castor sugar

6 peaches, halved and stoned

Place the verjuice, water and sugar in a stainless steel saucepan and boil for 20 minutes to make the sugar syrup. You should have approximately 875 ml if it is the right consistency.

Place the peaches cut-side down in a saucepan or deep frying pan. Pour the sugar syrup over and poach over medium heat for 20 minutes.

Stewed blood plums with yoghurt and muesli (see opposite)

PLUMS

THE PLUM IS NOT A FASHIONABLE FRUIT – THOUGH I AM NOT sure why. There are so many varieties, each offering a different flavour fresh as opposed to cooked. Yet only a few types are available in season (January to April). As with many fruits, if you have access to some of the old-fashioned varieties found in long-established orchards you have a treat in store. Of all my summer fruiting trees, the blood plums are those least attacked by birds. Perhaps it is due to their position against a stone wall away from the other trees, or the fact that the birds have simply left the area by the time the plums ripen. Both points may be handy for any gardener frustrated by birds eating their plums, especially when it becomes obvious how much of the crop has been part-eaten as the damaged fruit continues to ripen.

Blood plums make the best crumble, as much due to their delicious flavour as the intensity of the deep-burgundy juices that seep through the streusel topping. A friend also candies these plums to great effect. Their slight tartness balances the sugar used in the candying process, and the fruit keeps quite plump through the year sealed in a glass jar.

As much as I like blood plums fresh, and particularly a little warm from the sun, I also enjoy them stewed, served on muesli with yoghurt for breakfast. Baked halved blood plums make another simple dessert: I fill them with homemade almond paste and serve them with cream or, if I'm feeling creative, an almond tuile.

The ruby blood plum is the one we used to use for our Maggie Beer Blood Plum Paste and Blood Plum Jam; it is intense in flavour and colour and with that edge of piquancy that makes a really vibrant jam. However, they became more difficult to get so sadly we no longer make the jam.

The prettiest plums I have in my home orchard would have to be the damsons. Hidden by the leaves, the oval fruit is small and grows in clusters like grapes. Damsons have a spicy tang when cooked and are particularly good in a sauce to cut the richness of seasonal game meat. Damsons are also very successful in a paste (see page 115), made similarly to quince paste, and make great jelly.

Every greengage I pick I'm excited about – they are such beautiful plums. Though I'd planted my greengage coincidentally near my D'Agen prune plum, which, according to Louis Glowinski in *The Complete Book of Fruit Growing in Australia*, should have helped it to pollinate, in truth it wasn't until I planted a goldengage next to it that I had any real success. The goldengage is ordinary in comparison, but helps the notoriously shy green-gage to bear fruit.

Greengages make beautiful poached fruit and tarts. Topping a frangipane mix with halved greengages which have first been baked (not poached) with a little butter makes a great tart, as the flavour of the greengages marries well with almonds. However, the lovely pale green colour I had envisaged for a greengage jelly didn't quite transpire.

As plums and almonds go so beautifully together, add ground almonds to a crumble mixture; combine 100 g ground almonds, 125 g plain flour, 100 g sugar and 175 g unsalted butter. Use this mixture to top, say, 1 kg halved plums, dotted with 75 g butter and 1 tablespoon sugar then baked (add a little water or verjuice to the baking dish so they do not burn). Scatter the crumble mixture over then bake at 200°C for 25 minutes. Serve with fresh cream, mascarpone or vanilla ice cream.

The D'Agen plum, a member of the prune plum family, is a favourite of mine, fresh as well as dried. It has a very high sugar content and is relatively solid, which is why it holds its shape well during cooking and drying. The dark-purple skin and fairly insipid translu-cent yellow flesh of the fresh fruit transform when baked: the flesh turns a deep-golden hue and the colour of the skin intensifies tenfold, making them irresistible for open tarts.

I have only just discovered the Moya plum, a large, round prune plum. I recently started drying them in my small kitchen dehydrator. By not extracting excessive amounts of moisture, the flavour of the plum is simply intensified – the struggle then is to stop every-one pinching them. As much as I love prunes, the Moya plum handled like this adds a whole new dimension to dried prunes.

For years now I have made a plum tart using prune plums, beginning with Sour-cream Pastry (see page 184). I bake the tart shell, then fill it with thick mascarpone while it is still a little warm. I also bake the plums, first cutting them in half and dotting them with butter, in a separate dish until their flesh becomes an intense ochre-yellow; I then layer them over the mascarpone. The same method can be used for any plum. These baked plums are also great on their own with a bowl of mascarpone flavoured with a little plum brandy, or as the basis of a crumble.

While I delight in using dried prunes in many forms of cooking, the prune would have to come near the top of that list of foods people either love or hate. There is nothing like adding the word 'prune' to the menu to see the orders slow down. For months I included the thin-nest, richest chocolate tart on the Pheasant Farm Restaurant menu – shiny with just-made ganache, its superfine pastry melted in the mouth – and I served it alongside alcohol-soaked prunes. It was a chocoholic's dream, yet we almost had to give it away. So we re-worded the menu, omitting any mention of the prunes, and it sold like hot-cakes (so to speak). The really interesting thing was that the prunes, which still came with the tart, were seldom left.

If you were one of those people I had to trick, at least I might have given you a new view of this much-denigrated fruit. If this has whetted your appetite, try making your own sweetmeats by soaking prunes in port overnight, then draining them. Chop the prunes with some roasted almonds or walnuts, then fold through dark couverture chocolate melted with a little cream and pour into a tin. When set, cut into tiny cubes and serve with coffee. Rich, dark chocolate and prunes are a combination that is meant to be.

I have a friend with a love of rice pudding with prunes. Knowing her mother to be a good cook, I understand this comfort food, but secretly feel that this dish, when cooked by a less-interested cook, could be one of the main offenders on the prune-hater's list.

It is perhaps in savoury dishes that I most love prunes. Not too long ago I wrote about how I was addicted to French/American food writer Madeleine Kamman's prune mustard; well, I am on another bent now. This time it is a variation on a theme from Patricia Wells' book, *At Home in Provence*.

Here she gives her version of a prune and fig chutney made with red-wine vinegar and cinnamon sticks, traditional fare in southwest France, where prunes are much used. I extended the idea and poached prunes and figs in red-wine vinegar with Quatre-Épices (see page 184), then folded through a good wholegrain mustard. I keep finding uses for this prune and fig mustard, as I call it, such as in a sandwich thick with crisp local double-smoked bacon and rocket.

Talking about prunes and bacon, where have devils on horseback gone? I dare you to bring out these treats from the 1960s (or was it the '70s?). As long as you use good-quality bacon to wrap plump prunes, you will have everyone coming back for seconds.

Prunes go as well with pork as they do with bacon and they are good with lamb too. Moorish tagines combine prunes, lamb and couscous. And the Scottish cock-a-leekie is a perfect cooler-weather dish. Here, a piece of stewing beef (best with the shin attached), a boiling fowl, a bunch of leeks and another of herbs are simmered slowly, then pitted prunes are added for the last 20 minutes of cooking. This is serious comfort food, and not only for the flavours: the smells that waft through the kitchen are heartening in themselves.

If you are lucky enough to have a goose to cook, you can't go wrong if you stuff it with lots of onion, herbs, the goose liver, walnuts, bacon or pancetta, and prunes. Try making pies – for the filling, cook chicken, duck or rabbit on the bone, then cube the meat and toss it with the ingredients given for the stuffing above, adding some reduced pan juices or stock.

The sad thing is that Australian farmers are pulling plum trees out. A grower today tells me he has booked the bulldozer to pull out six varieties of choice plums, some of those only three to four years old, because not enough people relish these wonderful fruit. The prices can be rock bottom one year, okay the next and, if the growers are lucky, a good return comes one year in three.

There is, however, a property called Budgi Werri in Young, New South Wales, with a beautiful orchard of mature prune plum trees. This wonderful place is far more than just picture-postcard beautiful. The owners, Cheryl and Doug Heley, produce a variety of gourmet prune products using sustainable farming methods. The quality of this fruit is so close to that found in the southwest of France that this is a product well worth seeking out. For more details, visit their website www.budgiwerri.com.au.

PRUNE GNOCCHI
(TO SERVE WITH POT-ROASTED MEAT)
Serves 4 as an accompaniment

Thoughts of slow-cooking lead me to think of a leg of mutton cooked in a heavy-based casserole with lots of rosemary, roasted garlic and just enough stock or wine to keep it all from sticking. I would use saltbush mutton for its distinctive flavour and the melt-in-the-mouth quality it develops when cooked slowly, but it is an idea that could be applied equally well to everyday lamb, a shoulder of pork or even veal. Instead of adding prunes to the pan, serve the meat with this prune gnocchi – yet another way of utilising the very delicious prune.

20 prunes, stoned	sea salt flakes and freshly ground
squeeze of lemon juice	black pepper
400 g waxy potatoes, unpeeled	pinch ground cinnamon
60 g butter, plus extra for cooking	handful sage leaves
125 g plain flour	

Soak the prunes in lemon juice and water overnight. Next day, drain and set aside. Cook the potatoes in a saucepan of boiling water until tender. Drain well and press through a mouli or potato ricer back into the saucepan, then stand the pan over low heat for a minute to ensure no moisture remains. Spread the potato into a rectangular shape on your bench.

Melt the butter in a small saucepan. Meanwhile, season the flour with salt, pepper and cinnamon, then spread this over the hot potato. Drizzle over the hot melted butter and, using a pastry scraper or two knives, scrape the dough into a ball and knead for about 7 minutes. Roll the dough into a log about 2.5 cm thick and leave to rest.

Preheat the oven to 200°C. Smear a baking dish with butter and set aside. Cut off a 5 mm-thick slice of dough and flatten it out. Place a prune in the centre and roll dough around to enclose it. Repeat with remaining potato dough and prunes.

Place half the gnocchi in a saucepan of salted boiling water, and as they come to the surface, cook them for 1 minute. Remove with a slotted spoon and put into the baking dish, then repeat the process with the second batch. Dot the gnocchi with a little extra butter, add a handful of sage leaves and bake for about 10 minutes or until butter is golden brown.

DAMSON PASTE

It's not as time-consuming or dangerous making damson paste as it is quince paste, which spits furiously! I like to serve damson paste with a ripe, soft cheese or an aged cheddar. Just like quince paste, it can be cut into squares and rolled in castor sugar to be served with Turkish coffee. I'd also like to try it pressed into the centre of doughnuts and deep-fried, as I once saw demonstrated at the Croatian food stand at the Ovens Valley International Festival in Victoria's northeast.

damson plums, stalks removed and washed   **castor sugar**

Place the plums in a large, heavy-based preserving pan and cook for 30–40 minutes until soft, either in a 150°C oven, with a little water in the pan to avoid burning, or on the stove in just enough water to cover them.

Allow to cool slightly, then separate the flesh from the stones and purée the pulp in a food processor. Weigh the pulp and return it to the rinsed-out pan. For each kilogram of pulp, add 800 g sugar. Cook the paste over low heat to dissolve the sugar, stirring constantly. Increase the temperature and continue cooking, stirring frequently, until the greater part of the syrup has evaporated. By this time the pulp will have become quite stiff and require constant stirring to avoid burning. The paste is ready when it comes away from the sides of the pan. This whole process will take about 2 hours.

Coat a baking dish with a little castor sugar and add the paste, spreading it out to about a 1 cm thickness. Dry the paste in the sun on a warm afternoon or overnight in a warm place such as a gas oven with the pilot light left on. Remove from tray and wrap in baking paper, storing in the pantry, not the refrigerator, for up to several months.

PLUM SAUCE

Makes 1 litre

This is my interpretation of one of the many recipes for plum sauce in *The Barossa Cookery Book*, first published in 1917. This sauce is marvellous with barbecued pork sausages or grilled duck or kangaroo fillets.

3 kg blood plums

1 × 60 g piece ginger

500 g onions, roughly chopped

2 cloves garlic, sliced

extra virgin olive oil, for cooking

1.25 kg sugar

2 cups (500 ml) red-wine vinegar

2 teaspoons black peppercorns

½ teaspoon cayenne pepper

Halve the plums, leaving the stones intact. Bruise the ginger by pressing down on it with the flat blade of a knife. Sauté the onion, garlic and ginger in a little olive oil in a large preserving pan until softened. Add the remaining ingredients and cook for about 30 minutes or until the plum stones come away from the flesh. Strain the sauce and leave to cool. Fill hot sterilised bottles (see Glossary) with the cooled sauce and seal.

PLUM STREUSELKUCHEN   *Serves 8*

Streuselkuchen is the mainstay of Barossa bakeries, and plums make a wonderful addition. Freeze the plums whole until you need them, then cut them in half and place on top of the dough, sprinkling the streusel on top before baking – what great fruit flavour!

8 plums, halved and stoned
30 g unsalted butter, melted

DOUGH
15 g fresh yeast
2 tablespoons sugar
140 ml milk
250 g plain flour
grated rind of ½ lemon
2 eggs, beaten
50 g melted butter *or* cream *or* beaten
    egg white, for brushing

STREUSEL TOPPING
70 g brown sugar
½ teaspoon ground cinnamon
grated rind of ½ lemon
120 g unsalted butter, chopped
150 g plain flour

For the dough, mix the yeast in a cup with 1 teaspoon of the sugar, then leave in a warm place for 10 minutes or until frothy. Meanwhile, heat the milk in a small saucepan until lukewarm. Sift the flour into a warm, dry bowl, then add the remaining sugar and lemon rind. Make a well in the centre and add the yeast, then the beaten eggs and warm milk. Incorporate with a wooden spoon until mixture comes together to form a dough.

Knead dough for 20 minutes on a floured bench. Return to the bowl, cover with a tea towel and leave in a warm place until the dough doubles in size (this should take about 2 hours, depending on the weather).

Knock the dough back on a floured bench, then knead for another 1–2 minutes and form into a disc. Roll the dough to cover the base of a rectangular, shallow-sided biscuit tray. Leave to rise until it plumps up to size again. Preheat the oven to 165°C.

Meanwhile, to make the streusel topping, mix the sugar, cinnamon and lemon rind, then rub in the butter and flour, working the mixture with your fingertips, but do not incorporate the butter completely as you need some lumps for the streusel.

Brush the dough with the melted butter, cream or beaten egg white, then layer the plums over the dough, brush them with melted butter and liberally sprinkle the streusel topping over. Bake for 30 minutes. Serve warm with cream.

BAKED PRUNE PLUM AND MASCARPONE TART

Serves 6–8

1 × quantity Sour-cream Pastry
(see page 184)

1 kg fresh prune plums (about 25),
halved and stoned

60 g unsalted butter, chopped

2 cups (500 ml) mascarpone

2 teaspoons plum brandy (optional)

Make and chill the pastry as instructed, then roll it out and use to line a 20 cm tart tin with a removable base. Chill the pastry case for 20 minutes.

Preheat the oven to 200°C. Line the pastry case with foil, then cover with pastry weights and blind bake for 15 minutes, then remove the foil and weights and return the pastry case to the oven for another 5 minutes. Leave the pastry case to cool to room temperature and reset the oven to 210°C.

Arrange a layer of plums in a baking dish and dot with butter. Bake for 20 minutes or until cooked but still holding their shape, then leave to cool, reserving any juices.

Fill the pastry case with the mascarpone (if it is very thick, thin it with the brandy) and top with the plums. Transfer any reserved plum juices to a small saucepan and reduce over high heat, then drizzle over the tart. Serve immediately.

BAROSSA DRIED FRUIT COMPOTES

Serves 10

Amontillado is an aged dry sherry with a distinctively nutty flavour.

1 kg mixed dried Barossa fruits (prunes,
nectarines, apricots, peaches and apples)

3 cups (750 ml) Amontillado sherry

250 g sugar

50 ml pouring cream

double cream, to serve

Soak the fruit in the sherry for 24 hours. Line 10 individual heatproof cups or 100 ml moulds with foil. Make the caramel by boiling the sugar, pouring cream and 250 ml water together carefully over medium–high heat until very dark brown. Pour 1 tablespoon of caramel into each mould to coat the bottom. Half-fill each mould with fruit. Pour on some more caramel and then add another layer of fruit almost to the top. Finish with a final layer of caramel.

Preheat the oven to 180°C. Cover the moulds with foil, place in a roasting pan, then fill with boiling water to halfway up sides of mould. Bake in this water bath for 30 minutes or until set. Let the compotes cool a little, then turn them out on to plates and serve with the cream.

PRESERVES

THE VERY FIRST TIME I BECAME CLOSELY ASSOCIATED WITH THE Angaston Show was when I was writing my first book, *Maggie's Farm*, in 1992. Both Angaston and Tanunda in the Barossa Valley have an agriculture-based show each year, and I organised to be a fly-on-the-wall at the judging of the preserves section so as to better understand the process. What a delight it was watching the theatrical Mrs Stiller at work judging the many entries. Part of my satisfaction came from our sponsorship (with a modest sum, in business terms) of a prize for the preserves section – a feature of our local show that seemed to be dying out. Compared to the financial outlay, the joy we experienced made it the most pleasurable donation we have ever made. More small companies are following suit but not as many as are needed to keep this tradition alive. I have long wanted to see an 'unusual vegetables' category, to encourage growers of salsify, scorzorena, cavolo nero and other exotics that tend not to be grown commercially.

I persuaded the Tanunda Show to introduce a new category to their portfolio – 'open entry grape products' – and in sponsoring this I hope that it will be carried through to the Angaston Show too. As it happens, the Angaston Show is now held two weeks before the Tanunda Show so there is a fair bit of rivalry between the two. Everyone in the district, from restaurateurs to retail shops to families, benefits from these crafts being handed down to the younger generations, particularly here in the Barossa, where the life of self-sufficiency and barter was well established in the early days of settlement, and was still a part of daily life until sometime in the 1970s. It was such a privilege to see the final stages of setting up and the judging process, and highlighted the resourcefulness of Barossa Valley people. The source of our food is in the hands of country people, so we should encourage them and make it worth their while. I still live my life in such a rush that I seldom find the time to enjoy such occasions, but I plan to change that!

Both the Angaston Show, on the last Saturday in February, and the Tanunda Show, the second Saturday in March, make a great family day out. The local agricultural bureaus

get involved by displaying their produce – it's great to see what these small communities can achieve. As well as the agricultural emphasis, Tanunda has a very popular horse show. There are no expensive show bags, yet lots of things for children to do. Country shows such as these are held throughout the year in districts all over Australia. People like Mrs Stiller and her husband used to travel the show circuit and obviously immensely enjoyed the life they led. There are judges in every district who give so much of their time, but I've yet to meet anyone like Mrs Stiller, whose whole life seemed to revolve around 'judging time'.

One of the traditions we in the Valley hold dear is the annual making of dill pickles, so the Dill Pickle Championship is a hotly contested competition of the Tanunda Show, taken extremely seriously by both locals and judges. Having done my time many years ago as an Associate Judge, I was finally promoted one year to 'Chief Dill'. The judges of this competition have, over the years, been drawn from most of the top wine people of the Valley – the inimitable Peter Lehmann being the man who first led the charge. I can assure you that the white coats we wore and the spittoons provided were there for very practical reasons, as not every dill pickle is worthy of eating, particularly at 9 a.m. on a Sunday morning! I remember so well some of those judging mornings – there was a barricade to keep the judges and the 'dills' from the public, and those with a vested interest would hover around to see the reactions on our faces as we tested the dills. They were such good times for me.

It is so important to maintain these regional traditions, particularly in an area so steeped in food culture as the Barossa. As well as the Dill Pickle Championship, there is the German Cake Championship and the Rotegrütze Championship on the same day – all truly important traditional foods kept alive by the show society.

Getting a recipe out of any of the winners is understandably not on, given that there is many a small seasonal business on the side at stake. However, there is a wonderful book of Barossa recipes, *The Barossa Cookery Book*, put out by the Tanunda Soldiers' Memorial Hall Committee in 1917 (also the source of the Plum Sauce recipe on page 115). In its original form, this book had 500 recipes, and four or five years later it had 1000. It hasn't been altered in any way since that first publication and has sold well over 180,000 copies. There's no doubt that a lot of people here are interested in preserving, bottling and country cooking, as the recipes featured include dill pickles, grape and plum sauces, German cake and rotegrütze as well as so many others in which Silesian traditions have intermingled with the Mediterranean climate of the Barossa.

Mrs C. Kraft of Vine Vale submitted a recipe for cucumbers pickled in vine leaves to *The Barossa Cookery Book* in 1917. She gives us just a flavour of the book's tone when she writes: 'One cup salt, scalded with boiling water and cooled. Two cups water and a little dill, enough water to fill the tin. Use a benzine tin. Cover bottom of tin with vine leaves, then a layer of cucumbers and dill, another layer of leaves, and so on to the top. Last layer, vine leaves. Use young cucumbers. Cover with plate and weight for two weeks. Leave another week before using. Add more water if some should evaporate.'

PICKLED CORNICHONS   *Makes 5 litres*

As well as the traditional German way of preserving dill pickles, here is another method using the French cornichon, actually a baby dill about 5 cm long and best picked under-ripe with a little of the stem attached, then pickled in a straight vinegar solution. Using good-quality vinegar is important to this recipe; it must contain a minimum of 6 per cent acidity, as this affects the crispness of the pickle, which is its defining characteristic.

2 kg baby dill cucumbers	1 tablespoon allspice berries
300 g coarse sea salt	up to 2 litres quality white-wine vinegar
8 bay leaves	

Rub the cucumbers with a damp cloth, then place in a bowl and toss the salt through them. Leave overnight; the salt will draw out the moisture. Next day, rinse the cucumbers, drain and dry with a clean tea towel. Place them in a sterilised jar (see Glossary) or enamel crock with the bay leaves and allspice. Pour the vinegar over until the cucumbers are immersed, with several centimetres to spare (this stage is merely to measure the vinegar needed).

Pour off the vinegar from the jar into an enamelled or stainless steel saucepan and bring to the boil. Do not reduce but immediately pour over the cucumbers and seal the jar. They take 6–8 weeks before they are ready to eat.

MRS HEIN'S QUINCE JAM   *Makes 1.5–2 litres (depending on how long it is cooked)*

The first year we sponsored a prize in the preserve section at the Angaston Show, we were delighted to see that lifting the prize money for the winner from $1 to $200 lifted the number of entries as well, and has done so ever since. That year, two of the prizewinners were good enough to share their favourite recipes with me, and I include them here. With all respect to Mrs Hein, I halve the quantity of sugar stated below for my taste. By leaving the quinces whole, this recipe demonstrates a wonderfully simple way to make quince jam, as they are so hard to cut and core.

1 kg under-ripe quinces	about 2 kg sugar
1.5 litres water	

Rub and clean the quinces well with a rough towel. Cut the bumps off one end so they will sit flat in a large heavy-based saucepan. Place the whole quinces in the saucepan with the water and 125 g of the sugar. Boil gently, covered, for 1½–2 hours or until the quinces are light pink.

Carefully lift out the quinces on to a plate (an egg slice is good for this) and discard the cores, reserving the syrup. Chop the quinces roughly and return them to the saucepan.

Measure pulp and allow 1 cup of sugar to each cup of pulp. Re-heat slowly, stirring, until sugar is dissolved, then boil rapidly for another 20–30 minutes or until jam is set. Test this by placing a spoonful of jam on a saucer. Place saucer in the fridge for a few minutes, then test the jam by pushing it with your finger – if it wrinkles the jam is set.

MRS LOFFLER'S MUSTARD CABBAGE PICKLES   *Makes 2 litres*

This recipe can be made at any time of the year and served with cold meats and cheese or used for sandwiches.

½ small cabbage (about 1 kg)	1 cup (220 g) brown sugar, lightly packed
3 onions (about 500 g), sliced	2 cups (440 g) white sugar
2 green capsicums, seeded and coarsely chopped	1 tablespoon Keen's mustard powder
2 red capsicums, seeded and coarsely chopped	1 teaspoon ground turmeric
	1 teaspoon ground ginger
¼ cup salt	30 g flour
2 cups (500 ml) Seppelt's white vinegar	1 tablespoon celery seeds
	1 tablespoon yellow mustard seeds

Having discarded the old outer leaves and core, shred the cabbage, then combine in a bowl with the onions and capsicums. Sprinkle salt over and let stand overnight, covered, to draw out the moisture.

The next morning, cover vegetables with water, stir well to disperse the salt and leave to drain in a colander. Meanwhile, combine the vinegar and the brown and white sugars in a large saucepan. Stir over high heat until the sugar dissolves, then bring to the boil and add vegetables. Reduce heat to low and simmer for 5 minutes. (Cooking time may be different depending on the type of cabbage; for example, it may be less if you use a soft-leaf cabbage.)

Mix the mustard, turmeric, ginger and flour to a smooth paste with 125 ml water. Stir into the vegetable mixture and continue stirring until mixture boils and thickens. Reduce the heat and simmer for 10 minutes. Add celery and mustard seeds. Pour into hot sterilised jars (see Glossary) and cool before sealing.

QUAIL

I ONCE READ A LOVELY JAPANESE FOLK SAYING IN CHERRY RIPE'S column in *The Australian* newspaper, quoted from Max Lake's *Scents and Sensuality*: 'To find and enjoy a new flavour adds seventy-five days to your life.' Cherry was discussing the fervour with which the Japanese embrace new food flavours from other countries – sadly, in this case, McDonald's and Coca-Cola in particular. But it is possible to find variety in new foods that are not 'junk' foods, and that can be prepared so easily they could almost be called 'convenience' foods. Quail is one such food.

While quail used to be fairly standard fare in restaurants and have long been bred in the backyards of Greek and Italian families, it was not until more recently that they have been widely available to the home cook. Quail is incredibly tasty, and most often eaten just using your fingers, which makes it a much more casual meal. It is healthy, relatively inexpensive and can be prepared and cooked in less than 15 minutes (if you choose not to marinate it). It can be barbecued, pan-fried, pot-roasted, stuffed and oven-baked, and is equally tasty served cold at picnics as it is warm in salads or hot for dinner – after resting, of course. What more could you want for convenience?

There is a world of difference between a perfectly cooked quail and one that has been ruined by overcooking. The best tip I can give you for quail that is to be barbecued or pan-fried, is to prepare it by cutting along the spine and squashing it flat with the palm of your hand ('butterflying') for easier cooking. Make sure to tuck the wings in so the breast cooks evenly. In readiness for cooking you can coat the quail lightly with extra virgin olive oil, some freshly ground black pepper and fresh herbs, or make a marinade. Our favourite marinade for quail at the restaurant was made of fresh ginger, sliced garlic and equal quantities of honey and soy sauce. We marinated the butterflied quail overnight, skin-side down, and brushed it with the mixture while cooking.

If you prefer something simpler, try some honey and lemon juice, or just extra virgin olive oil, lemon juice and thyme. Be careful with the lemon, though, as it will actually begin

Grilled quail in a post-cooking marinade of verjuice, lemon peel, green figs, roasted walnuts and thyme (see page 126)

'cooking' the meat before any contact with the heat – hence whenever I use lemon juice in a marinade, I only leave the meat for about 20 minutes maximum. Another option is to rest the cooked quail in a post-cooking marinade of verjuice, lemon peel, small green figs cut in half, roasted walnuts and thyme for 10 minutes, then spoon the marinade out and serve with the birds.

Another important trick of the trade when barbecuing these small birds (particularly if they have been marinated in honey) is to turn them at 2-minute intervals. It may seem a bit of trouble but such small details make the difference between good and average cooking. If you don't turn them frequently, you will end up with a burnt offering. As they are such small birds, quail will dry out rapidly if overcooked, so, if barbecuing, allow about 8 minutes for cooking and then put aside to rest for 5 minutes before serving. The meat should still be a little pink on the breast (I don't mean raw) and will be juicy and delicious. If overcooked, they will be like cardboard.

When buying several quail, you will find at least some variation in their sizes: the plumper ones will need an extra minute or two of cooking time. This is another of those small details that make cooking more difficult, but also more rewarding when you get it right. However, you can elect to buy jumbo quail that are more consistent sizes.

If you wish to pan-fry your quail on the stove, allow closer to 12 minutes in total. The trick

here is to choose a pan large enough so that you do indeed fry gently (rather than poach) your food. For example, for two quails that have been butterflied you will need a pan measuring about 22 centimetres across. Warm 2–3 teaspoons of butter in the pan over medium–high heat, adding a dash of extra virgin olive oil so the butter doesn't burn. Make sure the butter turns golden brown before adding the quail, skin-side down. I then reduce the temperature to low, season the quail with a sprinkle of sea salt and freshly ground black pepper and wait until the skin is a light golden brown all over before turning.

The important thing is to adjust the flame so the butter doesn't burn. If you can keep the butter that lovely golden brown then you know the quail is cooking gently enough. It is also important not to sear the quail as, not only will it look unattractive, it will also toughen it. This is a simple principle of cooking I often see ignored.

Because you start with quite a high temperature to get the butter golden and need to turn it down to save the quail from burning, it's difficult to move far from the stove. If you prefer, you can just brown the birds on both sides and then place the pan in a 200°C oven to finish off. Cook the quail for about 4–6 minutes in the oven and leave it to rest for another 5 minutes on a plate on top of the stove. (As everyone's oven is different, it is only practice that will teach you the right cooking time.)

If you wish to serve one quail per person for a meal, you would probably need either to stuff them or serve them with Polenta (see below) – both are fabulous options. When we first opened the Farmshop I used to serve quail stuffed with rice, lots of diced onion softened in butter, orange rind, currants, almond slices and a little thyme. People would sit outside on the decking and devour them with their fingers and then want to buy fresh quail to take home, so I'd also supply the cooking instructions. It was tasty and filling and still stands up as a dish I would cook today. I would also glaze the outside of the bird with a little orange juice and extra virgin olive oil to caramelise the skin as it baked. The stuffed birds require about 10 minutes in the oven. Test if cooked by gently prising one leg away – if it resists being pulled, it is not ready.

My favourite way of eating quail is at late summer picnics and barbecues, when I stuff them with figs, and wrap them in either bacon or a thin slice of pork fat, fastened with a toothpick. These must not be prepared in advance, however, because if the fig is left in the quail for any period before cooking it has a most unusual effect on the uncooked meat and turns it mushy.

One notable dish that stood out during a recent trip to Paris was a quail salad. The quail was carved off the bone after cooking and served with grilled figs, onions, tiny beans and radicchio, then finished with a small amount of a fabulous glaze. The flavour of the quail, which was fattier than we are used to in Australia, was intense. I presumed the bird was dry-plucked, as I had discovered is often the case with poultry in Italy and France.

POLENTA TO TEAM WITH QUAIL
Serves 8

I particularly like a bowl of soft polenta served in a large dish, topped with pan-fried quail and its juices, and perhaps some caramelised onions.

1.75 litres Golden Chicken Stock (see page 55)	2 teaspoons salt
2 cups (340 g) polenta	100 g Parmigiano Reggiano, grated
	1 dessertspoon butter (optional)

Heat half the stock in a saucepan until simmering. In another saucepan, mix the remaining stock with the polenta while it is still cold, to make a paste. Slowly add the hot stock, stirring constantly over low heat to avoid clumping. Season with salt. Continue stirring over low heat until you see the polenta coming away from the sides of the saucepan (about 20 minutes). Add the cheese and the butter, if using. Serve with barbecued or pan-fried quail.

TART OF QUAIL WITH SAGE, BACON AND GRAPES

Makes 6 tarts

This is an old Pheasant Farm Restaurant dish that often appeared in the days when we reared our own quail. We made it with quail breasts to utilise any slightly damaged birds. Even though it's a more formal dish, it's actually very simple to make once you've made the Sour-cream Pastry (which is not only foolproof but also quick; if you're in a hurry, you can even manage without resting the dough for as long – with this recipe, some pastry shrinkage doesn't matter).

½ × quantity Sour-cream Pastry
   (see page 184)
120 g butter
extra virgin olive oil, for cooking
6 quails (cut along the backbone and
   pressed down flat to butterfly)
sea salt flakes and freshly ground
   black pepper

24 sage leaves
½ cup (125 ml) verjuice
2 cups (500 ml) reduced Golden Chicken
   Stock (see page 55)
3 slices sugar-cured bacon, halved *or*
   6 slices round pancetta
200 g seedless green *or* red grapes, stems
   removed and washed

Make and chill the pastry as instructed. Preheat the oven to 220°C. Using brioche or other small moulds, fit the pastry around the moulds, gently pressing it down on a baking tray, and cook for 10 minutes, then remove the pastry from the moulds and cook for another 5 minutes or until golden. (You can also mould the pastry around the base of an earthenware cup or heatproof glass upended on a baking tray, then bake until the pastry is golden.)

Heat 60 g butter in a frying pan over high heat until nut-brown, then add a dash of olive oil to prevent burning. Quickly season the quails with salt and pepper, then place in the pan and seal on both sides. Transfer the quail, skin-side up, to a roasting pan, drizzle with a little more olive oil, then place in the oven for 4–5 minutes. Wipe out the frying pan and heat the other 60 g butter, then add the sage leaves and gently cook until they are crisp but not burnt. Remove from pan and drain on kitchen paper. Remove the quail from the oven, transfer to a separate dish and rest them, turned skin-side down, for at least 10 minutes. When the quails are cool enough to handle, pull off the legs and, using a sharp knife, take each breast off the carcass.

Discard any excess butter from the roasting pan, then deglaze with verjuice, and reduce by half over high heat. Add the reduced stock and boil rapidly until the sauce reaches a syrupy consistency. Meanwhile grill or dry-fry the bacon or pancetta until crisp.

To assemble, place 2 legs and 2 breasts into each pastry case, followed by the bacon and sage. Place the assembled tarts in a hot oven for 2–3 minutes to warm through.

Bring the sauce back to the boil and throw in the grapes for about 30 seconds. Using a slotted spoon, place most of the grapes on top of the tarts, letting the rest cascade over. Pour the sauce around the base of the tarts and serve.

QUAIL WITH CELERIAC, APPLES AND PINE NUTS   *Serves 4*

On the last night of a trip to Paris with my friend Stephanie Alexander, we ate at Les Olivades and had the most memorable quail dish I have ever eaten. In attempting to replicate the quality of this dish, I've found jumbo quail works best.

100 g pine nuts

8 jumbo quails

hazelnut oil, for drizzling

1 tablespoon thyme leaves, finely chopped

sea salt flakes and freshly ground
   black pepper

½ cup (125 ml) reduced Golden Chicken
   Stock (see page 55), warmed

1 small celeriac

2 Granny Smith apples

juice of 1 lemon

2 heads witlof, leaves separated,
   washed and dried

2 red witlof *or* radicchio, leaves separated,
   washed and dried

1 bunch watercress, leaves picked,
   washed and dried

1 teaspoon aged balsamic vinegar

truffle oil, to serve

Preheat the oven to 200°C. Place pine nuts on a baking tray and dry-roast for 5–10 minutes or until golden brown. Place quail on their backs in a shallow heavy-based roasting pan. Drizzle them with hazelnut oil, then add thyme and season with salt and pepper. Roast quail for 10 minutes, then remove from oven, turn quail on to their breasts, pour in the warm chicken stock and leave to rest for another 10 minutes.

Meanwhile, peel and finely dice equal quantities of celeriac and apples and place in a bowl, then toss with lemon juice and hazelnut oil and season to taste.

Arrange the witlof and watercress on four plates, then spoon the celeriac and apple mixture onto the salad leaves, making a 'nest' for the quail. Place 2 cooked quail into each nest. Heat the reserved pan juices in the roasting pan over high heat, then add balsamic vinegar and the tiniest hint of truffle oil. Scatter the pine nuts over the salad greens and drizzle the pan juices over the quail and leaves. Serve immediately.

RASPBERRIES

THE HEAVENLY FLAVOUR OF PLUMP, RIPE, VELVETY SOFT raspberries is seldom as luscious as nature intended, unless you pick the berries yourself and eat them within hours. Although the hull separates itself easily from the berry, picking raspberries is still not the easiest work in the world. So, with that in mind, I think the rise of the pick-your-own fruit farm should be encouraged. While raspberry jam is easy to make at home (as the fruit has such a high pectin content), it's an extravagant jam to make if buying raspberries by the punnet. Often the raspberry farms sell their own jams that are so thick with fruit you'll never look at commercial jam again.

The other option is to grow your own – you'll need to prepare the ground properly and use a trellis, and your bird-deterring techniques will require some forethought. A cooler climate will undoubtedly always give the best results. My local nurseryman recommends adding sulphate of potash or manure to the bed, while that learned fruit expert Louis Glowinski asserts: 'The perfect spot would be open to the east and north, but shaded by a tree on the west. Soil needs to be free-draining and high in organic matter. Planting raspberries in rows north to south, plant out 30 cm apart along the rows, leaving 1.5 m between rows.'

Actually, I have always thought raspberry growers must be made of strong stock. I tried growing plants on canes for years but became too impatient; either the heat gets the berries, the plants fail to bear due to lack of water, or I miss the flush of fruit and find dried berries all over the canes. Luckily, we have a raspberry farm in the Barossa, which sells raspberries at our Saturday market when in season. Instead of just one short burst of fruit, raspberries come and go over a few months, so you can enjoy them with the fruits of early summer – the first white peaches, for example – then with late-summer figs, not to mention other summer berries. Berries will last only a few days in the fridge and if mould is present it spreads from berry to berry in the punnet, just as with lemons, so mouldy ones must be quickly discarded.

It is difficult to tire of eating raspberries raw, picked as fresh as possible and unwashed, so the pleasure of the velvety flesh is not diminished, then simply served with cream. Raspberries served with a sponge finger or almond bread need the least amount of attention. If you want something a bit more elaborate, try a raspberry and hazelnut meringue. Grind 125 g roasted hazelnuts to a coarse powder in a food processor. Whisk 5 large egg whites until stiff, then add about 250 g castor sugar, a little at a time, and fold in the ground hazelnuts. Divide the mixture in half and spread in two discs on baking paper. Bake for about 40 minutes at 175°C, then leave to cool in the switched-off oven with the door propped open. Spread one of the cooled meringues with whipped cream or crème fraîche, then add as much of a punnet of raspberries as you can. Top with the remaining meringue and sift over icing sugar, if you like. The chewy, nutty meringue, luscious raspberries and cream make the most wonderful combination.

If you have had a real bounty and have been able to make raspberry vinegar, a tablespoon added to a glass of water makes a refreshing non-alcoholic raspberry drink. Seppelt's recently made such a drop commercially – an adult soft drink, great for the hot weather. Then there is raspberries in a trifle, or with a moist lemon cake, or with grilled figs in a tart – I love all these, but best of all, I love raspberry ice cream.

When we used to own Charlick's Feed Store, our short-lived foray into the Adelaide restaurant scene, I stopped in with a friend to trial some new dishes during one of our seemingly endless heatwaves. When we went into the kitchen we found our freezer had broken down, leaving a parfait with layers of raspberry, vanilla and chocolate at the mercy of the heat. So much work had gone into this beautiful dessert! We all ate as much as we could while it collapsed before our eyes, particularly enjoying the intensity of the raspberry layer (only a small amount of sugar was used, with lime juice added to heighten the raspberry flavour, making a great counterpoint to the richness of the chocolate and vanilla). After that, we decided to replace this dessert offering with a safer option until the freezer problem was resolved.

Summer pudding is another favourite, preferably crammed with raspberries, blackberries and redcurrants. But if summer pudding is too fiddly for you, then make a panna cotta, a simple baked custard or a crème caramel served with raspberries alongside. Better still, for freshness and lightness, make a Blancmange (see opposite) and send it quivering to the table with a huge dish of raspberries and a little cream.

When the last raspberries appear in February, as they do in my neck of the woods, try them with fresh black or green figs, picked just before they burst. Serve the figs cut open and piled high with raspberries and a good dollop of cream – a sensational way to see out the summer. I used to have twelve heart-shaped moulds for coeurs à la crème, but they have disappeared, sadly. They were made of porcelain and had little holes in the base, which allowed a soft cheese like ricotta, sweetened with a little castor sugar, to be drained. When turned out, the cheese was light and fresh – a bowl of fresh raspberries (and cream too, perhaps) was all that was needed. Losing my little hearts was a pain, but I make do by buying fresh ricotta that comes with its own perforated bowl. I line the bowl with muslin (or even a new Chux), then press in the sweetened curd and leave it to drip overnight. It is not as romantic as the traditional hearts but the results taste every bit as good.

For all their fragility, raspberries freeze particularly well and can be used to make a jam out of season or a sauce for a dessert. Process the berries to a purée with just enough icing sugar to sweeten then pass through a sieve. (Allow about a tablespoon of sugar for each cup of fruit – the rarer yellow raspberry is sweeter, so it needs less sugar.) Serve the sauce with a rich chocolate cake or over ice cream, or add it to a cold, sweeter Italian style of sparkling white wine as an aperitif.

Whichever accompaniment you choose for your raspberries, enjoy the berries while they are at their best. They come in flushes – early and late summer, and even well into autumn in some years.

BLANCMANGE WITH RASPBERRIES   *Serves 4*

Recipes abound for almond blancmange. Instead of beginning by grinding your own almonds to flavour the milk, here an almond-flavoured liqueur is added to buttermilk, making this a very easy version.

vegetable oil, for greasing	200 ml warm water
2 cups (500 ml) buttermilk	100 g castor sugar
40 ml Amaretto	fresh raspberries, to serve
4 × 2 g leaves gelatine	
(see Glossary)	

Lightly grease four 200 ml moulds or ramekins with a flavourless vegetable oil. Combine the buttermilk and Amaretto and set aside. Soak the gelatine leaves in a little cold water for 5 minutes to dissolve. Bring the warm water and castor sugar to the boil in a saucepan, squeeze out excess water from the gelatine leaves, then stir them in to the sugar mixture and allow to cool.

Mix the flavoured buttermilk into the gelatine mixture and chill in the refrigerator for 10 minutes. Pour the mixture into the oiled moulds and refrigerate until set. Turn out just before serving by dipping the base of each mould into hot water before inverting. Serve with fresh raspberries.

PAN-FRIED FIGS WITH FRESH RASPBERRIES
AND EXTRA VIRGIN OLIVE OIL ICE CREAM   *Serves 4*

One of the most luscious ice creams I ever made was with extra virgin olive oil and ver-juice – a recipe given to me by my friend Ingo Schwartz, retired Master Pâtissier. As it was difficult to make without specific equipment, I began the journey of finding another way of incorporating extra virgin olive oil into an ice cream, as the mouthfeel of it is amazing.

This is a great dessert for non-sweet-tooths like me, as the tartness of the raspberries balances the hot fig/cold ice cream combination beautifully, and if the figs are ripe from the tree, you shouldn't need to add any extra sugar.

6 large ripe figs	ICE CREAM
60 g unsalted butter	250 g sugar
dash of extra virgin olive oil	100 ml water
1 tablespoon brown sugar	pinch salt
1–2 punnets raspberries	4 eggs
icing sugar (optional, to dust	200 ml extra virgin olive oil
raspberries if too tart)	200 ml full-cream milk

For the ice cream, make a syrup by placing the sugar and water in a saucepan and reducing by half over medium heat. Add the salt and swirl in, then leave this mixture to cool. Beat the eggs in a food processor, slowly adding the extra virgin olive oil in a thin and steady stream, as you would when making mayonnaise. Once the oil is fully combined, gradually add the cooled syrup and the milk, mixing as you go. Transfer to an ice cream machine and churn (following the manufacturer's instructions).

Cut the figs in half lengthways. In a frying pan heat the butter until nut-brown, then add a dash of extra virgin olive oil to prevent burning. Add figs to pan and sprinkle with brown sugar so that they caramelise quickly, and cook them for just a minute or two.

Serve 3 fig halves on each plate, piled with a generous helping of fresh raspberries and a scoop of ice cream. Dust with icing sugar if the raspberries are not as sweet as you would like.

HAZELNUT CAKE WITH FRESH RASPBERRIES *Serves 8*

This cake is not meant to rise, but instead will be a flat, cakey meringue, and it should be lovely and moist.

250 g hazelnuts	⅓ cup plain flour
⅔ cup castor sugar	rind of 1 orange
5 egg whites	2 punnets fresh raspberries, to serve
100 g butter	double cream *or* mascarpone, to serve

Preheat the oven to 200°C. Roast the hazelnuts on a baking tray for 10 minutes or until coloured but not burnt. Whilst still hot, rub the hazelnuts in a clean tea towel to remove the skin.

Adjust the oven temperature to 150°C. Once the nuts have cooled completely, transfer them to a food processor, add 2 tablespoons of the castor sugar, and process to a fine meal.

Grease a 26 cm springform cake tin. In an electric mixer, beat the egg whites until soft peaks form, then slowly add the rest of the sugar and mix in until dissolved.

In a small pan, heat the butter to nut-brown. Meanwhile, in a large bowl, mix the plain flour with the hazelnut meal, and add the orange rind. Fold in the egg white mixture, and then pour in the warm butter, leaving any butter solids behind in the pan.

Spread the batter into the cake tin and bake for 30–35 minutes. Serve with loads of fresh raspberries and double cream or mascarpone alongside.

ROCK LOBSTERS

 I ALWAYS THOUGHT, RATHER SMUGLY, THAT RESTAURANTS offering lobster were ill-informed. Knowing that our species lack the huge claw of the European lobster, I doggedly called them 'crayfish' and thought myself much more correct. But a few years ago the Fisheries Research and Development Corporation (FRDC) decided that what was colloquially called crayfish should be known Australia-wide as the rock lobster, with the location from which each species comes providing further identification (southern, eastern, western and tropical). *Marketing Names for Fish and Seafood in Australia*, produced by the FRDC, sets the record straight on many other species as well, in a bid to encourage uniform usage of names throughout the country.

There are few people I know who would not relish a meal of freshly caught rock lobster. Yet it is a luxury food, and each year supply and demand set different price parameters (these are always in the upper range, no matter the year, as rock lobsters are never in huge supply). Surprisingly, it is not always the Christmas market that is the key to pricing, even though the seasons during which rock lobsters can be caught (different in each state) all include it.

If you find you just can't live without lobster the rest of the year then look for companies such as Ferguson Australia, based on Kangaroo Island (www.fergusonaustralia.com). They provide lobsters all year round by holding them in tanks. They have won many awards for their innovative range of products, including medallions of rock lobster, lobster mustard, lobster oil and, my favourite, lobster sashimi. When I bought a pack of this sashimi (frozen but with the end flap of the tail included), instead of serving it raw, I melted 80 g unsalted butter in a small pan until foamy and almost nut-brown, then 'waved' the lobster flesh through the butter, just long enough for it to turn opaque. I then served it piled up in the tail with Sorrel Mayonnaise (see page 140), and it was as sweet and beautiful a lobster dish as I've ever had.

One of our family traditions is that we get to choose our favourite meal on our birthday. Both our daughters were born in November and no matter whether it is Saskia or Elli

Rock lobster with sorrel mayonnaise (see page 140)

celebrating, the choice is the same every time: rock lobster. I have a sneaking suspicion that one of the reasons for this is that they feel they are getting the most mileage out of the occasion since rock lobster is so extravagant. I'm not complaining, even though we've just had our younger daughter Elli's thirtieth birthday, which coincided with the early season, so rock lobster was on the menu for thirty people. I tried in vain to suggest an alternative but only lobster would do!

The best possible way to eat a rock lobster is to take it live straight from the 'craypot', as it is still known, to the cooking pot, but this is only possible for a very few people. The best rock lobster I have ever eaten was many, many years ago, on the only yachting holiday we've ever been on or are likely to go on. As we set sail to Kangaroo Island, my husband Colin found that he was a hopeless sailor, admittedly across one of the roughest stretches of water in the world. Things got better as we sailed in the lee of the island, but our plans of providoring by diving from the boat proved fanciful. It was with great luck that we met a fisherman on his way in after a fruitful stint at sea. We did a swap: cold beer for fresh rock lobsters. No other lobster has tasted quite so good since.

The next best thing is to buy from fishermen just after they come into port. Our family had a wonderful few days at Victor Harbor before Christmas some years ago and we called into a fish merchant there, Hinge and Ferguson. It was early in the day and they had no rock lobsters available but the boat was due in at 4.30 p.m., so we ordered two freshly cooked lobsters, to be picked up at their closing time of 5.30 p.m. We also requested that the rock lobsters not be refrigerated after they had been cooked, as refrigeration makes a remarkable difference to the flavour; we were eating them that evening so they would be fine to leave out for the short time involved.

On our return, I asked the fishmonger to cut the rock lobsters lengthways as we didn't have a knife in our lodgings; he then pushed the halves firmly together so they wouldn't dry out on the way home. My version of seafood sauce was the girls' choice, so cream, tomato sauce, Worcestershire sauce and Tabasco were duly purchased. For Colin and me it was just lemon juice, extra virgin olive oil and freshly ground black pepper. If I had had a kitchen I would have made a mayonnaise, to which I would have added the 'mustard', or digestive tract, from the rock lobster. Many reject the strong piquant mustard, washing it out, whereas I regard it as essential and use the lot.

If South Australia's Coonawarra and Limestone Coast regions are on your holiday wish list and you have a passion for rock lobster as well as for wine, then now is the time to get in on one of the area's best-kept secrets. For those in the know, almost all the vignerons and farmers in the area have holiday places at Robe and Beachport (from rudimentary beach shacks to more grand abodes) and you can bet if they have a shack then they also have a licence for a craypot.

South Australian licensing regulations have unwittingly created enmity between some families and neighbours, as the sharp-eyed ones heeded the call to apply for their recreational licences without reminding anyone else of the closing date. Only a limited number of licences are granted each year, so to lose one's licence can be pretty devastating to your foraging life. The allowed catch from these pots is four small lobsters a day, whether you have one or two licences; each licence allows one pot but the total for two licences for the one person is still four per day. Believe me, these licences are treasured, because although there is the sport of diving for them yourself, this might still seem a bit too adventurous for many. We are talking here of expensive creatures of the sea and ones that punters get tremendously excited by, almost without exception.

Don't despair if you have no personal connections to those in the know as you can still go to the local pubs and restaurants. More often than not, they have local lobsters on the menu, served with absolutely no fuss – rock lobster with little adornment, which is just as it should be. The real treat is experiencing a freshly caught and cooked rock lobster, eaten as soon as it cools down. Their sweet firm flesh is at its absolute best this way, and because it is very rich you need little of it to satisfy you.

If you decide to try diving for lobsters, then my insider tip is that the locals use fish or sheep heads for bait. When the sea is really calm at Robe you can access a reef that makes diving seem like child's play. Then, if you manage to catch some lobsters, why not try a local vigneron's cooking tip: 'take very fresh uncooked green tails, diced up into bite-sized pieces, battered and deep-fried, really rich and sweet'. The batter would just be there to protect the flesh of the lobster.

The rock lobster you buy live to cook yourself will be better than any you buy already cooked; unless you tee up the fisherman to cook it for you and collect it immediately when it is ready.

It is simple to cook rock lobster: stun it first in the freezer for 30 minutes, then immerse it in a deep, large saucepan of furiously boiling water for 12–18 minutes (depending on whether the lobster weighs around 500 g or nearer 1 kg). Add bay leaves, thickly sliced lemon, dill and a few black peppercorns if you like. Fishermen always use sea water, so if that is not to hand it makes sense to salt the water generously as it comes to the boil.

I am the last one to heap scorn on a potentially great product, but I do feel the need to warn you that a little investigation is required before you buy rock lobster. So if buying a cooked rock lobster in the city, far from the coast, is your only option, look for a specimen that is tightly curled and that flips back into position after being straightened out. This 'snap' indicates a green lobster, which will have been snap-frozen straight away after being caught – an unfurled tail is a sure sign that the lobster was left to die before being cooked, which means that the digestive tract will have started to break down, releasing enzymes that spoil the flesh. Never, but never, buy a rock lobster (or any other crustacean) that has a musty or pungent smell of ammonia – it will be off.

There is a premium trade in first-grade green tails that are snap-frozen for the fastidious Japanese market. These same tails can be bought fresh on the local market but usually only if ordered in advance. Their price – often twice as much per kilo as a whole rock lobster – may seem totally out of reach, but a calculation based on the amount of meat per dollar spent actually equates to less than the retail price for a whole rock lobster.

If rock lobster doesn't suit your budget but you love eating with your hands, look for what we call 'spiders' in South Australia – the heads of rock lobsters. Tossed in a wok with oil, onion and aromatics, these make a good feed – and don't forget the 'mustard'. A good number of spiders can also be chopped into tiny pieces to make a well-flavoured stock for soup.

Rock lobster will never be cheap, but it takes little effort to present, which can be an advantage in itself. However, it can also be extended wonderfully by the addition of really good pasta (see opposite) and a few carefully chosen ingredients: diced ripe tomatoes, artichokes preserved in good olive oil, roasted garlic cloves or caramelised fennel and a sprinkle of basil, dill, flat-leaf parsley or chervil will all give you a very special dish.

You can prepare a live rock lobster for the barbecue by stunning it in the freezer for 30 minutes and then blanching it for 2 minutes in boiling water to kill it. My favourite way is to take the tail, cut it in half lengthways and barbecue it with lots of extra virgin olive oil and lemon juice for about 4 minutes each side. Or you can cut the tail meat out of the shell, then steam or poach it and serve with the rind and juice of a lime, kaffir lime leaves, a little extra virgin olive oil and a dash of coconut milk.

If you have a cooked rock lobster, make a salad by removing the tail and cutting it into medallions. Moisten the meat with fruity extra virgin olive oil and lemon juice and toss in a little fresh dill. Boil small yellow waxy potatoes in their skins, then halve them and add warm to the rock lobster, with wedges of ripe tomato and sorrel leaves. Make a vinaigrette with more of the olive oil, a little wholegrain mustard, lemon juice and dill, then season and toss through the salad.

SORREL MAYONNAISE *Makes 375 ml*

I still prefer the simplest of all accompaniments with rock lobster and nothing beats home-made mayonnaise. The piquancy of the sorrel in this version cuts the richness of the lobster beautifully. For perfection, I would serve half a rock lobster, cut as close to eating as possible to prevent it drying out, with a good dollop of this mayonnaise, boiled waxy potatoes and a salad of bitter greens.

2 egg yolks
1 cup trimmed sorrel
pinch salt
juice of ½ lemon

½ cup (125 ml) mellow extra virgin olive oil
½ cup (125 ml) grapeseed oil
freshly ground black pepper

There is no need to chop the sorrel if you are using a blender, though you may need to if using a mortar and pestle. Blend the egg yolks with the sorrel and salt, then add a squeeze of lemon juice. When amalgamated, pour in the combined oils very slowly with the motor running until the mixture becomes very thick. Add a little more lemon juice, if required, and grind in some pepper, then continue pouring in the oil (it can go in a little faster at this stage). When the mayonnaise has emulsified, check whether any extra lemon juice or seasoning is required.

PASTA WITH ROCK LOBSTER *Serves 4*

1 × 1 kg live rock lobster
1 fennel bulb
salt
350 g fresh pasta sheets
extra virgin olive oil, for cooking
2 cloves garlic, finely chopped

5 peeled ripe tomatoes, chopped
pinch sugar
sea salt flakes and freshly ground
   black pepper
2 teaspoons freshly chopped basil

Chill the rock lobster in the freezer for 30 minutes to stun it. Remove any damaged outer leaves from the fennel and cut away the core, then slice the fennel finely. Reserve the fennel off-cuts. Fill a large saucepan with water, add the off-cuts, and bring to the boil. Salt the water once it is boiling.

Immerse the stunned rock lobster in the boiling water, then cover and cook for 4 minutes only. Drain the lobster and allow it to cool (do not plunge it into cold water, otherwise the meat will become soggy). When cool enough to handle, cut the lobster in half lengthways and extract the meat and the mustard. Cut the meat into medallions, then crack the legs and remove the meat.

Bring another large saucepan of water to the boil, then salt it and cook the pasta sheets for 3 minutes. Strain the pasta and drizzle olive oil over it to prevent it sticking, shaking it constantly to help stop the cooking process.

Fry the garlic gently with the sliced fennel in a little olive oil in a heavy-based saucepan over low heat until softened. Add the tomatoes, sugar and a little salt to the fennel mixture and reduce to the desired consistency. Add the rock lobster meat and 2 tablespoons olive oil and season with pepper. Remove the pan from the heat once the lobster has just warmed through. Warm the pasta by steaming it over boiling water for 2 minutes or cover it with plastic film and reheat it in a microwave oven on high for 1 minute. Toss the pasta and sauce together with the basil and serve immediately.

SALAD GREENS AND HERBS

 OVER THE PAST FEW YEARS, THERE HAS BEEN A QUIET revolution in the salad market that has taken us so far from the humble iceberg lettuce we all know that it is hard to keep up. Many still love the iceberg though, and, particularly when just picked from an organic garden, it is still worth its place on any table.

We can now choose from mignonettes, butterhead lettuce, oak leaf lettuce, curly endive, cos lettuce or baby cos (or gem) lettuce, and the list goes on. Added to that, we have rocket (whose peppery leaves are an essential part of my salad bowl), mizuna, tatsoi, radicchio, witlof, sorrel, lamb's lettuce (or mâche), baby spinach leaves and watercress, land cress, curled cress and mustard cress. And that's not an exhaustive list. We also have herbs of every imaginable variety available to us in almost any greengrocer and now micro herbs in great profusion. Many people plant herbs in their own garden as a matter of course and just-picked herbs add so much to your dish. Not only can you have herbs in perfect condition easily to hand, but in the spring you also have that profusion of mauve or purple flowers of thyme and sage to add to your cooking, whether it be a herb pasta dish, or pan-fried brains in nut-brown sage butter, using both the flowers and leaves.

Many of the lettuces mentioned above are soft and don't form a heart in the same way as an iceberg does (although cos does have an inner heart and it is the brilliant 'apple-green' inner leaves that I use; these days you can buy just the cos heart with all the outer leaves plucked off). These soft lettuces, so often grown hydroponically, are fragile and need to be transported home with care.

My big challenge is planting the right number of lettuces (indeed the right number of any vegetable). I tend to get carried away and plant three rows of the same lettuce instead of three different varieties, so they end up going to seed before I can use them, even though we eat salad every day. I obviously need more discipline!

Nurseries now have mixed punnets of lettuces where you can pick just the outside leaves for use as they grow. And rocket grows well from seeds, so well it could almost be a weed. I like to pick it very young; its peppery flavour can stand alone in a simple dish of freshly shaved Parmigiano Reggiano with slices of fresh pear, just on its own with a really good vinaigrette, or of course with ripe tomatoes or olives. You need to do so little when you have good ingredients. Even though I often grow rocket myself we have a grower in the Valley who delivers to us three days a week and the rocket is both peppery and sweet for being so fresh.

Salad burnet has a fresh cucumbery taste and makes a great addition to salads. One plant will produce all summer, with the long outside stems yielding larger and larger petals.

Sorrel is one of my favourite herbs (or is it a salad leaf?). It has such a strong piquant flavour that goes so well in sauces or savoury tarts. The baby leaves in a salad mix

shine through when teamed with something rich like smoked mackerel. I'll warn you, though: sorrel attracts snails like no other plant in my garden and I now grow it in pots off the ground.

Witlof is so versatile as a salad leaf and vegetable. Braise witlof in butter with some sugar – it will caramelise and become bittersweet, and is then great teamed with game. Just as radicchio, either grilled on the barbecue or braised in some butter and deglazed with vino cotto, is yet another flavour dimension I enjoy. Though more in season in autumn and winter, it is now available year-round.

Mesclun mix is widely available, but before buying make sure there are no brown marks at the base of the leaves, a sure sign that the mix isn't fresh. And, to me, this is a last resort.

As well as herbs, there are many sprouts to give extra texture and flavour to salads. Snow pea sprouts, sweet with a crunch, or snow pea shoots, could both be tossed through a warm salad of quail with pancetta, garlic croutons and other bitter greens.

In a salad, I would mix watercress with other, less strong leaves but, when abundant, watercress puréed with a little cream makes a really peppery sauce to serve with grills.

The vinaigrette most often used in our house, proudly my husband Colin's creation, is a mixture of 4 parts extra virgin olive oil with 1 part acidulant (a mix of ⅓ vino cotto and ⅔ red-wine vinegar), some sea salt flakes and freshly ground black pepper.

If I need a delicate vinaigrette I'll use verjuice mixed with perhaps walnut oil tempered with some grapeseed oil. While I use vino cotto rather than balsamic vinegar, this is simply because we make it ourselves. Quality red-wine or sherry vinegar, lemon or lime juices all make a great vinaigrette. Mustard is a variable, but often used. My great friend Peter Wall always uses mustard, adding a little cream and even a touch of sugar to his vinaigrettes, and for years, I always left making the vinaigrette to him whenever we ate together.

It is vital when serving salads to use quality ingredients, particularly the extra virgin olive oil. You must also wash, refresh and spin all lettuces dry; salad spinners are one of the essential kitchen tools. Other tricks are to rub a clove of garlic around the salad bowl for just that hint of flavour, as chef Damien Pignolet taught me to do; to choose the right-shaped bowl and salad servers; and to have the salad prepared but only dress it when ready to serve. The right salad servers are those that can be crossed over each other halfway up the bowl. They act as a raft for the salad vegetables to sit on until ready to serve – that one's a Stephanie Alexander trick, and used by us every day. Another idea is to toss the leaves with your fingers, making sure there is just enough vinaigrette to loosely grab onto the leaves. Drain any excess as you don't want your salad limp with vinaigrette.

A salad should have colour, flavour and crunch. A wonderfully fresh salad will make a difference to practically any meal.

WATERCRESS, WITLOF, BOCCONCINI, WALNUT AND GRAPE SALAD

Serves 4

100 g walnuts
2 teaspoons finely chopped shallots
2 red witlof, bases trimmed and
    leaves separated
handful picked watercress,
    washed and dried
handful salad burnet, washed and dried
¾ cup each red and green grapes, halved
1 lemon, thinly sliced and cut into
    small pieces

extra virgin olive oil, for drizzling
4 bocconcini balls
1 tablespoon roughly chopped
    lemon thyme leaves

VINAIGRETTE
¼ cup (60 ml) walnut oil
¼ cup (60 ml) verjuice
freshly ground black pepper

Preheat the oven to 220°C. Roast the walnuts on a baking tray for about 5 minutes or until just starting to brown, shaking the tray to prevent the nuts from burning. Rub the walnuts in a clean tea towel to remove the bitter skins, then place in a sieve and shake away the skins. Leave to cool.

Lightly fry the shallots in a little olive oil, and reserve. Toss the salad leaves together in a bowl, then divide them among 4 plates. Mix the walnuts, grapes and lemon slices and scatter over the leaves. Pour a little olive oil over the bocconcini, then roll them in the lemon thyme. Slice thinly and add to the salad leaves, along with the shallots.

To make the vinaigrette, whisk the walnut oil and verjuice until amalgamated, then add the pepper. Dress the salads just before serving.

PRESERVED LEMON, ROCKET AND GREEN BEAN SALAD *Serves 6*

4 quarters preserved lemon, flesh removed,
   rind rinsed and thinly sliced
½ cup (125 ml) verjuice
500 g green beans *or* flat (Roman) beans,
   topped and tailed
4 ripe roma tomatoes, sliced

½ cup (125 ml) extra virgin olive oil
sea salt flakes and freshly ground
   black pepper
½ red onion, finely sliced
½ cup basil leaves
1 cup rocket leaves, washed and dried

Soak the preserved lemon rind slices in verjuice for 30 minutes. Bring a saucepan of salted water to the boil, then blanch the beans until tender. Refresh in a bowl of iced water and set aside.

Put the tomatoes in a large bowl, drizzle with a little of the olive oil and season with salt and pepper. Drain the preserved lemon rind, reserving the verjuice, and add to the tomatoes, along with the drained beans and red onion. Whisk the verjuice and remaining olive oil together and season with pepper to taste. Pour the dressing over and toss to combine, then leave for 10 minutes. Add basil and rocket leaves and serve immediately.

PURSLANE AND BREAD SALAD *Serves 4*

This rustic salad teams perfectly with fish or chicken. Or you could add goat's cheese for a substantial luncheon dish for two.

3 thick slices wood-fired white bread,
   crusts removed
½ cup (125 ml) extra virgin olive oil
1 clove garlic, halved
2 tablespoons verjuice
4 handfuls purslane, washed, dried and
   snipped into 3 cm lengths

2 quarters preserved lemon, flesh removed,
   rind rinsed and thinly sliced
4 large anchovy fillets, torn into small pieces
sea salt flakes and freshly ground
   black pepper

Preheat the oven to 220°C. Brush both sides of the bread with half the olive oil. Toast on a baking tray in the oven until golden brown, turning after the first side has coloured. Rub the toast with cut garlic, then rip into bite-sized pieces and transfer to a bowl. Sprinkle with 1 tablespoon verjuice to moisten for just a few minutes; it is important that the bread is not soggy.

In a large bowl, toss the toast with the purslane, preserved lemon rind and anchovies. Whisk the remaining olive oil and verjuice and season with salt and pepper. Toss the salad with the dressing and serve immediately.

SKYE GYNGELL'S TORN BREAD SALAD WITH ROCKET, SOUR CHERRIES, CAPERS AND VERJUICE *Serves 6*

Hearing that I was to be in London in January 2006, the local Slow Food chapter asked me to present a masterclass on verjuice at Petersham Nurseries Cafe in Surrey, one of the city's absolute hotspots, with their chef Skye Gyngell, a very talented Australian. I was thrilled to accept, and even though it was to be held the day after a big Australia Day affair for 300 at Australia House (which I developed and oversaw the menu for), I knew I couldn't miss the opportunity.

The day was separated into two parts. First, a class for forty or so people, which was held in one of the greenhouses. I remember it being freezing cold and rugging up with scarves and an overcoat of some sort, but nothing could diminish my enthusiasm for sharing all I knew about verjuice, demonstrating its diverse uses, tasting and talking about it until I had no voice left. The second part was an even greater thrill. Months before, Skye had sent me copies of her menus, and they evoked in me such a sense of déjà vu: here was a produce-driven cook, surrounded by amazing bounty and working with the philosophy that only the best would do. Skye created a menu for lunch, and one dish after the other all included verjuice. It was a truly exceptional lunch; in fact, one of the great days of my food life, where the sum was even greater than its parts. Skye's dishes – so simple yet creative – simply sparkled. What generosity there was at that table! Here's one of my favourite dishes from that day.

¼ cup dried sour cherries
¼ cup (60 ml) verjuice
2 red onions, thickly sliced
2 tablespoons sugar
2 tablespoons red-wine vinegar
⅓ cup (80 ml) extra virgin olive oil
6 slices slightly stale sourdough bread,
   torn into bite-sized pieces
handful rocket leaves
small bunch chervil, sprigs picked
small bunch marjoram, leaves picked
   and chopped

2 tablespoons chopped preserved
   lemon rind
2 tablespoons salted capers,
   washed and dried
finely chopped rind of 1 unwaxed lemon

VINAIGRETTE
1 tablespoon Dijon mustard
¼ cup (60 ml) verjuice
sea salt flakes and freshly ground
   black pepper
¼ cup (60 ml) extra virgin olive oil

Place cherries in a bowl with ¼ cup verjuice and leave overnight to reconstitute. Drain before use.

Preheat the oven to 200°C. Combine the sliced onions, sugar, red-wine vinegar and 2 tablespoons olive oil, then arrange in one layer on a baking tray. Roast until soft and slightly caramelised.

Heat remaining 2 tablespoons oil in a frying pan and shallow-fry bread until golden and crisp. »

For the verjuice vinaigrette, place the mustard and verjuice in a small bowl and whisk to combine. Season with a little salt and pepper, then slowly whisk in the olive oil until emulsified.

Place all the ingredients, except the dressing, in a bowl, then lightly toss together with your hands. Pour over the dressing and toss thoroughly together. Taste for seasoning, adjusting the flavour with a little more salt and pepper if necessary.

HERB PASTA WITH SORREL BUTTER AND THYME   *Serves 4*

100 g flat-leaf parsley leaves	SORREL BUTTER
5 duck egg yolks	½ cup flat-leaf parsley leaves
dash extra virgin olive oil	1 cup sorrel leaves
pinch salt	250 g unsalted butter, slightly softened
300 g strong flour (see Glossary)	juice of 1 lemon
10 sprigs thyme, to serve	freshly ground black pepper

First, make the pasta. Blanch the parsley quickly – straight in and out of a saucepan of boiling water – and drain well but don't refresh. Purée the parsley in a food processor and add egg yolks immediately, so they take up the maximum colour from the parsley, then add the dash of oil and the salt. Add the flour to the food processor and pulse until the dough starts to combine. Take out and knead by hand until shiny. Rest the dough for 20 minutes, then roll through the pasta machine to angel-hair size.

Now make the sorrel butter. Process the parsley and sorrel leaves together and then add the butter and lemon juice. Add pepper if required. Roll into a cylinder, wrap in plastic film and place in the refrigerator. Strip thyme leaves from the sprigs.

Cook the pasta in salted boiling water. Drain, transfer to a serving bowl, and moisten with slices of sorrel butter. Toss with thyme leaves, dot with a few thyme flowers if available, and serve.

CHIVE FLOWER FRITTERS   *Serves 6 as a main course*

20 g butter	125 g plain flour
⅓ cup (80 ml) milk	extra virgin olive oil, for frying
¼ teaspoon white-wine vinegar	1 large egg white
pinch salt	24 chive flowers

Heat the butter, milk and ⅔ cup water in a small saucepan over medium heat, until just bubbling. Add the vinegar and allow to cool. In a bowl, mix the salt and the flour, then add the liquid slowly to avoid lumps. Leave the batter to rest for at least 20 minutes.

Heat about 2 cm of olive oil in a heavy-based saucepan until it is hot enough for a piece of stale bread to turn golden brown in a few seconds. Beat the egg white until stiff and fold into the batter. Dip a few chive flowers at a time into the batter then drop them into the hot oil and fry for a minute or two, or until golden brown. Transfer to kitchen paper to drain, then repeat with remaining batter and flowers. Serve immediately.

LEMON VERBENA ICE CREAM   *Makes 600 ml*

This recipe is based on the cheat's method of making anglaise (the custard that forms the basis of the ice cream) in a microwave. As each microwave will cook differently, the times may need to be adjusted.

8 unsprayed sprigs lemon verbena in flower	1 cup (250 ml) cream
	½ cup (110 g) sugar
1 cup (250 ml) milk	4 egg yolks

Finely chop the leaves and stalks of the lemon verbena, reserving the flowers. Place the milk and cream in a saucepan over medium–high heat, stirring in the sugar, then add the leaves and stalks and bring almost to the boil. Whisk in egg yolks, then transfer to a microwave-proof container and cook in the microwave on medium power for 8 minutes. Remove and whisk, then return to the microwave on medium–high power for another 4 minutes or until the mixture begins to thicken. Whisk again and leave to cool. Churn in an ice cream machine (following the manufacturer's instructions) and then add the lemon verbena flowers.

TOMATOES

FOR THE GARDENER, THE SCENT A TOMATO BUSH RELEASES on a summer's day, and the tingle on the skin as you brush past it, is worth any amount of time spent watering. Although it has a thousand culinary possibilities, picked ripe from the garden the tomato needs no more attention than a drizzle of good extra virgin olive oil, a turn of freshly ground black pepper and a sprig of its companion in life, basil. This is the tomato as I know it, the tomato I eat as if it were an apple – not fussed by the juice running down my arm!

Unfortunately, in the 1980s, the European trend of growing a nondescript tomato acceptable to a wide range of tastes became a worldwide practice, and the rise of the supermarket ensured its survival. Supermarkets have become huge buyers of vegetables, and as their interest is in products that last a long time 'looking good' on the shelf, this trend suited them perfectly.

This led to a rise in the practice of gassing tomatoes, already common in Queensland, and these tomatoes have infiltrated most parts of Australia in a big way. Harmless ethylene gas, the natural ripening substance fruit produces, is used to change the colour of tomatoes. By gassing their tomatoes Queensland farmers give themselves a price advantage, as it means they can pick their crops at varying stages of maturity. The CSIRO tells me that there is no difference in taste between a tomato that has been gassed and one that has not. The problem is that tomatoes picked before natural ripening has begun will not have the flavour that vine-ripening ensures. Because Queensland farmers rely on gassing they may well be picking their tomatoes before they have reached a sufficiently mature stage to guarantee flavour. The enzymes that cause fruit to soften are also those that produce flavour so, picked too early, the hard-skinned variety so loved by supermarkets (and designed to be handled as roughly as a tin of tomatoes) will never be able to produce the goods. If the farmers took the CSIRO's advice, they would let the tomatoes sit in a ripening room before gassing them and would reject any that didn't start to colour up naturally.

A rising consumer backlash is evident, with more discerning, flavour-driven people moving towards specialised greengrocers, organic grocers and farmers' markets – but even then it's a real search to find naturally ripened tomatoes. Semi-commercial growers who don't have to transport their crop far from their doorstep can fill these markets with the older varieties in the natural season but I suspect it will be a while before any solution filters through to the supermarkets.

A great surprise to me is that really good glasshouse tomatoes are grown in Murray Bridge near Adelaide during the winter. These are golf ball-sized with a thick skin like most commercially grown tomatoes, but this is one time when the skin doesn't detract from the flavour – even in winter, it's incredibly intense. The same variety is field-grown during the summer and is better still. Though these come from a large commercial grower, I've never seen them in supermarkets; instead I seek them out at our Central

Market in Adelaide. Here is a commercial tomato grown out of season that is amazingly full of flavour – so there is hope yet for better supermarket tomatoes, if the public demands it.

It is not just the ripeness of the tomato that affects its quality; flavour is closely tied to variety. Though season also has such a bearing (in that nothing is better than late summer tomatoes), I'm taken aback at how good these golf ball tomatoes are in winter. Am I going against my own philosophy of eating what's in season? I guess I am if the flavour is there.

While many people grow their own tomatoes in an effort to regain that flavour of old, my experience with buying plants from nurseries is that the varieties on offer are in the main disappointing. Happily there are other avenues. Heirloom varieties are available by seed only from The Digger's Club at Dromana, Victoria (see www.diggers.com.au). You can buy open-pollinated varieties from their mail-order catalogue so you can save your own seeds for future years. Their Tommy Toe, bearing fruit the size of an apricot, is a good bearer and stands out in the flavour stakes. If you're able to find oxheart, black oxheart (Russian) or Rouge de Marmande, they make great eating. Some small commercial growers specialise in these heritage varieties and they are becoming more readily available.

I belong to the Rare Fruit Society in South Australia but am sadly always too busy to go to their meetings. However, I read their newsletters religiously and, as I'm sure is the case in other states, there is a lot of seed saving and swapping going on. This year another member gave me a dozen tomato plants of a variety he has been propagating from American stock brought in legally thirty years ago. In taking them I had to accept responsibility to keep them separate from any other tomato plants and to agree to keep a quantity of seeds to share. The plants are tall and vigorous and the fruit makes very good eating. Even more exciting is a member who is growing eighty different varieties of heirloom tomatoes, and turning it into a semi-commercial enterprise – so it can be done. An important point of contact for seed saving is the Australian Seed Savers Network, run by Michael and Jude Fanton. View their website at www.seedsavers.net or email them on info@seedsavers.net for more information. Another contact I have come across, for those interested in sourcing less commonly available seeds for produce such as heirloom tomatoes, is The Italian Gardener. Their website is www.theitaliangardener.com.au and they can also be emailed at info@theitaliangardener.com.au.

I used to think that tomatoes had to be left on the vine until totally ripe, but having been challenged on that theory, I now realise that green-shouldered tomatoes, grown in full sun and coloured pinkish-red, will ripen to a really good tomato as long as they're not refrigerated (and may even rival those picked totally ripe). The only exception to this rule of not refrigerating tomatoes is when you've bought a large quantity of tomatoes for making sauce that are already riper than ripe and you need time to get organised to make the sauce – but only do it if it's essential.

I seldom plant less than twenty tomato plants at a time as there are good and bad years and I want to be assured of my own crop. This means some years I'll have more tomatoes than I could possibly use for home, but it never fazes me. Nor does it faze American cookery writer Joanne Weir, whose book *You Say Tomato* runs to almost 300 pages on this one subject alone. As well as containing recipes, it is also full of tips for preserving, slow-roasting and drying; these tips come from cooks from all around the world, including our own Phillip Searle, who as a chef makes more of a tomato than anyone I've known, and he's shared all of this knowledge with Joanne.

More years ago than I prefer to remember, I was lucky enough to see Phillip in action when he ran Oasis Seros restaurant in Sydney. Not only does he never waste a tomato, he uses every part of it in a series of processes. Firstly he cores them, then blends them until coarsely chopped, then cooks them in a stainless steel pot for 20 minutes. Once strained, he reduces the juice to one-tenth of the original volume over a low flame to give an essence that can then be used to add intensity to sauces. Then Phillip puts the leftover pulp through a mouli on its finest blade, adds a good olive oil, and cooks the pulp with a touch of sugar until very thick, resulting in a really concentrated purée. But there's still another process – no need to throw out the pulp left behind in the mouli. It is baked on a baking sheet at a low temperature until it's completely dry, then cooled and processed in the spice grinder. Now that's taking advantage of your crop!

I first learnt of *'strattu*, an intense and pure tomato concentrate, from Mary Taylor Simeti's book *Pomp and Sustenance*. For this, tomatoes are puréed and salted and then dried in the sun, where they are stirred frequently until all moisture has evaporated. Mary talked of it becoming a rare practice in Italy and I had always meant to try it, but never quite got around to it. Then at the Yalumba Harvest Picnic during the 1995 Barossa Vintage Festival

Pasta with tomatoes, basil and extra virgin olive oil (see page 156)

I found that the parents of a valued staff member (the Fantos) were not only making *'strattu* for themselves but had been persuaded by the organisers to sell small amounts. I couldn't believe my luck – I might not have learnt about it if the Picnic, designed to encourage small growers to value-add and show off their produce, hadn't taken place. The day opened my eyes to the wealth of tradition in this family, who had for years supplied me with the best asparagus and eggplants imaginable – and yet I had been too busy to delve any further; a salient lesson. I've since experienced bread from their backyard brick oven, have taken part in the pig-killing and sausage-making rituals, and, because of them, finally managed to hang the last of my cherry tomato crop in our shed for later use in winter dishes, to which they add an amazing intensity.

If you preserve your own tomatoes from the end-of-year crop you'll never have to use tinned tomatoes again. (Not that tinned tomatoes can't be ripe and flavoursome if you buy well, but they can have a taint that disagrees with me.) My first serious tomato-bottling took place in late summer 1996. So excited was I by the outcome that first year, when I rationed them to the dishes in which they would really make a difference, that now I preserve many more, always at the very end of the season. It is such a simple process, although it's worth checking the thermometer annually on your preserving 'outfit'. One year, while preserving with a friend, we had two kettles on the go the whole time; my thermometer wasn't registering properly and after all that work exactly half of the tomatoes fermented and bubbled over. Not only was it a dreadful waste of effort and tomatoes, it was a terrible, terrible mess to clean up.

To preserve, cut away the entire stem area from very ripe but firm tomatoes, then halve the tomatoes and pack them tightly, with the skins on, into no. 31 preserving jars (1-litre capacity); no water is added, as the tomatoes make their own juice (this is the vital part). Seal the bottles with lids and clips and then place in a preserving pan for 1 hour 15 minutes at 92°C (between settings 4 and 5 on older units). When they're done, I stand the bottles on a wad of newspaper for a minimum of 24 hours before storing them, or up to 48 hours if you can. I don't bother sterilising jars when making sauces, condiments or jams if I'm able to bottle the product in a preserving 'outfit' at near to boiling temperature, and then I invert the jar immediately – in this case an unsterilised lid presents no problem, as the heat from the contents also sterilises the lid. Don't worry that the tomatoes are not peeled when you come to use them: the skins will fall away as you remove them from the jar. And don't hide these beautiful tomatoes away in a cupboard if you have space to display them on a kitchen shelf. They glow like jewels!

Rather than waste over-ripe tomatoes too squashed for bottling, cut them into quarters and put them in a large baking dish with a drizzle of good olive oil (make sure you reject any mouldy or 'off' tomatoes in the process). Leave them overnight in an oven set on its lowest temperature or with the pilot light on so that they caramelise without burning. These tomatoes can be stored in a jar of olive oil for up to a week and added straight to any dish without puréeing.

Sun-dried tomatoes were thrown into every conceivable dish during the early 1990s, but, used in moderation, they are still a force to be reckoned with. I still find them essential in my duck egg pasta with smoked kangaroo, extra virgin olive oil and pine nuts or pasta with eggplant and pine nuts. Sun-dried tomatoes are also wonderful with fresh goat's cheese on bruschetta. More to my taste are tomatoes semi-dried in the oven: brush them with extra virgin olive oil infused with garlic and thyme, then season and roast them at 110°C for about 2 hours. These have a shorter shelf-life, but when covered with extra virgin olive oil and refrigerated they last for weeks. And if the tomatoes were really good to start with, these tomatoes become almost like sweetmeats that can be pinched from the fridge as a snack.

Probably my favourite way of serving tomatoes is to slice them thickly, drizzle them with extra virgin olive oil, sprinkle them with freshly torn basil leaves from the garden, sea salt flakes and freshly ground black pepper and leave for an hour before using them. Then take some good crusty bread and perhaps some more extra virgin olive oil and, loading it up with the sliced tomatoes, dip the bread back into the juices. Not far behind this favourite is a breakfast consisting of a good piece of toasted sourdough bread with lots of unsalted butter, really ripe tomato sliced thickly, sea salt flakes and freshly ground black pepper. Or a cold pasta dish, with tomatoes cut into chunks and marinated for a while in plenty of basil, sea salt flakes, freshly ground black pepper and lots of fruity extra virgin olive oil, then served with cooled, oiled penne. You need to do so little with tomatoes in their prime.

TOMATO SAUCE   *Makes 1 litre*

I prefer to make my tomato sauce with these extra ingredients, so that when I reach for a bottle from my pantry, it needs no further preparation for use in pasta sauces (though being the indulgent person I am, I often gild the lily with an extra flourish of olive oil).

1.5 kg very ripe tomatoes	½ teaspoon–2 tablespoons sugar
1 large onion, chopped	(depending on the ripeness of
1 carrot, chopped	the tomatoes)
1 stick celery, chopped	¼ cup (60 ml) verjuice *or* white wine
½ cup (125 ml) extra virgin olive oil	freshly ground black pepper
sea salt flakes	2 large basil leaves

Wash the tomatoes, then cut them into quarters, discarding the calyx, or base of the green stem, from each and cutting away any blemishes, and put them into a large preserving pan. Add the onion, carrot, celery and olive oil to the tomato, tossing to coat well. Add salt and sugar and stand the pan over a fierce heat. Stir the mixture constantly, watching that it does not catch and burn, until it starts to caramelise and the liquid has evaporated, about 20 minutes. Deglaze the pan with the verjuice or white wine, then check for seasoning, adjusting with salt and sugar as necessary. Grind in black pepper, then add the torn basil. Fill sterilised, hot jars or bottles (see Glossary) with the sauce and seal. The sauce keeps for months.

TOMATO SOUP FOR VINTAGE

Serves 4

This soup was inspired by Richard Olney's Grape Harvester's Soup from his book *Simple French Food*. I first made it to feed my restaurant staff when we closed up shop to hand-pick the semillon grapes in our vineyard. I wanted something tasty and easy to transport, a meal in itself. I used about double the tomatoes and a lot less water than the original recipe and I loved it so much that it always went back on the menu at the Pheasant Farm Restaurant during vintage.

6 medium tomatoes, very ripe yet firm

1 kg onions, thinly sliced
   (I use brown onions)

⅓ cup (80 ml) extra virgin olive oil,
   plus extra to serve

4 cloves garlic, finely chopped

sea salt flakes

½ teaspoon sugar (optional), or to taste

½ cup (125 ml) verjuice *or* dry white wine

1 litre boiling water

4 slices stale wood-fired bread

Cut out the core of the tomatoes – for this rustic soup I do not peel or seed them. Cut each tomato in half and then into quarters or eighths. Using a large, heavy-based saucepan, cook the onions gently in the oil, stirring over low heat with a wooden spoon for about 10 minutes or until they are uniformly light golden and very soft. Add the garlic and salt to the pan and cook for 5 minutes. Add the tomatoes, and sugar to sweeten if you wish; the sugar merely enhances the flavour of the tomatoes and gives a boost if they are not in perfect condition.

Cook for 10 minutes and then add the verjuice or wine and water. (For an over-the-top soup you could leave out the water altogether; this is also wonderful as a topping for a hot or cold pasta dish.) Simmer, covered, for 45 minutes before serving. Drizzle a little olive oil over each slice of bread and place a slice in each serving bowl. Ladle the soup over the bread.

AVOCADO AND TOMATO JELLY   *Serves 6*

Unless you have good tomatoes to work with, it is better to add extra avocado to this dish rather than diminish it by using lesser tomatoes. If making the jelly in advance (say the day before), use 2½ × 2 g gelatine leaves, but if using straight away use 3 × 2 g leaves.

3 ripe tomatoes
1½ cups (375 ml) verjuice
1 teaspoon castor sugar
2 sprigs tarragon
3 × 2 g leaves gelatine (see Glossary)
1 large ripe reed avocado *or* 2 medium hass
   avocados, peeled and cut into cubes

sea salt flakes and freshly ground
   black pepper
extra virgin olive oil and delicate
   greens such as snow pea tendrils
   or mâche, to serve

Wash the tomatoes, remove stalks and make an incision in the top of each tomato. Blanch very briefly in boiling water until the skin starts to pull away. Peel and dice the tomatoes, removing the seeds.

Heat the verjuice, castor sugar and one sprig of tarragon in a saucepan over low heat until it starts to simmer; do not boil, or the verjuice will become cloudy. Remove from heat and set aside to infuse. Meanwhile, soak the gelatine leaves in cold water for 5 minutes. Remove the sprig of tarragon from the warm verjuice, then squeeze out the excess liquid from the gelatine and add to the verjuice.

Once verjuice has cooled, layer tomatoes and avocado in six 135 ml-capacity dariole moulds or tea cups, adding a leaf of tarragon to each mould. Season to taste. Gently pour some of the verjuice mixture to the top of each mould. Refrigerate overnight or until set.

Either dip each mould quickly in a bowl of hot water or use a knife to separate the jelly from the edge of the moulds. Gently turn out onto plates and drizzle with a little extra virgin olive oil, then season with some sea salt and serve with some delicate greens to garnish.

LITTLE BLANCHE'S RIPE TOMATO CHUTNEY

Makes 7 litres

A close friend from Tasmania kindly passed on her family recipe for tomato chutney. I have played with the quantities, added onions and changed the vinegar. I have to admit it's so heavy in sugar I temper it to my taste with a little less.

1.5 kg Granny Smith apples, peeled,
  cored and roughly chopped
2 kg onions, finely chopped
4.5 kg vine-ripened tomatoes,
  cut into eighths
750 g raisins

125 g salt
1 kg sugar
3 cups (750 ml) red-wine vinegar
6 cloves garlic
80 g grated ginger

Cook the apples, onions and tomatoes in a large heavy-based saucepan over medium heat for 10 minutes. Add the remaining ingredients and simmer gently over low heat for 2–3 hours. Reduce any excess liquid at a high temperature. Transfer to sterilised jars (see Glossary) and seal. Unopened jars of this tomato chutney will keep for years.

RUSTIC TOMATO AND BREAD SALAD

Serves 4

4 thick slices sourdough bread,
  crusts removed
½ cup (125 ml) very good-quality
  extra virgin olive oil
sea salt flakes
6 ripe tomatoes, cut into chunks

2 small red onions, thinly sliced
1 Lebanese cucumber, peeled and chopped
½ cup basil leaves, torn
½ cup loosely packed marjoram leaves
2½ tablespoons red-wine vinegar
freshly ground black pepper

Tear bread into small chunks and toss in a frying pan over high heat with 75 ml of the olive oil until golden and crisp. Place the bread in a large salad bowl (preferably wooden), season with salt to taste, then add the vegetables and herbs. Toss with remaining olive oil and red-wine vinegar, season to taste and mix well.

TUNA

THE BLUEFIN TUNA IS A COLD-WATER FISH AND IS CAUGHT in the waters off southern Western Australia through to Tasmania. The local bluefin is available from January until some time in March. The season's end date depends entirely on quotas: once they are filled, the season ends. Most of the fish available in Adelaide comes from Port Lincoln and is caught by pole boats, although there are some lobster fishermen who line-fish in their off-season. The sashimi market in Japan demands long-line fishing, but most of the top-quality pole-caught tuna from Port Lincoln also goes to Japan. It is hard to believe that in the 1990s it was often difficult to get local tuna in South Australia. Although yellowfin is certainly more widely available now, bluefin is much harder to find as the best always gets exported.

The process of tuna fishing is fascinating. First, the fishermen go out two to three nights in advance to catch sardines, which are kept alive in tanks on the boats. (The sardines out of Port Lincoln are apparently very sweet, but there is still no local commercial fishery for them.) Spotter planes are then sent out to locate schools of tuna. The planes radio the boats, directing them to the schools, which are marked by 'fast boats' for the following pole boats. The schools are then encircled with nets and the tuna excited by the live sardines. A line is run with large, bare hooks which shine through the water like the sardines, and the tuna take the unbaited hooks. These days the boats are big business and carry automatic poling machines.

The main requirement for quality fish is that they are killed immediately and humanely. The treatment of the fish after catching is what dictates the price, and this processing depends on the boat's facilities. Some boats are sophisticated enough to have a freeze-chill operation on board; tuna caught by these boats is shipped straight to Japan. The yellowfin fished off Cairns is killed and gutted on board and put in a brine to chill so as to avoid deterioration.

Prime-quality tuna farmed for the Japanese sashimi market take three to four months to reach the required size. Once they reach 30 kg they are harvested, killed quickly and efficiently, and placed in an ice-brine mixture to bring down their body temperature, which conserves their prime quality; they are flown to Japan daily.

Of Australia's tuna harvest exported to the Japanese market, 75 per cent is sent by sea, frozen at super-low temperatures (–60°C), and 25 per cent is sent fresh by air. The fish are held in the ice-brine from the harvest pontoon to the processing plant to preserve them, while the air-freighted fish are generally sent with two average-sized (40 kg and above) tuna in one box.

When thinking about tuna, I find it difficult deciding which particular way I like it best: raw, cured, just seared or, surprisingly, slow-cooked. If pressed, I would have to say my most outstanding tuna experience took place in Tokyo – ironically, we were eating bluefin tuna from South Australia. This was tuna at its least adorned; not just plain old raw tuna, but *toro*, or fatty tuna belly, the most amazing delicacy. For this, tuna needs to be top quality; since it is the fat that makes the *toro* so exceptional, the bluefin is preferred over the yellowfin, which is not as fatty.

The purity of this fish was extraordinary and it made me realise that I had eaten a lot of less-than-perfect raw fish in my life. The answer lies in how the fish is handled from the minute it is caught to the moment it is served. I have since learnt from Australian chefs

Neil Perry and Tetsuya Wakuda that, as fish don't have kidneys, they are particularly fragile and subject to stress. If a fish is stressed, it produces lactic acid, which means it virtually self-combusts, or 'cooks' from the inside out; so there goes any chance of perfection.

Tuna is such a versatile fish, so easy to prepare and cook. Grilling or barbecuing tuna are the easiest options of all. Rather than marinating before cooking I simply brush with extra virgin olive oil, have the barbecue really hot and salt the fish just before it goes on the fire. The vital cooking tip is that the tuna should be seared quickly on both sides and left to rest, then served rare, ranging from pink to almost totally raw, depending on your personal taste and the quality of the fish. Never cook it until it's 'done' right through. Slip the resting fish into a dish with whatever fresh herbs you have to hand, some slices of lemon and extra virgin olive oil, so it is 'relubricated' as it rests in the post-cooking marinade. Tuna is also sensational served as a thick steak, seared on each side, rested and accompanied by a sophisticated reduced red-wine sauce.

Serve a really fresh piece of tuna raw, chopped into little cubes and tossed with diced cucumber, tomato, avocado and extra virgin olive oil, then add a touch of chervil and a final squeeze of lemon juice or verjuice.

SALADE NIÇOISE   *Serves 4*

500 g piece raw tuna
200 ml extra virgin olive oil
sea salt flakes
2 handfuls fresh herbs (chives, basil,
    flat-leaf parsley), chopped
4 small waxy potatoes
12 quail eggs
16 baby green beans
12 cherry tomatoes, halved

12 yellow plum tomatoes
8 baby artichokes, preserved in vinegar
½ teaspoon Dijon mustard
2 tablespoons lemon juice
freshly ground black pepper
1 baby cos
2 tablespoons top-quality capers
    (preferably Australian)
12 small Niçoise olives

Cut the tuna into steaks of approximately 2½ cm thickness. Drizzle with a little olive oil, sprinkle with salt and sear on a hot grill or barbecue plate for about 1 minute on each side. Transfer to a plate to rest, drizzle with 2 tablespoons of the olive oil and add half the fresh herbs.

Boil the potatoes and set aside. As soon as they are cool enough to handle, cut in half lengthways and drizzle the cut side with a little olive oil. Boil the quail eggs for 2 minutes until just soft. Drain, then put into cold water and peel.

Plunge the beans in boiling water for about 2 minutes or until cooked but still bright green. Drain and refresh. Add the potatoes to a bowl with the tomatoes and drizzle with more olive oil. Remove any excess vinegar from the artichokes by patting dry with kitchen paper, and cut in half. Cut the quail eggs in half.

Make the vinaigrette by combining the balance of the oil, mustard and lemon juice with the remaining herbs. Season.

Distribute the lettuce between the serving plates. Cut the tuna into chunks and pile in the centre of the lettuce. Arrange the potatoes, tomatoes, quail eggs, beans, artichokes, capers and olives evenly over the plate, then pour over the vinaigrette and serve.

TUNA PASTA   *Serves 4*

Many people are nervous about serving anything rare. The following recipe is delicious, and because the tuna is thinly sliced, the warmth of the pasta cooks it enough.

1 red onion, thinly sliced
100 ml extra virgin olive oil
juice of 1 lemon
2 tablespoons top-quality capers
    (preferably Australian)

sea salt flakes and freshly ground
    black pepper
200 g piece raw tuna, thinly sliced
2 tablespoons finely chopped flat-leaf parsley
300 g dried angel hair pasta

Sweat the red onion in a small saucepan over medium heat in olive oil until translucent, then add lemon juice (it will turn very pink), capers, salt and pepper. Check the vinaigrette for balance and toss through the raw tuna and parsley. Cook the pasta in a saucepan of boiling salted water. Drain and moisten with olive oil. Pour the vinaigrette over the hot pasta and toss through, then serve immediately. To achieve the dish's full effect it needs to be served once everyone is seated and ready, as the pasta has to be hot enough to cook, or 'set', the tuna.

CURED TUNA

The next step up from raw tuna is cured; a simple but satisfying way to serve this fish, as it is with salmon too. The difference between these two fish is that, depending on what cut of tuna you are curing, you will often be managing a much thicker piece of flesh than for salmon, meaning that the curing time will be longer. Even though tuna fillet seems expensive, you don't need to buy a large quantity of it and there is no waste.

500 g sugar

500 g sea salt

dried dill *or* coriander seeds, to taste

1 kg fillet of tuna (of uniform thickness)

Mix the sugar and salt together and flavour with the dill or coriander seeds. Line the base of a large rectangular ceramic or plastic dish with half this mixture. Lay the fish on top and cover with the remaining sugar and salt, ensuring the fish is covered in a thick, even layer. Cover with plastic film and put a tray or plate on top to weigh it down (or you could use cans as weights). Transfer to the refrigerator for 12 hours (if you like it lightly cured like I do), or 24 hours for a drier result. The timing will depend greatly on the thickness of your fillet.

Wipe the curing mixture from the fish, then slice it thinly. Toss these slices with equally thin slices of ripe avocado, a minced golden shallot, a little extra virgin olive oil, lemon juice and flat-leaf parsley. If you have meyer lemons that are beginning to ripen, thinly slice, then cut each slice into eighths and toss these through too. Alternatively, you could omit the olive oil and make a very thin mayonnaise instead. Covered well, the cured tuna keeps for up to 1 week in the fridge.

YABBIES AND MARRON

FORAGING FOR FOOD IS A TIME-HONOURED BAROSSA TRADITION, and the poaching of yabbies (freshwater crayfish) from dams has long been a popular pastime for country people, especially kids! Yet these days poaching is becoming less tolerated. We're in the lucky position of having our own yabby dam at the farm so I have had years of experience of cooking the yabbies caught by my family.

The smellier the bait used to catch your yabby, the better. However, I well remember the way my children, when quite small and bored by my preoccupation with the restaurant, would tie pieces of soap or bread on a line to dangle over the balcony of the house, which jutted out over a pond. In a year of plenty they had no trouble catching yabbies. I could always tell when they had success by the squeals of delight intermingled with fear as they tried to haul the yabby up and grab it before it fell through the cracks of the verandah timbers. There is quite an art to picking up a yabby by the back of the head, and it is an art worth learning.

When we left this tiny house at the farm – which was really just two small bedrooms, a bathroom and an open living room, as our kitchen was the restaurant kitchen next door – we weren't prepared for our girls' reluctance to move to our present home. Although not huge, it is at least double the space, and has great character; even though it initially lacked some basic mod cons, we soon rectified that. We made a deal with the girls, that, as they were losing the dam at the farm to swim in, we would build a swimming pool between the new house and the dam at the bottom of the garden. While that was a bit of a coup for them, more important to their settling in was that the dam happened to be full of yabbies. Each night for those first few summers, the girls would lay nets for the yabbies, pulling up such great feeds that we would eat outside almost every night, starting the meal with a great pile of yabbies to share.

City friends love yabbying expeditions. One treasured day, with a refrigerator full of Christmas leftovers and a promise of yabbying, the only 'bait' was a plate of fresh quail.

Given the full net of yabbies we feasted on later, the quail was a sacrifice well worth making. There's no need to be quite so extravagant though, as the feeding response of the yabby is induced by odour. So, as I said, the smellier the bait the better.

Sadly, the home dam, either through us eating it dry, the local tradition of poaching or years of drought in the 1990s, is now empty of yabbies, so our yabby feeds are now few and far between.

It is best to yabby at night when yabbies move about to feed. If your pond is really turbid, however, you'll be able to trap them during the day too. The best net of all is an 'opera' net. They are illegal in rivers but can be left baited the night before in a dam, so you can be sure of a catch.

Not all traditional farmers are keen on the yabby (*Cherax destructor* by name and nature). Yabbies burrow into the sides of dams when the water is low, digging down to the water table, and then return to the surface when the dam refills. This digging can cause leakage through the dam walls. Legend has it that yabbies can be found 7 metres down; when farming them, it is imperative that the water level be kept constant to stop burrowing.

There is a real demand for yabbies in Europe, although this is, in large part, being satisfied by American crawfish farmed commercially in Louisiana, and also now in big numbers in China. Also, European freshwater crays were decimated after the American crawfish was introduced there some fifty or sixty years ago, carrying with it the crayfish plague. Our yabby is larger and much fuller in flavour than the crawfish, so there is hope that it can be pushed as a quality product to the discerning customer, given that it's expensive to produce and export.

There are four producers in Western Australia who already export to Europe, and indeed that state's yabby industry is a much larger concern than South Australia's. I've been told there was a law by which every paddock in Western Australia must have a turkey-nest dam in it (this is a dam where the dam walls are above ground level). Farmers harvest their own yabbies and these are collected live for export, and then held in dams, waiting for orders from all over Australia, or to be shipped to Europe (mostly Germany). They are graded and purged before being shipped.

It is the introduced South Australian yabby that Western Australian farmers are harvesting, although two indigenous species, the gilgie and koonac, are also sometimes available. It is something of an irony that the South Australian yabby is providing such an export opportunity to Western Australia, while the introduced Western Australian marron is thriving on Kangaroo Island. The red claw is also part of the yabby family; this variety has been very successful in parts of Queensland, where the farming of it is quite an industry. While very similar to look at, its harder shell makes it more difficult to peel.

Farmers purge their yabbies by holding them in fresh water so that the customer is presented with a yabby with a clean intestinal tract (it's actually still there but it's free of grit and rubbish so doesn't need to be removed). This is done to extend their shelf-life as they are transported live, stunned on ice; given the choice, I find an unpurged dam-caught yabby has much more flavour. I err towards a 110 g yabby, as it has such a presence on the plate. However, the best weight-to-tail ratio actually comes from a smaller 80 g yabby.

Yabbies should be stunned on ice or in the freezer for 20 minutes before cooking. On no account should they be left to die by the side of the dam. The dead yabby, cooked by mistake, will have an off smell and a peculiar mushy texture.

Yabbies are usually only available cooked at fish markets. During summer you will often find live yabbies in the Barossa markets, and probably at other farmers' markets in yabby territories, which will be much better eating than those caught commercially in the wild, as in many cases these will not have been handled well and are likely to be overcooked. However, nothing will taste as good as those you have caught and cooked yourself.

If you have caught your own yabbies, there are two ways of dealing with them after stunning them in the freezer: cooking them entirely, or par-cooking them in preparation for pan-frying or barbecuing. For the first (and simplest) method, bring a stockpot of salted water to the boil with dill seeds and a lemon wedge or two in it. Toss in 6–10 stunned yabbies at a time, then allow the water to come back to the boil (this usually takes a couple of minutes – if it seems to be taking longer, cover the pan with a lid to encourage boiling, as the yabbies will overcook other-wise) and cook the yabbies for 2–3 minutes, depending on size. I use a wire 'cage' I have had made especially that is very similar to one for boiling pasta. This way I can pull the yabbies out easily. Spread the cooked yabbies out on a bench to cool. Wait until the water comes back to the boil before cooking the next batch.

For preparing yabbies you want to pan-fry or barbecue, follow the same instructions but only immerse the yabbies in the boiling water for 1 minute. At this stage you can lift the flap of the tail up and carefully pull the intestinal tract out in one piece, if you like. The yabbies are still not more than just 'set' so can cope with the balance of cooking; overcooked yabby flesh becomes stringy and unpalatable.

The claw of the yabby is delicious. Rather than bash it with a mallet and risk splintered shell spoiling the delicate flesh, take the small part of the claw and pull it until it is loose. If the yabby is fully cooked, it will release the sweet claw whole.

Brush tiny par-cooked yabbies in their shells with extra virgin olive oil and barbecue them for about 1 minute per side. If the yabbies are large, halve them lengthways and toss in a frying pan with extra virgin olive oil and a splash of Pernod for a minute or two. The flavour of the Pernod and oil on your fingers as you peel and eat the yabbies is incredibly more-ish. For a change, try using walnut oil, and then deglaze the pan with verjuice. Or cook the yabbies in nut-brown butter with a good squeeze of lemon juice and lots of freshly ground black pepper.

A traditional lemon mayonnaise or a verjuice beurre blanc is pretty special served with a large platter of freshly boiled yabbies and lots of crusty bread. To be honest, though, you need nothing more than extra virgin olive oil, lemon wedges, freshly ground black pepper and a dish of sea salt flakes to make a memorable meal from yabbies.

Eating yabbies outside has a special cachet. At home we spread a table with lots of newspaper, position an old-fashioned washstand alongside and fill it with warm water as a communal finger bowl, then offer a pile of serviettes. A bottle of extra virgin olive oil, wedges of lemon, sea salt, freshly ground black pepper and crusty bread complete the picture – along with plates stacked ready for people to make their own dipping sauce. So if you have cooked a huge tub of yabbies, let people shell their own. You'll find those driven by flavour sucking the juicy 'mustard' from the heads after devouring the tails. (My husband Colin sets the tails aside until he has enough to make a great sandwich, but I'm never patient enough to do this.)

If you tire of yabbies served à la naturel (though who would?), then they can be thrown together in so many ways. Think summer, think yabbies cooked, peeled and set in jelly in the bottom of coffee cups used as moulds, using either verjuice or a stock made from yabby shells or a mixture of both, then topped with peeled, seeded and diced ripe tomatoes and some basil. Turn them out on a bed of baby lettuce leaves and make an unctuous mayonnaise to serve alongside.

While yabbies have a great affinity with tomatoes and basil, the most ambrosial yabby dish I've ever cooked involved pan-frying yabbies with wild boletus mushrooms from a nearby pine forest. I cooked the young, dense mushrooms and the halved yabbies in the same pan in nut-brown butter and a little walnut oil with lots of freshly ground black pepper and some basil. Given the earthiness of the wild mushroom, I suspect yabbies would also be amazing pan-fried with fresh truffles, if one had the chance. Teaming globe artichokes with the first yabbies of the season, a mayonnaise flavoured with Pernod and a salad of peppery rocket would also make the most of these earthy flavours.

Don't waste the shells; find a recipe for lobster bisque and make a yabby version, although expect a more delicate flavour. Consider a yabby consommé made in the same manner as a crab consommé – even better, jelly it.

JANET'S SEA URCHIN ROE DRESSING
TO SERVE WITH YABBIES   *Makes 500 ml*

We prepared this dish for a very special wedding for Bronny Jones at the Pheasant Farm Restaurant in the early 1980s. Janet Jeffs, now a lauded restaurateur in Canberra, was so important in the restaurant's early days; she opened my eyes to so much and gave me confidence in my own ability. This dish was very much Janet's, and eating it was the first time I had experienced sea urchin, although it is now one of my favourite foods ever.

Bronny, a regular performer at the musical evenings we used to hold in the restaurant, had been studying and playing clarinet in New York and Paris and was to marry an

American astronomer. Her memories of the Pheasant Farm Restaurant were as special to her as her playing had been to us. (The musical evenings had featured Susan Hackett, the instigator, on flute, Stephen Walter on piano, Suzannah Foulds singing and Peter Jenkin and Bronny on clarinet – each of them serious professionals with a love of food and wine. They were such special occasions, and just done for the love of it all.)

The wedding was a great feast, with Janet, Bronny's close friend, designing the menu and cooking the meal with some help from me. I remember Janet organising a friend to gather the sea urchins – they certainly weren't on the general market in those days. I was bowled over by the flavour.

½ lemon	2 teaspoons mirin
2 egg yolks	2 teaspoons light soy sauce
2 tablespoons white-wine vinegar	sea salt flakes and freshly ground
400 ml peanut oil	white pepper
roe from 2 sea urchins	

Juice the lemon and blend it with the egg yolks and white-wine vinegar in a food processor, then add the peanut oil in a slow, steady stream with the motor running to make a thick mayonnaise. Mash the roe and stir it into the mayonnaise with the mirin and soy sauce. Check the flavourings and season. Serve immediately.

YABBY SAUCE
Makes 500 ml

If your guests are too polite to suck the heads when eating freshly boiled yabbies, put the discarded shells aside to make the following sauce as soon as possible after shelling. The sauce is great with freshly boiled yabbies, but it also makes a wonderful base for a soup, and can be tossed through pasta with boiled and peeled yabbies and fresh basil.

40 yabby heads, well crushed	⅓ cup (80 ml) Cognac
6 cloves garlic, finely chopped	150 ml tomato paste
2 carrots, finely chopped	1 cup (250 ml) white wine
2 leeks, white part only, finely chopped	2 cups (500 ml) verjuice (optional)
1 large onion, finely chopped	sea salt flakes and freshly ground
½ fennel bulb, finely chopped	black pepper
100 ml extra virgin olive oil	60 g unsalted butter (optional)

Sweat the crushed yabby heads and all the vegetables in the olive oil in a large saucepan over high heat for about 15 minutes or until the vegetables are cooked. Pour the Cognac into the pan and allow it to evaporate, then mix in the tomato paste. Add the wine and 250 ml water (or just the verjuice instead) and simmer gently for 1 hour.

Strain the sauce into a clean saucepan through a conical sieve or similar, pushing on the contents as you do so to extract as much flavour as possible. Reduce the sauce to the desired consistency, then season and add the butter to make it more velvety, if desired. This sauce should be used as soon as possible but can be kept refrigerated for a couple of days.

YABBY RICE PAPER ROLLS WITH ROASTED TOMATOES, ROAST GARLIC AÏOLI AND SNOW PEA SPROUTS

Makes 24

Yabbies were well and truly on the menu for my Paris jaunt in June 2001, where my brief was to devise a cocktail party menu for 500 (though on the night 700 people turned up). My first thought was to do yabby tails wrapped in vine leaves, then pan-fried in nut-brown butter and verjuice, but the logistics of organising 1000 perfect tender vine leaves from afar were nightmarish. Next we thought of herby risotto-encased yabby dolmades using pre-served vine leaves, but the leaves retained too much of their briny flavour no matter how many times I soaked them. Little brioche balls filled with lemon myrtle-scented yabby bisque were next, but these too were rejected as we worried about the delicious yabby juices oozing all over the well-dressed guests.

In the end, the yabby tails in rice paper wrappers we prepared were far simpler than any of the above, and the dish was a great success! I got a huge kick out of serving one of my favourite ingredients so simply and so far from home. Being able to go with the flow topped off the event – that is, after all, what good cooking is all about.

24 raw yabby tails
butter, for cooking
sea salt flakes and freshly ground
    black pepper
½ cup (125 ml) verjuice
½ cup (125 ml) extra virgin olive oil
12 sunrise limes (a type of native lime)
    or 3 meyer lemons
24 large square rice paper wrappers
    (available from Asian grocers)
2 punnets snow pea sprouts

AÏOLI
1 head garlic
sea salt flakes and freshly ground
    black pepper
30 ml lemon juice
30 ml verjuice
2 large egg yolks
1 cup (250 ml) extra virgin olive oil

ROASTED TOMATOES
24 cherry *or* truss tomatoes
sea salt flakes and freshly ground
    black pepper
1 sprig thyme
extra virgin olive oil, for drizzling

To make the aïoli, preheat the oven to 180°C. Wrap the garlic in foil and bake until soft (depending on the size, it could take between 30 minutes and 1 hour). Leave to cool, then squeeze out the garlic into a food processor. Add 2 pinches salt, a little pepper, the lemon juice and verjuice. Amalgamate in the food processor, then add the egg yolks and process until well combined. Begin to add the oil in a very slow stream, then move to a steady stream as the aïoli begins to accept more oil and emulsifies.

Reduce the oven temperature to 120°C. For the roasted tomatoes, cut the base of the tomatoes with a cross, then drop them into a saucepan of boiling water for a few seconds to loosen the skins, then dip them in iced water. Remove skins and cut tomatoes in half. Place in a baking dish, season and add the thyme. Drizzle generously with olive oil and bake for 1 hour or until tomatoes collapse. Remove from the oven and add a little more olive oil to moisten, then set aside.

Peel the yabby tails, leaving the shell on the end intact. The simplest way is to place your thumb under the end of the tail and, using the thumb of your other hand, remove as for a prawn. Insert a skewer through from the tail to the end of the flesh to keep the tails straight.

Heat a little butter in a frying pan over medium–high until nut-brown and quickly pan-fry the yabby tails, then season to taste and deglaze the pan with a splash of verjuice. Rest the tails in a marinade of olive oil, half the finely sliced sunrise limes (or half the meyer lemons cut into thin slices widthways, then cut into tiny triangles) and salt and pepper, for at least 30 minutes.

Soak the rice paper wrappers in cold tap water until the edges are pliable; you can do this a couple at a time. Lay them out flat on a tea towel, then pat dry and place on a chopping board. To assemble the rolls, place a line of snow pea sprouts down the centre of each wrapper, then add a little thinly sliced lime or lemon and some roasted tomato halves. Add one yabby tail and 1 teaspoon roasted garlic aïoli. Fold one end in and roll so that the yabby tail and snow pea sprouts are exposed at one end.

MARRON

Marron may originate from Western Australia, but Kangaroo Island in South Australia has become their second home. There are now so many marron naturalised in its streams that farming them is becoming big business.

Commercial production on the island ranges from catching wild marron in streams and dams to farming them in an amazingly sophisticated way, as John Melbourne, from near Vivonne Bay, does. Originally from Adelaide, John spent most of his working life in London. He tells the story of having dinner in England with Australian friends who talked about marron, and it was as if a light bulb switched on in his head. He had just sold his business in London, the water connection made sense (he had been working in water treatment and water quality instrumentation), and he was looking for a new project.

John's initial research took him to Western Australia, but he ended up on Kangaroo Island. He made a huge investment in a mammoth turkey-nest dam, breeding ponds and growing-out dams, all wire-netted to keep the birds out and with an expansive underground network of pipes and valves to control water flow. It is a meticulously managed property and John has now opened a stylish café on the site, serving marron in many

different guises each day of the week – a must for any visitor to beautiful Kangaroo Island.

A decent-sized marron can constitute a main course, but size is dictated by age. Marron are a lot slower growing than their yabby cousins, so a perfect main-course marron may be three years old – and a lot harder to find.

The simplest way of preparing marron is to stun them in the freezer first for 20 minutes, then blanch them in a large saucepan of rapidly boiling water for up to 1 minute (depending on size) after the water returns to the boil. Plunge the marron briefly into iced water and then cut them in half, remove their intestinal tract and reserve the 'mustard' in the head for adding to a sauce or mayonnaise. Toss the marron in a saucepan with whatever flavouring or herbs you wish to use.

Marron accept highly perfumed oils such as truffle and walnut particularly well and make a great warm salad with heads of frisée, witlof, baby rocket, basil, salad burnet, flat-leaf parsley and some fresh asparagus. Make a vinaigrette of truffle or walnut oil and verjuice, and toss through the salad.

Mushrooms and marron are a surprisingly successful combination (see below). Try packing the head cavity of halved marron with sautéed diced mushroom and spring onions, then drizzle the lot with just a little real truffle oil. It is a delicious way to present marron, whether you are serving several small specimens or a large one per person.

One memorable meal at our old restaurant Charlick's was a marron poached in an aromatic fish stock with star anise, kaffir lime leaf, crushed lemongrass, coriander stems and white peppercorns. The meat was taken from the shell and tossed with cucumber, green papaya, coriander, mint and a touch of ground-up dried shrimp, all in a little extra virgin olive oil. Then a dressing was made from black rice vinegar, lemon juice with sugar to balance, peanut oil and a touch of grapeseed oil, so as not to overpower the peanut oil. What a dish!

MARRON WITH MUSHROOMS AND VERJUICE   *Serves 4*

I cooked this recipe in Tokyo a few years ago, at the Shinjuku Park Hyatt. I had the luxury of taking really large marron with me, and having the fresh markets of Paris at my disposal (via the airways, of course) to order fresh cèpes to accompany the dish. While I use pine or boletus mushrooms here, dried cèpes or porcinis reconstituted in verjuice make a very satisfactory alternative.

4 × 240 g live marron
4 golden shallots, finely chopped
150 ml walnut oil, plus extra for brushing
1 sprig thyme, leaves picked
195 ml verjuice, plus extra for brushing
sea salt flakes and freshly ground black pepper

4 fresh pine *or* boletus mushrooms, stems trimmed and caps quartered
butter, for cooking
4 large fresh vine leaves

Prepare the marron as described above. Preheat the oven to 180°C. Combine the shallots, walnut oil, thyme leaves and 70 ml of the verjuice to make a vinaigrette, then season with salt and pepper to taste.

Brush quartered mushrooms with walnut oil and verjuice, then dot with a little butter and season well. Bake mushrooms, turning once, for 10 minutes or until golden on all sides. Set aside. Reset oven to 220°C.

Poach vine leaves in a saucepan in the remaining 125 ml verjuice until cooked through (about 2 minutes for mature leaves); dry well. Heat a shallow, heavy-based roasting pan in the oven.

Brush cut surface of marron with vinaigrette and bake for 5–6 minutes. As the marron rests, pour remaining vinaigrette into the pan and stir in the mushrooms and their juices. Dot the vine leaves with butter (top-side up) and crisp in the oven for 2 minutes. Place a crisped vine leaf on each plate, top with 2 marron, then spoon over the vinaigrette. Serve immediately.

ZUCCHINI

THE ZUCCHINI IS ONE OF THE MOST ABUSED OF ALL VEGETABLES. Sadly, many are grown thick and long. Large zucchini means old zucchini: the water content is higher, the flesh is less dense, the flavour diminishes and shelf-life is impaired. These zucchini wither and become unattractive very quickly, and are often bitter to eat.

This is one vegetable I like to eat when it's really small, so for me the best zucchini is about the size of a small cigar. Specialty farmers are now selling them at this size with the flowers attached – it's a great step forward.

Zucchini is probably the easiest of all vegetables to grow yourself, and anyone who does so will know that they grow while your back is turned. If you've missed one hidden under the umbrella of leaves, before you know it you can have a giant on your hands. I've grown four zucchini plants this year from seeds I got from my supplier The Italian Gardener (I chose the paler, ridged variety, my favourite). I've never ever had plants this large (they look more like elephant ears), and whilst at the beginning of the season I thought I should have planted at least four more, now I've decided to plant only two next year, as I'm absolutely swimming in zucchini, even when picking every second day. I can afford to be fussy, so anything longer than 12 cm goes to the chooks!

I remember clearly the days when zucchini, also referred to as baby marrows or courgettes, particularly in English and French books, were considered exotic. My mother had come to live with us in 1975 when my second daughter Elli was born. A city person, she took to gardening with a vengeance. As money was scarce, Mum would present us joyfully with baskets of vegetables she'd grown herself. Zucchini were enough of a novelty that size didn't seem to matter then, although Mum seldom picked them smaller than 18 cm. They were usually consumed the day they were picked and as such made great eating. When larger ones that had been missed were finally picked we were not allowed to waste them; instead, Mum stuffed and baked them, usually with minced meat. These days it is easy to be seduced by 'new' vegetables. But don't lose sight of the everyday ones – instead, enjoy them at their best by growing and picking (or buying) them at their optimum size and age.

The most common types of zucchini you are likely to come across are the dark-green zucchini, a paler-green striped one and a yellow zucchini. Essentially all variations on a theme, they have slightly different flavours. I find the pale-green zucchini sweeter than the dark-green, while the yellow tastes a little of tea leaves to me, like yellow squash.

The zucchini gives us the first triumph of the season, with its deliciously delicate flowers. Growing zucchini, even if it is in containers in a courtyard, is a cinch – it also means you don't have to worry about how you transport the fragile blooms home from the markets. In my garden, the long, golden blossoms are so beautiful to gaze upon, and stuffed zucchini flowers have become a firm favourite.

Now for some anatomy: the zucchini bears both male and female flowers. The male flower is much larger and particularly suited to stuffing. The female flower can also be stuffed but, as it becomes the zucchini itself in due course, it is a shame not to let it develop.

The fresher the flower, the easier it is to stuff (before the petals close up), so pick or buy them just before you plan to use them. Beware: earwigs, ants and millipedes tend to love the moist interior of these blossoms, but are highly undesirable guests to have at the table, to say the least. Make sure you check each flower very carefully before you begin cooking.

The filling for zucchini flowers depends on what you have at hand. Cheeses, from bocconcini to goat's cheese, Gruyère or Parmigiano Reggiano, cut into tiny dice so they melt in the very short cooking time and mixed with chopped anchovy and flat-leaf parsley, are delicious. Tiny cubes of peeled ripe tomato with minced garlic and flat-leaf parsley made into a paste with some olive oil is another idea. A simple dob of Pesto (see page 19) or Salsa Agresto (see page 20), with or without cheese, makes a fresh and more-ish filling.

The important points to remember are to prepare your ingredients ahead of time and to work very quickly. You can make a light batter or dip the blossoms into a dish of beaten egg, then dust them in flour or polenta before frying. Once each flower is battered, you need to cook it immediately. I tend to shallow-fry the zucchini flowers using a bulk extra virgin olive oil. This way I achieve the desired crispness while the flavour imparted by the oil is a positive one, rather than just leaving a 'fatty' aftertaste.

Young zucchini specimens, by the way, are perfect to eat raw – just make sure you do so as soon as they have been picked. Wash and slice them very thinly for the best flavour. You will be surprised by just how sweet the zucchini is – raw, washed zucchini make a great salad when sliced as thinly as possible lengthways, then dressed with a vinaigrette of extra virgin olive oil, lemon juice, garlic and basil or marjoram, and seasoned. Leave the salad for a good half an hour before eating, tossing it every now and then. Alternatively, toss thinly sliced zucchini in a little melted butter and extra virgin olive oil in a hot frying pan for just a minute, then season and add freshly chopped flat-leaf parsley.

When you take young zucchini from the garden and treat them this simply, it's a specialty all of its own. Slice 1 small zucchini into slices as thin as possible. Heat some butter with a dash of olive oil until nut-brown, toss in the zucchini with a good pinch of sea

salt, a couple of grinds of black pepper, a pinch of nutmeg and some freshly torn basil and serve immediately. The zucchini should still have a small amount of crunch and, fresh from the garden, is as sweet as sweet can be.

Small zucchini can be boiled whole for just a few minutes, then drained and left to cool a little. Sliced lengthways and served with good extra virgin olive oil, a generous squeeze of lemon juice or verjuice and freshly ground black pepper, they are delicious. If you grow zucchini, try cooking the tiny ones with their flowers still attached. I use a frying pan with a little boiling water, salt and a knob of butter added to effectively braise the zucchini, turning them over carefully with a slotted spoon.

Try pan-frying equal quantities of zucchini and eggplant cut into 1 cm pieces. Sauté the eggplant first in extra virgin olive oil, then set it aside on a warm plate and quickly cook the zucchini in fresh oil. Toss the warm vegetables together with more extra virgin olive oil and some lemon juice and fresh basil leaves, then grind on black pepper.

Chargrilling zucchini on a barbecue adds another dimension. Slice the zucchini lengthways into three or four strips, then brush with extra virgin olive oil and season with fresh thyme and freshly ground black pepper. Sear each side until coloured, then squeeze on a little lemon juice, add a drizzle of olive oil and season with salt and pepper.

Zucchini also pickle well but have to be exceptionally crisp specimens to start with. Bring 500 ml water and 500 ml white-wine vinegar to the boil and cook sliced zucchini for just a couple of minutes. Drain and dry the zucchini and transfer to a clean jar with freshly chopped herbs and garlic. Pour in enough extra virgin olive oil to cover the zucchini – you will need to top up the oil for the first few days. I store this pickle in the refrigerator for a few weeks before using it. The olive oil does not preserve the zucchini – you need an acidic component to do that – but, along with the cold of the refrigerator, it delays spoiling for a few weeks once opened.

ZUCCHINI IN AGRODOLCE   *Serves 4*

I found this recipe in Elizabeth David's *Italian Food*, but I use verjuice rather than white-wine vinegar and sugar. Look for small zucchini for this dish.

⅓ cup (80 ml) fruity extra virgin olive oil	pinch ground cinnamon
450 g small zucchini, cut into thick rounds	sea salt flakes
freshly ground black pepper	¼ cup (60 ml) verjuice

Heat the olive oil in a large frying pan with a lid and gently cook the zucchini, covered, for about 5 minutes over low heat, then remove the lid and season with pepper and cinnamon, and salt if needed. Turn up the heat to high and add the verjuice, then cook for a few minutes more until the sauce is syrupy. Serve immediately with grilled fish or pan-fried chicken breasts.

COCKTAIL ZUCCHINI FRITTERS   *Makes 16 cocktail-sized fritters*

I have four Italian zucchini plants in my garden this year (the pale-green, ridged variety). I've never grown these before and they are the best I've ever eaten. However, they yield so much once they're truly established that I have to be more and more inventive in coming up with ways to use them.

Getting my grandchildren to eat greens hasn't been the easiest thing, but one evening my daughter Saskia made zucchini fritters to serve with drinks, and it was touch and go as to who ate the most – the adults or the kids.

My version of these are cocktail-sized and feature labna, a staple in our household. The acidity in this works well for my palate.

160 g grated zucchini

1 teaspoon sea salt flakes

2 teaspoons chopped basil

2 teaspoons chopped mint

70 g labna (see Glossary)

½ egg (I know it seems a waste, but it's all you
   need for this recipe, so whisk the egg and
   halve it, or double the recipe depending on
   how many you want to serve)

2 tablespoons plain flour

squeeze of lemon juice

freshly ground black pepper

3 tablespoons extra virgin olive oil

Spread the grated zucchini out on a perforated dish, and sprinkle with the salt. Leave for a minimum of half an hour to allow the moisture to be drawn out.

Wring out the grated zucchini with your hands to extract as much liquid as possible. Transfer to a bowl and add the chopped herbs, labna, egg, flour, lemon juice and a grind of pepper, and mix through. Spoon out portions of the mixture to make fritters ½ cm thick and 2 cm round.

Choose a frying pan large enough to hold eight fritters at a time. Add half the olive oil to the pan, and when the oil is hot, add the first batch of fritters to the pan. Quickly seal the fritters on one side and when golden, flip over and cook on the other side. Remove them from the pan and set aside to rest on kitchen paper before quickly cooking the next batch in the remaining oil. Serve hot – they are absolutely scrumptious.

GILL'S ZUCCHINI AND APPLE SALAD

Serves 2 as a side dish

Gill Radford, a chef and caterer from the Barossa, helps keep me sane during the long filming seasons for the ABC TV series *The Cook and The Chef*. Together we discuss ingredients, mull over recipe ideas and taste dishes, and so often Gill's ideas add another dimension that I hadn't thought of. This dish, using fresh ricotta, is the perfect example – the fresh green apple giving that little something extra.

1 small green apple
verjuice *or* lemon juice, to dress
160 g baby zucchini
100 ml extra virgin olive oil
¼ cup firmly packed fresh herb leaves
   (marjoram, thyme, flat-leaf parsley, etc),
   washed and well-dried

juice of ½ lemon
½ teaspoon sea salt flakes
1 teaspoon sugar
2 tablespoons fresh ricotta *or*
   fresh curd cheese
freshly ground black pepper

Slice the apple into very thin strips, then toss in a small bowl with a touch of verjuice or a squeeze of lemon juice.

Bring a large pan of salted water to the boil, add the zucchini and blanch for 2–3 minutes, then remove from the water and set aside. Heat the extra virgin olive oil in a small pan until hot (but not smoking), then toss in the herbs and fry until crisp. Remove the herbs and drain on kitchen paper, retaining the oil.

Mix 60 ml of herb oil from the pan with the lemon juice, then add the salt and sugar and adjust seasoning if necessary.

Once cool enough to handle, slice the zucchini in half lengthways and drizzle the cut sides with any leftover herb oil. Toss these with the apple, then mix through the vinaigrette until well coated. Serve immediately, topped with crumbled cheese and season to taste.

ZUCCHINI FLOWERS IN BATTER WITH
GRUYÈRE AND ANCHOVIES

Serves 4

You can batter just the flowers, as in this recipe, or you can batter whole baby zucchinis with the flower still attached. Just slice the zucchini with two parallel cuts, almost to the top, leaving the flower attached. This allows the zucchini to cook at the same rate as the flower. Then stuff the flower and batter the whole lot.

Even though using extra virgin olive oil for deep-frying seems extravagant, you can use the same oil many times over.

200 g Gruyère (I use Heidi Farm
    Gruyère), grated
18 anchovy fillets, finely chopped
18 zucchini flowers
extra virgin olive oil, for deep-frying
sea salt flakes and freshly ground
    black pepper

BATTER
200 g self-raising flour
pinch salt
1½ cups (375 ml) chilled water

Mix the Gruyère and anchovy fillets in a bowl. Check each zucchini flower for insects and remove the stamen. Distribute the cheese stuffing evenly between the flowers and gently squeeze the petals together at the top to seal.

Heat a good quantity of olive oil in a deep-fryer to 180°C, if you have one, or in a deep saucepan (about 20 cm across) until hot; the pan must be large enough to contain the hot oil as it bubbles up when the flowers are dropped into it. Test the temperature of the oil by frying a small chunk of bread in it: if the bread turns golden brown immediately, the oil is hot enough.

Make the batter just before you start cooking the stuffed flowers. Sift the flour with the salt into a bowl, then quickly stir in the cold water until just mixed (the batter will look a little lumpy). Dip the flowers into the batter, then carefully lower 3 flowers at a time into the hot oil until golden, turning them with a spoon to ensure even cooking. They will take about 5 minutes. Remove the cooked flowers and allow them to drain on kitchen paper, while cooking the remaining ones. Season to taste and serve immediately.

BASICS

DUCK EGG PASTA

$3\frac{1}{5}$ cups (500 g) strong flour (see Glossary)   4–5 duck eggs, depending on their size

To make the pasta, tip the flour onto a bench and make a well in the centre. Whisk the eggs together and pour into the well, and gradually incorporate them into the flour, following the method described on page 57. Add an extra yolk if needed. Knead the pasta dough until it forms a shiny ball and is firm to the touch. Cover the dough with plastic film and rest it in the refrigerator for 30 minutes. Cut the pasta dough into about 8 equal portions.

Before beginning to roll the pasta, bring a large saucepan of salted water to the boil. Set the pasta machine on a bench, screwing it down firmly. Working in batches, take one piece of dough and press it as flat as you can with the palm of your hand, then feed it through the rollers set on their widest aperture. Fold the rolled dough in thirds, and then pass the narrow end through the machine again. Repeat several times, preferably until you hear a sound that I can only describe as a 'plop' – this is the tension of the dough releasing as it goes through the rollers.

Adjust the machine to the next setting and pass the dough through. Repeat this with every setting until you get to the second to last. As the dough moves through each setting it will become finer and finer and the sheets will become longer and longer; you may need to cut the sheets to make them more manageable. Adjust the machine, selecting the widest cutter, and run the pasta through to cut into strips. Hang the pasta ribbons over the back of a chair to dry.

Slide the pasta gently into the boiling water, then partially cover with a lid to bring back to a rapid boil. Stir the pasta gently to keep it well separated. Fresh pasta only needs to cook for 3 minutes or so. Drain the cooked pasta, reserving a little of the cooking water in case you need it to moisten the completed dish. Do not run the pasta under water or you will lose the precious starch that helps the sauce or oil adhere. Generously drizzle the pasta with olive oil immediately.

SOUR-CREAM PASTRY
Makes enough to line a 20–24 cm tart tin

This recipe makes a very short, flaky pastry with a light, melt-in-the-mouth texture. It is a great all-rounder and can be used in a whole variety of dishes, both sweet and savoury. I like to chill the pastry case in the freezer, as this ensures it is really well-chilled before it goes in the oven.

This pastry rises beautifully and is really light and flaky, which is great if you're making a tart or a pie, but if you want a flat pastry, like a thin pizza dough, a good trick is to 'inhibit' the pastry as it cooks. To do this, carefully open the oven halfway through the cooking (when the pastry is beginning to rise), take out the tray for a moment and press down on the pastry with a similar-sized tray or a clean tea towel, then return the tray to the oven. This will stop the pastry rising too much.

200 g chilled unsalted butter, chopped into small pieces

250 g plain flour

120 g sour cream

Put the butter and flour into the bowl of a food processor, then pulse until the mixture resembles coarse breadcrumbs. Add the sour cream and pulse again until the dough just forms a ball. If shrinkage worries you, gather the dough into a ball with your hands and bounce it on the bench. Carefully wrap the dough in plastic film and leave to rest in the refrigerator for 15–20 minutes.

Roll out the dough until it is 5 mm thick, then use it to line a 20 cm tart tin with a removable base. Chill the pastry case for 20 minutes.

To blind bake, preheat the oven to 200°C. Line the pastry case with foil, then cover with pastry weights. Blind bake the pastry case for 15 minutes, then remove the foil and pastry weights and bake for another 5 minutes.

QUATRE-ÉPICES
Makes 1 tablespoon

This spice mixture is used for pâtés, rillettes and terrines. Although meant to be made of four spices, it can be modified to suit personal taste. Spices are much better freshly roasted and used straightaway than stored for a long period.

10 cloves
1 tablespoon white peppercorns
1 cinnamon stick

¾ teaspoon ground ginger
¾ teaspoon freshly grated nutmeg

Grind all ingredients to a fine powder in a spice mill.

ROUILLE
Makes 400 g

A pungent and particularly more-ish way of using garlic is to make this paste to serve with a fish soup, stew, braised oxtail, lamb shanks or with a crudité of fresh vegetables. For those who like spicy heat, it can be adjusted by including a chilli with the red capsicum. Rouille is French for 'rust' – and this should be the colour of your sauce.

1 large, very red capsicum	4 cloves garlic
200 ml extra virgin olive oil, plus extra for roasting	50 ml red-wine vinegar
2 slices bread, crusts removed	a few saffron threads (optional)
milk, for soaking	3 free-range egg yolks
½ teaspoon cayenne pepper	sea salt flakes and freshly ground black pepper

Preheat the oven to 200°C. Cut the top off the capsicum and remove the seeds. Rub with some olive oil and roast in the oven until it collapses and seems to be burnt – usually about 20 minutes. Take the capsicum from the oven and let it rest for a few minutes before putting it in a plastic bag to sweat. When it is cool enough to handle, peel, removing all traces of blackened skin.

Soak the bread in a little milk for 10 minutes, then squeeze it thoroughly.

Place the capsicum, cayenne pepper, garlic, bread, vinegar, saffron threads, if using, and egg yolks in the bowl of a food processor and purée well. Season, then with the motor running, slowly pour in the olive oil in a stream as you would for mayonnaise, processing until emulsified.

SALSA VERDE
Serves 4

Salsa verde, an Italian green sauce, is often served with boiled meat (it is the traditional accompaniment to *bollito misto*), poached chicken breasts, fish or offal, and is especially good with tongue or brains.

1 boiled potato, peeled and chopped	extra virgin olive oil
1 cup firmly packed flat-leaf parsley leaves	1 tablespoon red-wine vinegar
3 anchovy fillets	sea salt flakes and freshly ground black pepper
1 clove garlic	
2 tiny cornichons (see Glossary)	

Combine the potato, parsley, anchovies, garlic and cornichons in a food processor. With the motor running, add enough olive oil, a little at a time, to make a thick sauce, then blend in the vinegar, salt and pepper. This sauce is best served on the day it is made.

BABY ONIONS ROASTED IN VINO COTTO   *Serves 4 as an accompaniment*

500 g baby onions, outer skin removed

¼ cup (60 ml) extra virgin olive oil

½ cup (125 ml) vino cotto (see Glossary)

sea salt flakes and freshly ground
black pepper

sprigs of lemon thyme, to garnish

Preheat the oven to 180°C. Cut the onions in half. Line a roasting pan with a large piece of foil (enough to fold over the onions), then place the onions in the centre of the foil. Whisk together the oil and vino cotto and pour over the onions, then season. Fold the foil over the onions and seal to form a parcel, then roast for 1 hour or until the onions are soft.

Increase the oven temperature to 200°C. Open the foil parcel then return the pan to the oven for a further 10 minutes, to caramelise the onions. Garnish with lemon thyme and serve as an accompaniment to roasted or grilled meats or fish, or dot with goat's cheese and flat-leaf parsley and serve with crusty bread.

CARAMELISED ONION SALAD   *Serves 4 as an accompaniment*

Although the onions for this dish need long, slow cooking, they can be prepared in advance and left at room temperature. This salad is wonderful with tongue or grilled steak or sausages. If you are using the caramelised onion in a tart or in the recipe on page 8, exclude the dressing. You might need to warm the tart without the cheese first if the onion is at room temperature rather than hot.

5 large onions

2 sprigs rosemary, leaves stripped

100 ml extra virgin olive oil

1 clove garlic, finely chopped

2 teaspoons balsamic vinegar

2 tablespoons freshly chopped
flat-leaf parsley

sea salt flakes and freshly ground
black pepper

Preheat the oven to 150°C. Trim the ends of each onion, leaving the skins on, then cut the onions into 1 cm-thick slices. Mix the rosemary with 2 tablespoons of the olive oil.

Line a shallow, heavy-based roasting pan with baking paper, then brush this and both sides of the onion slices with the rosemary oil. Bake the onions for 30 minutes, then check whether they are starting to colour. When the onions are a deep caramel colour turn with a spatula and discard any burnt pieces. Remove the pan from the oven when all the onion has caramelised on both sides. This can take between 1 and 2 hours. Allow the onions to cool a little, then remove the skins and place the onions in a serving dish.

Mix the remaining olive oil with the garlic, vinegar, parsley, salt and pepper and pour over the onions while they are still warm. Serve at room temperature.

GLOSSARY

Wherever possible, I've explained any less familiar ingredients and techniques in the relevant recipes, but I've also included brief notes here on some ingredients and procedures that are used throughout the book.

Arborio rice
What distinguishes this pearly-white, short-grained rice is the amount of starch it releases during cooking, and it is this starch that makes a risotto creamy. Arborio rice should be cooked until it is *al dente*, which takes about 20 minutes, depending on the quality of the rice.

Blind baking
Baking a pastry case 'blind', or without its filling, helps to stop the filling from making the pastry soggy. Lining the pastry case with foil and holding it down with pastry weights prevents the pastry case from rising and losing its shape as it cooks. Special pastry weights are available at kitchenware shops, but dried beans work just as well.

Cheese
see Labna; Parmigiano Reggiano

Chocolate
The flavour of chocolate is determined by the amounts of chocolate liquor and cocoa solids it contains.

Bitter chocolate has the highest percentage of cocoa liquor and no added sugar, so it has a strong chocolate flavour, which adds depth to savoury dishes.

A good bittersweet chocolate may contain 65–70 per cent cocoa solids, and the best even more. Because it has sugar added, it is mostly used for sweet dishes – or eating.

Couverture chocolate is the name given to high-quality chocolate that melts well and dries to a glossy finish, making it perfect for covering cakes and for making fine desserts. It can also be used in any recipe calling for chocolate, since its high cocoa butter content gives it a fine flavour and texture.

Cornichons
Cornichons are tiny, crisp gherkins pickled in the French manner: picked when they are 3–8 cm long, and pickled in vinegar or brine. They are crunchy and salty, and are perfect to serve with rillettes, pâtés or terrines, to accompany a charcuterie plate, or as part of a ploughman's lunch.

Cream
In Australia, most cows are kept to produce milk rather than cream, so the fat content of their milk needs to be supplemented at various times of the year to bring it up to the 35 per cent fat content that is needed for pure cream. With nothing else added, this cream is good for enriching sauces.

Any cream labelled 'thickened cream' also has a thickener such as gelatine added. Because of the extra stability that the thickener provides, this is the best cream for whipping – just remember that reduced-fat thickened cream (with around 18 per cent fat) cannot be whipped successfully.

Double cream is very rich, with a fat content of 45–60 per cent. Some of the thicker ones are perfect for spooning alongside a dessert. Try to find farmhouse versions that have been separated from unhomogenised milk.

Flour

Strong flour, also known as bread flour or baker's flour, is my staple flour. What differentiates strong flour is its high gluten content, which allows dough to stretch rather than break during kneading and rolling, making it particularly suitable for making pasta and bread. The gluten in strong flour also helps to ensure an extensive and even rise in bread.

Flours are further classified according to the percentage of wheat grain present. Wholemeal flour contains the whole grain, and so has a wonderful nutty taste, while brown flour contains about 85 per cent of the grain and white flour between 75 and 80 per cent. The flour industry is moving to predominantly unbleached flour; bleached flour must be specially requested. I prefer unbleached flour as it contains slightly more nutrients; it also has a more robust texture, which works well in breads and pizza bases.

Self-raising flour is plain flour with baking powder and salt added during the milling process, in the proportions of about 1¼ teaspoons of baking powder and a pinch of salt for every cup of flour.

It is used for making pancakes, cakes and muffins.

Gelatine

Gelatine leaves have a better flavour and texture than powdered gelatine. However, confusion can arise from the fact that the gelling strength of gelatine leaves is measured by their 'bloom' rather than their weight. All my recipes have been developed using Alba brand Gold-strength leaves, which weigh 2 g each and have a bloom of 190–220 g.

As gelatine will set more firmly over time, you may be able to use less gelatine if you can make the jelly the day before it is needed. A couple of other things to note: gelatine takes twice as long to dissolve in cream or milk as it does in water; and sugar can inhibit setting, so the higher the sugar content, the softer the set will be.

Labna

Also referred to as yoghurt cheese, labna in its purest form is simply thick drained yoghurt. You can make it yourself by stirring 5 g salt into 500 ml plain yoghurt (the kind with no pectin, gums or other stabilisers) then placing it in a sieve lined with muslin or a clean Chux and leaving it to drain for at least 4 hours or overnight – the longer you leave it, the thicker it will get. Commercial labna is tart and tangy: some versions are thick enough to hold up a spoon, while others are more like soft sour cream.

Oils

As you will probably have gathered by now, I use extra virgin olive oil liberally in my cooking, and consider it vital to my food – and, indeed, my life. The only other oils I occasionally use are nut oils to flavour a salad dressing, and refined grapeseed oil in dishes where a more neutral-flavoured oil is desirable, such as in desserts, or to combine with extra virgin olive oil when making mayonnaise, to avoid a bitter after-taste.

Parmigiano Reggiano

Authentic aged parmesan cheese made in Italy according to specific traditional practices, Parmigiano Reggiano is my first choice for use in risottos, polenta, soups, and sauces such as pesto. I also love it as part of a cheese board or freshly shaved in salads. Grana Padano has a similar flavour to Parmigiano Reggiano, but has not been aged for as long, so can be a useful, less expensive alternative.

Pastry weights *see* Blind baking

Rice *see* Arborio rice

Sterilising jars and bottles

To sterilise jars that are to be used for storing or preserving food, wash the jars and lids in hot, soapy water, then rinse them in hot water and place them in a 120°C oven for approximately 15 minutes to dry out. This method also works for bottles.

Sugar syrup

Sugar syrup is a simple solution of 1 part sugar dissolved in 1–2 parts water (depending on its intended use) over low heat. It is great to have on hand if you are keen on whipping up your own cocktails at home!

Tomato sugo and passata

These dense, slow-cooked tomato sauces originate from Italy. They are usually made with just tomatoes, but herbs and spices may also be added. Sugo is coarser as it is made from chopped tomatoes, whereas the tomatoes for passata are sieved, making it more like a purée. Both can be used in soups, stews sauces, or any dish where a tomato flavour is desired, but without the texture of acidity of fresh tomatoes.

Vino cotto

Literally meaning 'cooked wine' in Italian, this traditional Italian preparation is made by simmering unfermented grape juice until it is reduced to a syrup. The one I produce is finished with traditional red-wine vinegar to make it truly *agrodolce* (sweet–sour). With a much softer flavour than vinegar, vino cotto can be used to make sauces for meat or salad dressings or even drizzled over strawberries. In fact, it can be used anywhere you would normally use balsamic vinegar.

LIST OF SOURCES

The author and publisher would like to thank the following people and companies for allowing us to reproduce their material in this book. In some cases we were not able to contact the copyright owners; we would appreciate hearing from any copyright holders not acknowledged here, so that we can properly acknowledge their contribution when this book is reprinted.

Extracts

Alexander, Stephanie, *Stephanie's Australia*, Allen & Unwin, Sydney, 1991; Alexander, Stephanie, *The Cook's Companion*, Lantern, Melbourne, 2004; Grigson, Jane, *Jane Grigson's Vegetable Book*, Penguin, Harmondsworth, 1980; Lake, Max, *Scents and Sensuality*, Penguin, Melbourne, 1991; Pepin, Jacques, *La Technique*, Hamlyn Publishing Group, New York, 1978; Waters Alice, *Chez Panisse Café Cookbook*, Random House, New York, 1999.

Recipes

Gooseberry pavlovas: Tina Duncan; Peter Wall's raspberry vinegar: Peter Wall; Rose's pressed eggplants: Rose Fanto; Skye Gyngell's torn bread salad with rocket, sour cherries, capers and verjuice: Skye Gyngell; Upside-down apricot tarts: Ferguson, Jenny.

BIBLIOGRAPHY

Alexander, Stephanie, *The Cook's Companion* (2nd edition), Lantern, Melbourne, 2004.
—— *Cooking and Travelling in South-West France*, Viking, Melbourne, 2002.
—— *Stephanie's Journal*, Viking, Melbourne, 1999.
—— *Stephanie's Seasons*, Allen & Unwin, Sydney, 1993.
—— *Stephanie's Australia*, Allen & Unwin, Sydney, 1991.
—— *Stephanie's Feasts and Stories*, Allen & Unwin, Sydney, 1988.
—— *Stephanie's Menus for Food Lovers*, Methuen Haynes, Sydney, 1985.
Alexander, Stephanie and Beer, Maggie, *Stephanie Alexander & Maggie Beer's Tuscan Cookbook*, Viking, Melbourne, 1998.
Anderson, Ronald, *Gold on Four Feet*, Ronald Anderson, Melbourne, 1978.
Andrews, Colman, *Catalan Cuisine*, Headline, London, 1989.
The Barossa Cookery Book, Soldiers' Memorial Institute, Tanunda, 1917.
Beck, Simone, *Simca's Cuisine*, Vintage Books, New York, 1976.
Beck, Simone, Bertholle, Louisette and Child, Julia, *Mastering the Art of French Cooking, Volume One*, Penguin, Harmondsworth, 1979.
Beer, Maggie, *Maggie's Table*, Lantern, Melbourne, 2005.
—— *Cooking with Verjuice*, Penguin, Melbourne, 2003.
—— *Maggie's Orchard*, Viking, Melbourne, 1997.
—— *Maggie's Farm*, Allen & Unwin, Sydney, 1993.
Beeton, Mrs, *Mrs Beeton's Book of Household Management*, Cassell, London, 2000.
—— *Family Cookery*, Ward Lock, London, 1963.
Bertolli, Paul with Waters, Alice, *Chez Panisse Cooking*, Random House, New York, 1988.
Bissell, Frances, *A Cook's Calendar: Seasonal Menus by Frances Bissell*, Chatto & Windus, London, 1985.
Boddy, Michael and Boddy, Janet, *Kitchen Talk Magazine* (vol. I, no's 1–13), The Bugle Press, via Binalong, NSW, 1989–92.
Boni, Ada, *Italian Regional Cooking*, Bonanza Books, New York, 1969.
von Bremzen, Anya and Welchman, John, *Please to the Table: The Russian Cookbook*, Workman, New York, 1990.
Bureau of Resource Sciences, *Marketing Names for Fish and Seafood in Australia*, Department of Primary Industries
    & Energy and the Fisheries Research & Development Corporation, Canberra, 1995.
Carluccio, Antonio, *A Passion for Mushrooms*, Pavilion Books, London, 1989.
—— *An Invitation to Italian Cooking*, Pavilion Books, London, 1986.
Castelvetro, Giacomo, *The Fruit, Herbs and Vegetables of Italy*, Viking, New York, 1990.
Colmagro, Suzanne, Collins, Graham and Sedgley, Margaret, 'Processing Technology of the Table Olive',
    University of Adelaide, in Jules Janick (ed.) *Horticultural Reviews* Vol. 25, John Wiley & Sons, 2000.
Cox, Nicola, *Game Cookery*, Victor Gollancz, London, 1989.
David, Elizabeth, *Italian Food*, Penguin, Harmondsworth, 1989.
—— *An Omelette and a Glass of Wine*, Penguin, Harmondsworth, 1986.
—— *English Bread and Yeast Cookery*, Penguin, Harmondsworth, 1979.
—— *French Provincial Cooking*, Penguin, Harmondsworth, 1970.
—— *Summer Cooking*, Penguin, Harmondsworth, 1965.
De Groot, Roy Andries, *The Auberge of the Flowering Hearth*, The Ecco Press, New Jersey, 1973.
Dolamore, Anne, *The Essential Olive Oil Companion*, Macmillan, Melbourne, 1988.
Ferguson, Jenny, *Cooking for You and Me*, Methuen Haynes, Sydney, 1987.
Field, Carol, *Celebrating Italy*, William Morrow, New York, 1990.
Fitzgibbon, Theodora, *Game Cooking*, Andre Deutsch, London, 1963.
Glowinski, Louis, *The Complete Book of Fruit Growing in Australia*, Lothian, Melbourne, 1991.

Gray, Patience, *Honey From a Weed*, Prospect Books, London, 1986.

Gray, Rose and Rogers, Ruth, *The River Cafe Cook Book*, Ebury Press, London, 1996.

Grigson, Jane and Fullick, Roy (eds), *The Enjoyment of Food: The Best of Jane Grigson*, Michael Joseph, London, 1992.

Grigson, Jane, *Jane Grigson's Fruit Book*, Michael Joseph, London, 1982.

—— *Jane Grigson's Vegetable Book*, Penguin, Harmondsworth, 1980.

—— *Good Things*, Penguin, Harmondsworth, 1973.

—— *Jane Grigson's Fish Book*, Penguin, Harmondsworth, 1973.

—— *Charcuterie and French Pork Cookery*, Penguin, Harmondsworth, 1970.

Halligan, Marion, *Eat My Words*, Angus & Robertson, Sydney, 1990.

Hazan, Marcella, *The Classic Italian Cookbook*, Macmillan, London (rev. ed.), 1987.

Hopkinson, Simon with Bareham, Lindsey, *Roast Chicken and Other Stories*, Ebury Press, London, 1994.

Huxley, Aldous, *The Olive Tree*, Ayer, USA, reprint of 1937 ed.

Isaacs, Jennifer, *Bush Food*, Weldon, Sydney, 1987.

Kamman, Madeleine, *In Madeleine's Kitchen*, Macmillan, New York, 1992.

—— *The Making of a Cook*, Atheneum, New York, 1978.

Lake, Max, *Scents and Sensuality*, Penguin, Melbourne, 1991.

Manfield, Christine, *Christine Manfield Originals*, Lantern, Melbourne, 2006.

McGee, Harold, *The Curious Cook*, Northpoint Press, San Francisco, 1990.

—— *On Food and Cooking*, Collier Books, New York, 1988.

Ministero Agricoltura e Foreste. D.O.C. *Cheeses of Italy* (trans. Angela Zanotti), Milan, 1992.

Molyneux, Joyce, with Grigson, Sophie, *The Carved Angel Cookery Book*, Collins, 1990.

Newell, Patrice, *The Olive Grove*, Penguin, Melbourne, 2000.

del Nero, Constance and del Nero, Rosario, *Risotto*, Harper and Row, New York, 1989.

Olney, Richard, *Simple French Food*, Atheneum, New York, 1980.

Peck, Paula, *The Art of Fine Baking*, Simon & Schuster, New York, 1961.

Pellegrini, Angelo M., *The Food Lover's Garden*, Lyons & Burford, New York, 1970.

Pepin, Jacques, *La Technique*, Hamlyn Publishing Group, New York, 1978.

Perry, Neil, *The Food I Love*, Murdoch Books, Sydney, 2005.

Pignolet, Damien, *French*, Lantern, Melbourne, 2005.

Reichelt, Karen, with Burr, Michael, *Extra Virgin: An Australian Companion to Olives and Olive Oil*, Wakefield Press, Adelaide, 1997.

Ripe, Cherry, *Goodbye Culinary Cringe*, Allen & Unwin, Sydney, 1993.

Santich, Barbara, 'The Return of Verjuice', *Winestate*, June 1984.

Schauer, Amy, *The Schauer Australian Cookery Book* (14th ed.), W.R. Smith & Paterson, Brisbane, 1979.

Scicolone, Michele, *The Antipasto Table*, Morrow, New York, 1991.

Scott, Philippa, *Gourmet Game*, Simon & Schuster, New York, 1989.

Silverton, Nancy, *Nancy Silverton's Pastries from the La Brea Bakery*, Random House, New York, 2000.

Simeti, Mary Taylor, *Pomp and Sustenance*, Alfred A. Knopf, New York, 1989.

Stobart, Tom (ed.), *The Cook's Encyclopaedia*, Papermac, London, 1982.

Studd, Will, *Chalk and Cheese*, Purple Egg, Melbourne, 2004.

Sutherland Smith, Beverley, *A Taste for All Seasons*, Lansdowne, Sydney, 1975.

Sweeney, Susan, *The Olive Press*, The Australian Olive Association, Autumn 2006.

Symons, Michael, *One Continuous Picnic*, Duck Press, Adelaide, 1982.

Taruschio, Ann and Taruschio, Franco, *Leaves from the Walnut Tree*, Pavilion, London, 1993.

Time-Life Fruit Book, Time-Life, Amsterdam, 1983.

Wark, Alf, *Wine Cookery*, Rigby, Adelaide, 1969.

Waters, Alice, Curtan, Patricia and Labro, Martine, *Chez Panisse Pasta, Pizza and Calzone*, Random House, New York, 1984.

Waters, Alice, *Chez Panisse Café Cookbook*, Random House, New York, 1999.

—— *Chez Panisse Menu Cookbook*, Chatto & Windus, London, 1984.

Weir, Joanne, *You Say Tomato*, Broadway Books, New York, 1998.

Wells, Patricia, *At Home in Provence*, Scribner, New York, 1996.

Wells, Patricia and Robuchon, Joël, *Simply French*, William Morrow, New York, 1991.

Whiteaker, Stafford, *The Compleat Strawberry*, Century Publishing, London, 1985.

Wolfert, Paula, *The Cooking of the Eastern Mediterranean*, Harper Collins Publishers, New York, 1994.

—— *The Cooking of South-West France*, The Dial Press, New York, 1983.

—— *Mediterranean Cooking*, The Ecco Press, New York, 1977.

Zalokar, Sophie, *Picnic*, Fremantle Arts Centre Press, Perth, 2002.

ACKNOWLEDGEMENTS

This extract from *Maggie's Harvest* represents the culmination of a life's work to date, so how can I possibly conjure up all the people who have been instrumental in so many ways over the years?

My husband, Colin, is my rock – a true partner in every sense of the word. My daughters, Saskia and Elli, have grown into strong, independent women and we share regular boisterous meals with their partners and our much-loved grandchildren, Zöe, Max, Lilly, Rory, Ben and Darby.

The indomitable Julie Gibbs, originally suggested an update of *Maggie's Farm* and *Maggie's Orchard*, an idea which developed over time into *Maggie's Harvest*. I always had faith in Julie's extraordinary ability to know just what will make a book special.

Photographer Mark Chew effortlessly captured the essence of the produce in the book – it feels so Barossan! Daniel New, the book's designer, weaved his magic with the design. Marie Anne Pledger not only helped out on the shoots, but provided paraphernalia from her own kitchen and that of her friends for us to use.

There are so many in the team at Penguin I'd like to thank. My editors Kathleen Gandy and Virginia Birch and Nicole Brown for keeping us all on track, Anouska Jones for proof-reading, and Jocelyn Hungerford and all at Penguin for eleventh-hour assistance.

Over the years I have had an incredible array of staff who have contributed so much to both my business and my life. First and foremost was the lovely Hilda Laurencis, who sadly died as I wrote the very last pages of *Maggie's Harvest*.

From the Pheasant Farm Restaurant days, Sophie Zalokar, Steve Flamsteed, Nat Paull and Alex Herbert remain part of our extended family, and more recently Victoria Blumenstein and Gill Radford have both done much to ease my daily life.

The friendly, hard-working team at the Farmshop are the public face of our business and help to keep the tradition of the farm alive. I have so much to thank them for. Our customers, from the early days of the Pheasant Farm Restaurant, to those who buy our products all over the world today, have believed in us and what we've done.

I would also like to thank Brian Jeffries, Director of the Tuna Boat Owners Association of South Australia for updating me on the status of tuna.

INDEX

LANTERN

UK | USA | Canada | Ireland | Australia
India | New Zealand | South Africa | China

Penguin Books is part of the Penguin Random House group of companies whose
addresses can be found at global.penguinrandomhouse.com.

Penguin
Random House
Australia

First published by Penguin Group (Australia), 2015
This material was originally published as a section of *Maggie's Harvest* by Maggie Beer

1 3 5 7 9 10 8 6 4 2

Cover and text design by Daniel New © Penguin Group (Australia)
Design coordination by Hannah Schubert
Typeset in Cochin by Post Pre-Press Group, Brisbane, Queensland
Colour reproduction by Splitting Image, Clayton, Victoria
Printed in China by 1010 Printing International Limited

National Library of Australia
Cataloguing-in-Publication data:

Beer, Maggie.
Maggie Beer's summer harvest recipes / Maggie Beer ;
Mark Chew (photographer).
Notes: Includes bibliographical references and index.
ISBN 9781921384240 (pbk.)
Subjects: Seasonal cooking.
Cooking, Australian.
Other Creators/Contributors:
Chew, Mark, photographer.
641.564

penguin.com.au/lantern

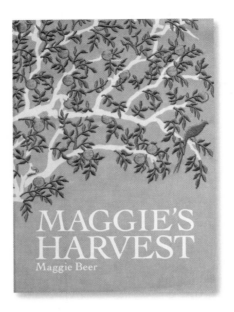

This landmark book from one of Australia's best-loved cooks
was first published in 2007 and will be available
as four seasonal paperbacks.

ISBN 9781921384257   ISBN 9781921384226   ISBN 9781921384233